How To Buy Sp
and Move To S

How To Buy Spanish Property and Move To Spain ... Safely

NICK SNELLING

First published in Spain in 2009 by Nick Snelling
This edition published in the United Kingdom
by Summertime Publishing

Edited by John Pointon

ISBN: 978-1-907498-80-0

DISCLAIMER

Praise

Yet again, Nick Snelling has transformed a bewildering and complex subject into a practical and authoritative guide. Information really is power, and How to Buy Spanish Property and Move to Spain – Safely should be required reading for anyone even thinking about buying property in Spain.

Martin Dell www.kyero.com

One by one, Snelling knocks down the barriers that everyone faces when relocating to Spain. Logical, useful and just the right amount of information on each subject. How to Buy Spanish Property and Move to Spain – Safely. [is] like a compass that will point you in the right direction at all times. Put this book in your back pocket before crossing the Channel.

Alfredo Bloy www.euroweeklynews.com

At last, a book about Spain that tells it the way it is! Unsparing in his judgments and advice, Nick Snelling has produced a book that is a critically important guide for anyone even considering coming to Spain. How to Buy Spanish Property and Move to Spain – Safely tells the unvarnished truth and reveals the dangers and benefits inherent in relocating or buying in Spain. Clear, concise and comprehensive, this book should be required reading …

Steve Hall www.thisisspain.com

A sound investment for both those thinking of upping sticks and the new arrival. How to Buy Spanish Property and Move to Spain – Safely gives a rounded game plan, explains the rules, and will take its readers' hand to lead them up the ladders and avoid the snakes. Written in plain English, this invaluable book ends rumour and speculation, and should help people avoid that bitter pill commonly known as hindsight.

Jack Troughton Round Town News

Anyone thinking of relocating to Spain should buy How to Buy Spanish Property and Move to Spain – Safely immediately! It is worth its weight in gold as a vital guide that will help avoid all the obstacles that lie in wait for the unwary. Penetrating and uncompromising it provides consistently clear, practical advice.

Mark Eastwood www.costablancauncovered.com

Thousands of Britons are seduced every year by the warmer climate of Spain and move here to build a better life. But the legal system and infrastructure are very different to the UK's. It can be a minefield of research and websites to gather all the information you need to relocate comfortably and without worry. So it's great that Nick Snelling has done all the hard work! How to Buy Spanish Property and Move to Spain – Safely covers everything you need to know, and is comprehensible and easy to follow.

Hannah Murray www.talkradioeurope.com

What a breath of fresh air – a moving to Spain book that actually tells it like it is and covers just about every subject that matters, and covers them in such detail that this has to be the most authoritative moving to Spain guide ever. I highly recommend that anyone looking to move to Spain reads this; it's like the "moving to Spain bible". Move to Spain without it at your peril.

Justin Aldridge www.eyeonspain.com

Nick Snelling steps forth and leads readers along the turbulent path of moving to Spain, smoothly and definitively. His book is packed to the seams with essential information, which is presented in a coherent and absorbable style. If you're considering a move here then you simply MUST read How to Buy Spanish Property and Move to Spain – Safely

Keidi Keating www.thesentinella.com

… up to date, informative and comprehensive …

Vanessa Rocchetta www.expatica.com

Acknowledgements

No book is easy to write when its aim is to provide authoritative details and advice about another country – let alone one as deceptively complicated as Spain. However, I have been blessed with significant assistance from a group of highly qualified professionals who have provided invaluable advice. Without their generous help, this book could never have been written. So, my grateful thanks go to:

Carolina Just Miro *(Lawyer)*
Practising lawyer who specialises in conveyancing.

Mark Paddon *(Building surveyor)*
British building surveyor permanently based in Spain.

Alberto Diaz Raya *(Ingenerio Superior)*
Spanish management consultant and property developer.

Dr Maria Soriano *(Paediatrician)*
Specialist in children's healthcare.

Beatriz Gonzalez Menendez *(Professor of Classics)*
A teacher working within the Spanish state school system.

John Pointon *(Marketing and management consultant)*
Director of an international construction consortium.

Sonia Garcia Fernandez *(Veterinary surgeon)*
A practicing veterinary surgeon specialist in domestic animals.

Jose Ivars Lopez *(Property and marketing expert)*
Specialist in international property development and marketing.

Robert Burns *(Chartered accountant)*
Expert in Spanish business practice and UK pensions.

For full details and contact information see **Contributors**.

Foreword

As the biggest free English language newspaper in Spain, at Euro Weekly News we constantly write about English speaking people's experiences in Spain. Unfortunately, all too often, we come across stories of people who have either bought property in Spain or moved here and then had an array of problems.

However, when we investigate the stories, often we find that the people concerned blundered into Spain with almost no preparation or prior knowledge about the country and how it functions. Indeed, a common thread is how carelessly many people buy property in Spain, thinking that everything is just the same as it is in the UK.

In fact, the glory of Spain is that it is very different from North European countries. For the most part this is a good thing and what sets Spain apart from other countries as somewhere wonderful in which to live.

However, property law in Spain is significantly different to that of Northern Europe. Indeed, as Nick points out, there are thousands of illegal properties in Spain or properties which have significant potential liabilities. So, whilst you can buy property in Spain safely – you really do need to know what you are doing beforehand.

The same is also true of where you buy and this is as true for holiday homes as it is for permanent living. Spain is a vast, complicated country with enormous variations of lifestyle on offer between its very different regions. This means that getting your location right is essential, if you are to take advantage of the terrific quality of life that exists in Spain.

The frustrating thing for most commentators is how easily problems can be avoided by people coming to Spain. With the right advice and sound knowledge your property purchase or move to Spain can be problem free. However, everything depends upon sound, practical advice – a commodity in short supply, given the vested interests sometimes tied up in the Spanish property industry.

The great thing about this book is that it has been written by a highly regarded writer who knows Spain intimately. Nick knows how the Spanish property industry works, what to buy and how. As importantly, he has raised his family in Spain and knows, first hand, how the education system works, the health system functions and what it is like to work and run a business in Spain. All of this means that Nick brings to this book objective, comonsense information that is absolutely invaluable.

As I have written many times, Spain can be a fabulous place in which to live or have a holiday home but everything depends upon laying sound foundations right from the start.

So, do take advantage of this excellent book, avoid unnecessary problems – and enjoy Spain to the full!

ALFREDO BLOY
Editor Euro Weekly News
www.euroweeklynews.com

Contents

Introduction

One of the extraordinary things about Britain is the consistently high proportion of people who say they would like to move abroad. Time and again surveys confirm this desire, which seems to exist irrespective of age or wealth. Indeed, it seems that someone leaves the UK every three minutes to move abroad.

Clearly there is a strong nomadic streak within us Britons. We rarely stay in one place for long *within* the UK and seem to be quite content to move from one area to another without a second thought. Then, given half the chance, we relish the opportunity of living in a foreign country. In fact, there are supposedly more Britons per capita living abroad than any other nation – albeit the highest density can be found in nearby France and Spain.

Of course, the motivations for living abroad are often as varied as the very characteristics of us British. Some people move abroad because they are bored and are seeking adventures; while others relocate because of disenchantment with the UK and the social changes that have occurred over the past few years. Meanwhile, many people simply want to settle down to enjoy a kinder climate, as well as a cheaper and better quality of life.

Irrespective of the reason, any relocation is a sensitive matter with every step critical to the long-term success of the move. Get it right and you can start a new life that will be incredibly enriching and fulfilling. Get it wrong and it will end up not just in acute disappointment, but also the loss of considerable money and, sometimes, the bitter break-up of relationships.

Certainly, moving house within the UK is, invariably, extremely stressful and the stakes high. It is hard to know

1

for sure whether your new area will be suitable, let alone whether the house you are buying is truly sound and good value. There are also all the imponderables, like whether the local people will be welcoming and the amenities workable. For those with children or perhaps looking for work, the risks and accompanying stresses are even greater.

Naturally, moving abroad is far more of a commitment than any move within the UK – not least, if you move to a country where you do not speak the language! This factor alone can make life extremely challenging and complicate even the simplest of actions. Indeed, although living in a country with a radically different culture and language is tremendously exciting, it is an experience requiring considerable thought and preparation.

So, the choice of where to live and exactly where to move to needs to be made with supreme care to ensure the dreams you have are achieved – and that the adventure of relocating is maximised, and rewarding.

I am, of course, biased towards Spain. This is a country to which I moved permanently with my family some years ago, after having researched numerous other options as far afield as South Africa, and several countries in South America.

To my delight, we have relocated to a country and specific area that has provided us with a fantastic way of life. Indeed, our expectations have been far exceeded and my family looks upon Spain as our home and our country by default. My children are now fluent in two of the three major world languages, have been superbly well educated and have enjoyed growing up in a safe, child-friendly environment.

Meanwhile, my wife and I speak tolerable Spanish and

have been enchanted by a way of life that, debatably, disappeared largely from the UK thirty years ago. We love the lively, Mediterranean 'feel' of Spanish towns and villages, the intimacy of village life and the all year round access to the outdoors. We adore sitting on cafe terraces throughout the year, the rhythm of *siesta* and the peculiarity of dining at ten or eleven o'clock at night.

Reasonably keen sportspeople, we have been seduced by the cheapness and sheer availability of activities. Within a radius of twenty minutes from our villa we can horse ride, climb, walk and bicycle in a stunningly beautiful area of protected mountains. Equally, we can drop down to some of the finest, blue flagged beaches in the world to swim, snorkel, sail, fish or scuba dive.

We have been enchanted by the excellent amenities and life provided by the nearby cultured town of Gandia, whose busyness is in sharp contrast to the traditional community life of our little mountain village. There we share in a life that has all the theatre and closeness of a society little changed for centuries. Meanwhile, an easy one-hour drive takes us to Valencia (with its international airport), a city renowned for its culture, stunning City of Arts and Sciences and (for my wife!) wonderful shops.

Put simply, we have a quality of life that is better than anything we could have aspired to in the UK. Life is more interesting, more challenging, more rewarding and more fun. Our money goes further, our overheads are lower and we are healthier than ever. Crime is lower, the streets safer and the options for activities outside of our home, far greater. We also feel enriched by living in a country that is both linguistically and culturally very different from the UK.

One of the most surprising aspects to living in Spain is how Spanish culture has retained its purity and depth, something that is rarely experienced by holidaymakers or the casual visitor. Almost every town and village has a *Casa de Cultura* (culture centre) from which are organised seemingly endless fiestas and numerous, often free, cultural events throughout the year. Invariably, these wonderful occasions have nothing to do with tourism and are aimed purely at the local population. They add a colour and texture to life that has no recognisable counterpart within the UK.

As for the Spanish themselves, they are hospitable, tolerant and kindly, and have an infectious *joie de vivre*. In fact, if we left Spain now, the memory we would treasure most would be the nature of the native people. It is one thing to move to another country because of the climate and beaches – and quite another to live amongst people who are friendly and actively enhance daily life. That is a rare quality indeed and one of the most notable and glorious aspects to living in Spain.

Of course, the climate and way of life differs enormously from one area to another. Indeed, the country is as complicated as it is fascinating and can veer between cutting-edge developed world and (albeit sophisticated) developing world. On the surface, Spain can sometimes look very similar to the UK but, in reality, the two (for better and worse) are very different.

However, Spain is not all 'paradise' and living here is far from problem free. There are significant land law issues and there have been some dreadful property-related abuses (like land grabs). Meanwhile, the infrastructure is variable, new construction is sometimes appalling and the economy rests on shaky foundations. There is significant corruption and some astoundingly poor regional and local planning and building control. Doing business can be challenging and the bureaucracy baffling.

Moving to Spain, therefore, can be easy and trouble free or it can turn into an utter nightmare – depending on either luck or your preparation. As luck is not something to rely on when the stakes are high, any move should be undertaken only with the right knowledge and after significant preparation. The aim of this book (complemented by my blog *Culture Spain* – *www.culturespain.com*) is to provide you with as much 'straight from the hip' information as possible to ensure that any move you make to Spain will be both safe and successful – for the long term.

To Move or Not To Move

It has been suggested that some 30% of all Britons who come to live in Spain return to the UK after three years. This is certainly consistent with my personal experience and I would not be surprised if this trend continues unabated. I suspect this phenomenon is true of virtually any other place to which Britons relocate – whether it is to France, Australia, Greece or the United States.

Why do so many people return to the UK? This is an extremely important question that needs to be looked at carefully, well before any move. If you know the potential problems, you can take an informed view as to whether relocating will suit you over the long term. It may be that, after having looked at the reasons why people often do not relocate successfully, you postpone your move or compromise on your choice of destination.

> *Know the common reasons for relocation failure*
> *and confirm that those factors will not affect you –*
> *or that you have a strategy in place to negate them*

Of one thing you can be sure: relocating to another country means committing. It is also stressful and, frequently, expensive. This is certainly not something to do unless you are determined, understand the potential problems and have a strategy to deal with these. Any reversal of relocation can often be difficult and sometimes very costly. This is particularly true if you have problems selling your foreign home or have to re-enter the UK job market having lost your previous contacts.

Some Common Reasons for Relocation Failure

There are a number of common reasons why relocation may not work in the long term:

Grandchildren

The draw of grandchildren should never be under-estimated. Many people come to Spain to retire *before* they have grandchildren. However, once grandchildren arrive, the desire to be an integral part of their lives may become very strong. Frequent trips back to the UK are sometimes not enough to satisfy every new grandparent.

Infirmity

The Spanish healthcare system is very good. There is also private healthcare in Spain as well as English speaking doctors, dentists and nurses. However, people with a long-term illness often feel more comfortable being back in the UK within a system they understand and where every aspect is in English.

Old age

Spain has an underdeveloped system of old-age residential homes. Indeed, those that do exist tend to resemble hospitals and are rarely places to which the British elderly would willingly retire. The call to be close to family also tends to mean that the elderly return home – most notably upon the death of one partner.

Money

Spain is no longer 'dirt cheap' and many people underestimate the money they require to live here. Initial over-spending can drain resources and any currency fluctuations (such as the 2008 sterling crash) can result in financial turmoil.

Work

Spain is not an easy place in which to find work and employees rarely receive anything resembling UK rates of pay. Few people allow sufficient time to develop a business and therefore end up having to retreat to the UK for a realistic income.

Wrong location/lifestyle

The choice of location for long-term relocation influences every aspect of life. A poor choice and thereby the lifestyle on offer can lead to a rapid disenchantment with Spain.

Unrealistic expectations

Spain is neither paradise nor does it hold the elixir to cure unstable relationships. Expectations of a dream lifestyle can be often impossibly high and when not achieved create a bitterness that grinds into daily life.

Property problems

Spain has a land law that is radically different to the UK's and can lead to appalling problems with property ownership. Structural defects can also occasionally render a property uninhabitable or be a drain on finances. A bad or unsafe property purchase can create enormous unhappiness and destabilise even the most robust of people.

Boredom

Frequently, people trap themselves within a 'gilded cage' that, after a period of time, simply lacks adequate stimulation. It is critical to be proactive in developing a social life, in work, or in activities that are involving and compelling.

Commitment

Some people try to live half their life in the UK and half in Spain. Though this can work, it tends to be disruptive and lacking in absolute commitment, to the point at which some people become unsettled about where exactly 'home' is.

Non-consensual

Any move is a risk and one that needs to be agreed on by both partners. Often one partner or the other is not really keen on relocating and only does so to 'keep the peace' or 'humour' their partner. This tends to be fatal for relocation as the less keen partner will be constantly negative and looking for every excuse to return to the UK.

Children

Relocating children successfully is a sensitive matter and is intimately bound up with their age and the type of education (both secondary school and advanced) available. If children are unhappy and cannot settle in a new country, they place almost unbearable pressures on their parents.

Elderly or infirm parents in the UK

Depending upon how close your relationship with your parents is, any increasing illness and dependency can place real pressure on you to return to the UK.

It is certainly more common for people to state that they "*have* to go back" to the UK – rather than they "want to go back". More often than not, financial, medical, family or property related issues – rather than a dislike of Spain or its lifestyle – force a return.

Avoiding The Problems

Many of the above problems can be resolved once you recognise their existence. For example, choosing the right location is far more complex than most people imagine and sometimes requires a good deal of compromise. Depending on your circumstances, you may have to settle, for example, somewhere that is not be your first choice, but *is* ideal for easy and cheap accessibility to the UK.

Many of the most common problems can be avoided through ensuring there is a consensus about the move among all members of the family. When one partner has been coerced into moving, this frequently results in that person, understandably, undermining the success of the move. Small problems may then be magnified until the only solution is a return to the UK.

Make certain there is a consensus between you and your partner about relocating and that you are both equally committed to the move

There is also often an innate flaw in the philosophy of many people wishing to move abroad. People frequently state that one of their aims is to do less than they are currently doing in the UK. In other words, they want to take things easy. To some extent this is obviously desirable but, in the long term, rarely works.

Certainly the most successfully relocated Britons in Spain are notable for their ongoing energy and their determination, right from the start, to do *more* than they did in the UK – albeit in a different way. Without doubt, life is more interesting when you are active and it is critical, when considering relocation, to recognise this. A busy social life and perhaps an element of work can make a huge difference to the long-term enjoyment and sustainability of life abroad.

As mentioned earlier, many people fall into the trap of the 'gilded cage' : buying a stunning property in the wrong location and losing sight of the primary reason for moving in the first place – to improve significantly their overall quality of life. However, as many industry professionals acknowledge, no sooner has someone's aeroplane landed than they start to focus solely on 'bricks and mortar'. Many people spend far more time looking at properties than they ever do studying the areas in which these are situated.

Properties are inanimate objects and, however fine, can rarely provide a fulfilling lifestyle in the long term. For that you need people, communities and activity. This is not to say that property is unimportant, just that many people's fixation on housing can result in the tail wagging the dog.

Ensure that your aim in relocating is to be more – not less – active in Spain than you are now, even if this is in a different way …

It is important to have a reasonably clear idea of why you want to leave the UK and what you both need and want from your intended move. This helps immeasurably when you are trying to assess where to go – whether a country or a specific area within that country. Once you know what you are seeking you can make a wish list. This can then be compared with any potential problem areas that you might have identified (for example, from the ones mentioned above).

Be clear and focused about what you want to achieve by relocating and the type of life you envisage leading

Relocating Choices

Getting specific about the following factors should help you narrow down the options best suited to you:

Distance from the UK
- ☐ One hour's flight
- ☐ Two hour's flight
- ☐ Three or more hours away

Language
- ☐ English speaking
- ☐ English as the secondary language
- ☐ Little or no English spoken

Climate
- ☐ Atlantic
- ☐ Temperate
- ☐ Tropical

Culture
- ☐ North European
- ☐ Mediterranean
- ☐ African
- ☐ Islamic
- ☐ Asian

Type of landscape
- ☐ Flat
- ☐ Mountainous
- ☐ Hilly
- ☐ Arid
- ☐ Green
- ☐ Forested
- ☐ Arable

Population density or distribution
- ☐ Urban
- ☐ Village
- ☐ Countryside

Demographics
- ☐ Expatriate area

☐ Native (i.e. high-density Spanish, French, Moroccan and so on)

Proximity of facilities like:

☐ Shops
☐ Major shopping centre
☐ Doctor's surgery
☐ Hospital
☐ Private healthcare
☐ Beaches
☐ Schools (both primary and secondary)

Activities

☐ Physical: such as riding, walking, diving, skiing, or cycling
☐ Social: such as clubs, associations, or gourmet food
☐ Cultural: such as theatre, cinema, architecture, or museums

Work

☐ Existing opportunities
☐ Skills shortage
☐ Size of potential market
☐ Acceptability of your qualifications
☐ Rates of pay/profitability
☐ Cost/route to market
☐ Corporate law
☐ Taxation levels

Communications

☐ Landline telephone
☐ Internet – high speed
☐ Motorway
☐ Railway
☐ International airport

Housing

☐ Minimum requirements: bedrooms, bathrooms, office, and so on
☐ Desired requirements: swimming pool, flat plot,

workshop, and so on
- ☐ Affordability
- ☐ Income earner: B&B, rentable apartment, and so on

Cost of living
- ☐ Value for money
- ☐ Day to day running costs

Political/economic stability
- ☐ European Union
- ☐ Democracy
- ☐ Dictatorship
- ☐ Strong economy
- ☐ Bureaucratic
- ☐ Corrupt
- ☐ Stable currency
- ☐ Inflation

Of course, deciding what you really want, and if your intended location will be suitable, is always going to be somewhat subjective. Reality is often quite different from any preconceived opinions and what appear to be 'facts' – and other people's experiences should not necessarily be relied upon.

> *No amount of theoretical research can beat*
> *actually seeing an area*

Finding Information That's True

There is a tremendous amount of information easily available to help you. For statistics and hard facts, the CIA World Fact Book is very good, and country reports by Amnesty International are well worth looking at. Obviously, there is a vast supply of information on the internet, although it is always worth double-checking what you've read. Much of what is available online is biased or has been written by someone with a vested interest (well-meaning or not). This is never more so than in the property industry where information relating to local housing (and lifestyle) is often far from impartial.

The best way to narrow down where you want to move is by visiting the potential area. This may sound blindingly obvious, but it is amazing how often people move – lock, stock and barrel – to a place they have not been before. Others move after having been there only briefly on holiday – during which time they may have barely moved away from their beach resort.

But, as they say in the British military, "a good recce is never a waste of time". The reconnaissance needs to be thorough and your research should establish whether the area you think is ideal, truly is appropriate for long-term living. This is often harder to establish than it appears, not least because being abroad quickly equates to 'being on holiday' for most people. It is easy to be half-hearted about doing the nitty-gritty research when the sun is out and the beaches enticing! It can also be difficult to 'read' a different country, let alone a particular area, correctly in this situation.

Effective Research

So, how is it best to do effective research?

- Make sure that you go to where you intend moving or buying property at least twice and at different times of the year – perhaps during the height of summer and again in winter. Holiday areas can be radically different in low and high season as they respond to the ebb and flow of sometimes enormous numbers of people. Some hilly or mountainous areas that are in full sun during the summer can be largely in the shade during the winter months.

- Always have a disciplined schedule that will keep you energised and focused on your prospective relocation.

Make some fixed appointments each day, while leaving sufficient free time to do your own research as new factors present themselves.

- Make sure that you travel widely around your desired area. Where possible, do this is in concentric circles until you reach at least an hour from where your proposed destination. An hour's radius will, in reality, become your 'neighbourhood' and you must have a reasonable idea of its pros and cons.

- Take time out to find some expatriate bars. These almost invariably exist and can be excellent places to pick up the latest information from people with no vested interest in seeing you move there. However, never rely on information from one source alone!

- Try to stay in a local B&B. B&B owners, particularly if they are expatriates themselves, tend to be a mine of information, and other guests might also supply further information about the area.

- Arrange appointments with a couple of real estate agents so that you can see examples of some properties – but be truthful and advise the agents beforehand that you are doing only preliminary research. Normally, agents will freely show you properties on this basis, and be more open than if they were chasing down a 'live' client.

Research is never truly effective unless you stay for a sustained time in the proposed location

Rental Rules

If you come to the conclusion that you have found an area suitable for your relocation it is an excellent idea to rent somewhere for a few months. Of course, this is not always possible, given your personal time constraints, but undoubtedly it is the best way of finding out, from day to day, whether the area will deliver what you want. Certainly, finding rental homes is no problem and there are several excellent web sites that have thousands of rental properties from which to choose.

If you decide to rent, try to:

- Rent for about three months. Any longer tends to be superfluous.

- Arrange your timing so that it crosses the seasons – perhaps from the end of the height of summer through to mid-autumn. This way you will gain a feel for the changing weather as well as any significant change in local population numbers.

- Stay in a property that is as similar as possible to the type you wish to buy. If you want to buy a farm, little is gained by renting an inner-city flat! Equally, it is pointless renting a villa when you want to live in a newly built townhouse.

- Rent a property that is located where you want to live i.e. on the same estate or within the same area of the town.

- Be constantly active and enquiring.

Why Move To Spain?

No country is perfect, of course. However, Spain provides a very fine compromise for someone intending to relocate and this is true irrespective of age. Equally, Spain is child friendly and can work well for those who want to live abroad while bringing up their children.

Positive Factors

The positive aspects of Spain can be summarised as:

Proximity to the UK

This is an important factor for those who need to be able to return regularly, quickly and easily to the UK. Elderly relations often need attention and any remaining business interests, occasional visits. Meanwhile, most people want to live somewhere that is cheap and accessible for grown-up children and friends. Flight times to the UK are normally just under two hours.

A kind climate

Spain is such a vast country that its climate varies considerably. However, almost everywhere has a gentler overall climate than the UK and marvellous long summers are guaranteed – whether you are in Atlantic Galicia, the Costa del Sol, Catalonia, the interior of Spain or along the Valencian coastline. That said, note that inland Spain can be quite cold in winter and annual snow is common.

Cost of living

Undoubtedly, Spain has become far more expensive than it was some years ago. However, it still offers remarkable value for money in comparison with the UK. A combination of the climate and the availability of leisure activities tend to mean that you spend less money to achieve a superior overall quality of life.

Variety of accessible activities

One of the joys of Spain is that it is a massive country with a relatively small population benefiting from excellent roads, railways and airportshe country has excellent beaches, mountain ranges and extensive natural parks. These are complemented by historic medieval and Moorish towns – *and* ultra-modern cities. It is a great place for those who enjoy the outdoors yet equally suitable for the ardent shopper.

Political security

It is almost inconceivable that Spain would revert back to a dictatorship or reject democracy. Spain has matured, so that politically it is not too dissimilar to the UK in having two main political parties (the PP and PSOE). Spain is also similar to the UK in that it has a constitutional monarchy (this led by a respected and sure-footed king).

The EU

Few things make relocation easier than moving to a country within the EU. Spain belongs to both the EU and NATO. This means that you have the same rights to live and work in Spain as you do in the UK.

Healthcare

Spain has a sophisticated and efficient national healthcare system with GP clinics in most villages and major hospitals (with A&E departments) in all large towns.

Education

Education is compulsory in Spain. The country has state schools, semi-private schools, private schools and a scattering of international schools – together with a comprehensive university system. The equivalent of the UK's A level qualification is the highly respected *Bachillerato*.

Language

This is both a positive and negative (see below) for someone who is relocating. Spanish is the second most spoken language in the world and therefore a superb language for children to learn. It is also Latin based and has many words that are similar to English – making it relatively easy to learn to a basic level. Thankfully, English is the obligatory second language for schools in Spain and some Spanish people now speak English.

Culture

Spain has a rich and fascinating culture that varies enormously from one region to another. Indeed, one of the surprises for most Britons is to discover how varied and complex it is. A long, complicated history has provided the country with great depth and an inheritance of wonderful architecture and influences that have extended from the Phoenicians to the Romans and then to the Moors and North Europeans.

Mentality

The Spanish are remarkably tolerant and generous. Intolerant of violence, naturally open and friendly, they are normally part of close-knit communities. They are used to dealing with foreigners and consider themselves as having much the same overall mentality as North Europeans.

Infrastructure

Spain, with some exceptions, has a modern, developed world infrastructure. The roads, railways and airports work well. Mains electricity, water and the telephone system are efficient and ADSL is available in most places. Commercial centres and major supermarket chains abound and it is rare to find it difficult to buy any commodity that exists in the UK.

Bureaucracy

Like any country, Spain has more than its fair share of bureaucracy, though once you are properly established this tends not to affect daily life greatly. In some areas (like Valencia), where power is devolved to village town halls, decision-making can be surprisingly efficient and quick. The secret lies in a good *gestor* (See *Money and Pensions*).

Child-friendly

Like many Mediterranean countries, Spain is child-friendly in a way that the UK is not. This is delightful for anyone wanting to raise their children in a caring environment where children are universally welcome and tolerated – whether late at night, at a fine restaurant or elsewhere.

Lack of political correctness

Spain is still reasonably robust about the most extreme and illogical aspects of 'political correctness' and health and safety. This is refreshing for most people.

Effective police force

Spain has three police forces (See *Police & Emergency Services*) with different remits. On the whole the police are considered efficient and fair and are generally respected.

High-density expatriate areas

The Costa del Sol and parts of the Costa Blanca and Catalonia have areas with many relocated expatriates, which provides a potentially instant social network.

Few dangerous creatures/diseases

Spain has five poisonous snakes, and some scorpions. However, none of these should kill you and there are few other life-threatening creatures or natural diseases.

Benign geography

Spain suffers minor earthquake tremors and some short-lived and violent rainstorms. Particularly in the interior of the country, it has extremes of heat and cold. You need to be careful of living within low-lying coastal areas that can be affected by flood run-off. But, on the whole, it is a country without any serious or regular dangers such as hurricanes, tsunamis or major earthquakes.

Longevity

Spain has some of the best rates of longevity in Europe!

Negative Factors

The negative aspects to Spain are:

Land laws

There have been many appalling abuses of the land law in Spain. Land grab is a complicated matter, has many grey areas and needs to be treated with great caution (through a first-class lawyer!).

Property prices

By early 2008, property prices in Spain were no longer (in many cases) providing value for money. Indeed, prices had risen to ludicrous levels compared to similar properties in the UK. This was particularly the case with, for example, villas and apartments on some golf complexes. The 'correction' of housing prices in 2008 and 2009 should redress this situation and make Spanish property more affordable and pricing more realistic.

Aesthetics

Rampant modern development within Spain has run in conjunction with poor planning and design. Coastal Spain, for the most part, has many developments that have done little or nothing to enhance the natural beauty of the country.

Poor build quality

Unfortunately, much of the new building undertaken over the past 10 years has been from mediocre to dreadful quality. This means that, as a house buyer, you need to pay close attention to any recently built properties. Some are good – but many are not.

Language

Unless you speak Spanish, you will encounter a barrier that can frustrate the simplest of actions. It will be also extremely difficult for your children to start successfully at a Spanish school if they are older than 12 or 13 and do not speak fluent Spanish already.

Currency fluctuations

If your pension or income is paid in sterling, be aware that fluctuations in the currency markets can adversely affect the purchasing power of your money. You may be fine one year and, possibly, in trouble the next.

Low levels of pay

Salaries in Spain and general rates of pay are much lower than those in the UK.

Legal action

The law courts are notoriously slow and cumbersome and the process of litigation, expensive and lengthy.

Work

This can be difficult to find if you compete directly with the Spanish in the Spanish marketplace. So, you need to bring a particular skill to the country or aim to service the expatriate population. Starting a business is no less difficult than elsewhere in the world. This is hazardous and can take time before it starts to make money.

Drug abuse

Thankfully, young Spaniards tend to drink less than young people in the UK and social drinking rarely results in violence or other unsavoury behaviour. However, casual use of cannabis, marijuana and even cocaine is quite common in Spain. Indeed, Spain has the highest use of cocaine per capita in Europe.

One of the most striking things about Spain is that it provides a fine way of life easily accessible to all. Certainly, there are more exciting places to live and areas boasting more dramatic scenery. There are also many other cultures that are more challenging and markedly different from Northern Europe. However, if you want somewhere close to the UK that is safe and fun, with a wonderful climate, that will provide an affordable, high quality of life for the long term, Spain is hard to beat.

The very fact that Spain is such a fine compromise has made it an enduringly popular country for Britons seeking to relocate. There are estimated to be some one million of us in Spain today. This alone should reassure you that Spain is both a sensible and good choice of country for relocation.

> *Good preparation and planning is the bedrock of successful relocation*

That said, there are dangers – the chief of which are choosing the wrong place for your long-term relocation and/or buying the wrong type of property. Either can be upsetting, but the latter can result in appalling stress and may lead to the loss of significant amounts of money. This is probably no different in many newly developed or developing countries. The answer is to to avoid any potential problems by being sufficiently knowledgeable before you make your move. Most issues need never have happened in the first place.

Location, Location, Location

Stressing the importance of location has become a cliché. However, it cannot be stressed often enough, as your location will define your future life. If you make a mistake with your choice of location within Spain, it may end your dreams of a new life and lead to a rapid and embarrassing retreat to the UK. Alternatively, if you decide to move again within Spain, this is bound to be an experience that is disruptive, unwelcome and expensive.

Financial Cost of Buying The Wrong Property

You should realise that any sale of property in Spain, depending on your personal classification, is likely to attract capital gains tax at 19%, even if you are selling your primary residence. Equally daunting is Spain's 7% purchase tax (8% on new builds), payable when you buy a property. Move twice in succession (2 x 7% purchase taxes and a CGT of 18%) and you may lose a lot of money to the taxman! So, it is important to make sure that any purchase of property or relocation is correct and does not result in further unnecessary moves.

Always concentrate more on the suitability of your proposed location than on searching for particular properties

There are some very good general guidelines about what tends to suit the majority of people when they relocate. These are really important to understand and deserve close attention for two reasons:

- If given guidelines work well for most successfully relocated Britons, sheer common sense suggests you should consider them carefully – especially given the amount of people who have relocated to Spain over the past 30 years.

- If you relocate outside the criteria required by most people, you may have problems should you choose to sell your property in the future. Certainly, one of the key guidelines to purchasing a foreign property is 'only buy what you can resell easily'. Therefore your choice of property location is critical and, wherever possible, should match that desired by the maximum number of people possible.

Critical Location Guidelines

The secret to choosing a location revolves around ensuring that you are:

- No more than a couple of minutes' drive away from a village with reasonable amenities. The village should be more than a 'one-horse *pueblo*' and have, for example, at least a couple of bars and restaurants, a small supermarket and perhaps a baker's and butcher's, a pharmacy and doctor's surgery. The village will be your community, your first line of security and an essential part of your social life and day to day network.

- A maximum of 15 minutes from a major town that has pretty much everything you need – from a new Mercedes garage through to 1 euro cheap goods shops. It should cater for your weekly shop and have a full range of banks, major supermarkets and services of all kinds – together with an A&E hospital. Also, it should be a lively working town that remains active all year round. Ideally, its main commerce should not come from tourism.

- One hour from an international airport with cheap flights. The proximity of the airport is vital in case of emergencies and to give you the freedom to fly easily back and forth between Spain and the UK. You will also find many friends and family coming to visit you and frequent long drives to an airport to collect and deliver them can quickly wear thin!

- A maximum of 20 minutes from the coast. The Spanish dream for the vast majority of people is defined by being close to the Mediterranean – irrespective of whether you like the seaside or not! If you buy a property far from the beaches, you will find it more difficult to sell or rent.

The factors above are uncontentious and logical. However, it is amazing how many people buy without understanding these points. They wonder then why life is so awkward and why they have so few friends – or why it is so hard to make any progress with integration in their local community.

> *Try to locate: two minutes from a village, 15 minutes from a large town, one hour from an airport and no more than 20 minutes from the coast.*

On holiday, it is not really too much of a problem to drive five or ten minutes to the nearest shop to buy a litre of milk or to have a drink. Equally, a half-hour drive for your weekly shop is no hardship. However, after six months – let alone a couple of years – not being within easy reach of amenities can leave you isolated and resentful.

Time and again, people buy in the '*campo*' (countryside) and defy the above guidelines – most often because one partner has wanted a large stretch of land. While looking at 20,000 m^2 of gorgeous olive groves may be enchanting for a month or two, it can make any meaningful social contact difficult. After a relatively short period, many find this inescapably lonely – and gallingly inconvenient despite the beauty.

There is much to be said for moving to a location in Spain that is not too radically different from your previous situation in the UK. If you have lived in a town most of your life, living in the depths of the countryside, in another country, can be too big a step to take in one bound. This is not to say it does not work for some people – but great caution should be exercised in taking the plunge.

Of course, a classic mistake made by many people is to confuse a holiday location with that suitable for long-term living. The two are very different. Indeed, it is all too easy to be suckered, after a delightful holiday, into thinking that a place that was so charming for a week or so would work equally well throughout the year.

Never mistake a holiday home and its location
for a permanent home

For a traditional holiday to succeed you need very little – pleasant scenery, a great beach, some basic shops nearby and a few lively restaurants and nightclubs. It is also handy if there is somewhere picturesque for a day out – though this rarely defines why you choose a holiday location. As for the property, it needs to be clean, neat and tidy, have a pretty view and, if possible, its own swimming pool. Blessed with great weather, this combination has all the potential to ensure a terrific couple of week's holiday.

In fact, you are likely to have such a great time that you may think that this is all you need for day to day life!

However, appreciate that what you experience on this type of holiday is almost entirely artificial. Most holiday areas die once the season is over. The lively bars, for example, often close down as do some – or all – of the local shops.

Indeed, the area that was once so enchanting may remain empty for as long as seven or eight months of the year. Meanwhile, your lovely rented holiday home may be surrounded both by other empty rental properties and second homes that are only used during the summer. Absent will be the friendly, relaxed 'community' present during the height of the season. Worse still, it may be that the 'ideal' villa or flat you rented lacks central heating, important utility areas, or a decent-sized kitchen, large master bedroom and living area – all so important for long-term, day to day living.

Finding a successful location is complicated and its long-term workability surprisingly fickle. It is not easy to 'read' another country and you need to focus very carefully if you are to make sure that a given location will provide you with a fine quality of life – irrespective of the season. To move to a holiday area with its significant ebb and flow of holiday-makers can be a mistake. It can be a real shock and deeply disappointing to see your beloved holiday area during the winter months – when the weather is poor, the wind gusting, the beaches empty, the bars locked up and the sea grey.

That said, the converse of a holiday area is a working Spanish village or town. These are very different from those in the UK. Despite appearances (particularly during *siesta*), they are rarely the place to live if you want a private and tranquil existence. Urban Spain is generally more lively and noisy than many other European countries – let alone Britain. Town is a place of socialising (often with children in bars), very late summer nights and an active and boisterous community life. This may not suit you any more than a holiday area deserted for much of the year would.

Without doubt, getting the balance right is difficult and deserves real time and attention …

The Tools for Success

You must choose your location carefully to ensure you have many potential 'levers' available. These will provide you with a full, interesting and convenient lifestyle throughout the year. Examples are:

Immediately around your potential property

☐ A permanently settled population
☐ A mixed society of those who work, have children and are retired (a 'real-life' community as opposed to one of just the retired expatriate or elderly)
☐ A mixture of nationalities, including a high proportion of Spanish nationals
☐ Non-tourist bars, restaurants and shops
☐ Some local parkland where you can walk freely

Within around 15 minutes' drive

☐ A large, populated centre with its own year-round economy (and one not dependent only on tourism) with an A&E hospital, dentists, vets, cinemas, high street, shopping centre and industrial estate
☐ A railway station that connects to a major city
☐ A good beach (your friends, children and grandchildren will want this to be nearby!)
☐ An extensive area of wild parkland
☐ A range of potential activities – diving, horse riding, cycling, go-karting, quad biking, fishing, climbing
☐ Clubs and associations (British Legion, local expat

associations, quiz night clubs, and so on)
- ☐ Fine and varied restaurants, nightclubs and bars
- ☐ Somewhere you can obtain English language newspapers and magazines
- ☐ A good selection of schools and sports centres (if you have school-aged children)

Within one hour's drive
- ☐ A major city
- ☐ A marina
- ☐ An international airport with cheap flights
- ☐ An alternative town – preferably with some inherent interest (perhaps a great castle or historic centre)

Minimum Amenities

The point of the above-mentioned factors is that for permanent living you must have:

- A comprehensive and accessible infrastructure nearby to support your overall requirements – whether this means well-stocked supermarkets or the availability of good dentists, vets, mechanics, discount warehouses, shops, cultural activities, concerts and shows.

- A social life that is generated by having people permanently living near and around you who have 'normal' (not only retired) lifestyles. Few things are more disruptive than having temporary neighbours, or living next door to properties that are used primarily as rented holiday homes. Equally, living among retired expatriates is not just a perversion of living in a foreign country, it can also lead to an agoraphobic, artificial and potentially boring lifestyle.

- A range of extensive activities and depth to the area to sustain your interest for many years to come.

Never underestimate the variety and extent of infrastructure, social ambience and amenities that you require for a successful, long-term relocation

Gilded Cages

A good example of a location that can sometimes deliver less than it promises at first sight is some of the large, newly built estates. These are often built on a hillside and can offer tremendous housing with beautiful views over the sea and surrounding countryside. They are often reached by a twisting road that winds its way up the hillside and around the houses. Quite often these estates have a bar (and sometimes a property sales office) at the lower entrance.

The problem is that the nearest village is often some five to ten minutes' drive away and therefore dislocated from life on the estate. In turn, most of the properties will have been built for the foreign buyer's market and have very few local Spanish residents. Accordingly, many estates are little more than up-market ghettos of expatriates (of whatever nationality) and, worse still, have a high proportion of rental/second homes.

You should be wary of buying into on this ese types of estates. They may provide a 'dream' lifestyle for a year or so, but are rarely satisfactory long term. The ever- fluctuating population is not conducive to developing a working community and the artificiality of the 'community' that does exist can be unsatisfactory. What's more, the drive up and down, or through the estate, to the nearest non-estate bar or shop can become very trying over time.

The Work Factor

Work is of course an important consideration for anyone relocating. This may well define your location both on a macro and micro basis. Spain is unlike the UK in that the population density of the country is highest along the coast with notable 'islands' of high population centres such as Madrid, Cordoba, Seville, and so on.

Depending on your work, you may have little choice but to locate near a major population centre. However, even this decision is more sensitive than it appears – particularly if you do not speak Spanish and your intended market is expatriates. If the latter, you will need to undertake some research to help you identify and locate the high density English or German, for example, expatriate market you wish to service.

Checking Demographics

Establishing specific Spanish demographics is not as difficult as it sounds. The Spanish government's National Institute of Statistics (*Instituto Nacional Estadística*) publishes annually a distribution record of the (properly registered!) population residing throughout Spain. This can be found on www.ine.es. From this (which is also in English), you can see not only how many people live in a given area, but also their nationality.

So, for example, if you looked up Gandia (in Valencia province), you would find the following demographics:

Population of Gandia	79,958
Foreigners (*extranjeros*)	20,840

Foreigners are then broken down into respective countries. For example:

From EU countries	9,876

Of these you would note that there are:

Germans	164
Britons	385
French	538
Italians	712

This is an exceptionally good way of researching an area on the basis of its demographics, if, for example, you want to avoid living among too many expatriates or if, for business purposes you need to locate near people of your own nationality or somewhere with a high density of non-Spanish people.

Once you have narrowed down a location it is time to start thinking about properties. In principle, this should be the easy bit – but is a process similar to treading your way through a minefield …

Basic Land Law

Before you start looking at individual properties, it is vital to realise how very different Spanish land law is from the UK's. The difference in the way that property has developed and is treated by the Spanish effectively defines:

- The type of property available to you
- The safety or danger of buying properties in certain locations
- The potential investment value of a property
- The resaleability of a property

By understanding Spanish land law through the following outline you will be able to buy safely – and thereby avoid many of the problems experienced by people when they move to Spain. Many of these problems are unnecessary and stem from ignorance or the naive belief that Spain and the UK share the same land law. In fact, Spanish land law is significantly different from the UK.

> *Do not think, for one moment, that Spanish and UK land law is the same*

The first matter to understand is that there are two *main* designations of land in Spain:

Urbanizado (Building) Land

This is land on which it is legal to build – subject to obtaining planning permission and abiding by the relevant regulations. This land will normally (but not always) have a complete infrastructure made up of roads with pavements and street lighting, mains water supply, mains drainage, mains electricity and landline telephones (generally with an ADSL facility). *Urbanizado* areas are clearly designated on the plans held by town halls and their designation is black or white – either an area of land is *urbanizado* or it is not.

However, it is critically important to know that *urbanizado* areas are not always *fully urbanizado*. This means that an *urbanizado* area may not have *all* its proper infrastructure in place.

So, for example, an *urbanizado* area (particularly on some estates) may have electricity, mains water and *some* of the roads made up with street lighting and pavements. Any missing elements of the infrastructure (such as, for example, where there are no pavements and street lighting) may at some stage be rectified by the local authority. If this occurs, the owners of the property on the relevant part of the *urbanizado* estate (*urbanización*) will have to pay for completion of the remaining works i.e. the installation of mains drainage or the surfacing of the roads or the installation of proper pavements and street lighting.

> *Always try to buy only a property that is classified as urbanizado and, preferably, fully urbanizado*

The safest property purchase in Spain is on land that is *fully urbanizado*. If this is the case then you should face no further liabilities for infrastructure costs nor face any possibility of land grab.

The signs that a property is *urbanizado* (and fully *urbanizado)* (subject to confirmation from your lawyer) are when the property has:

- Mains water
- Mains electricity
- Telephone landline
- Mains drainage

- A properly laid road
- Pavements
- Street lighting

If your intended property lacks any of the above then it is highly unlikely that it is both *urbanizado* and *fully urbanizado* – so be extremely wary if you are assured otherwise!

Normally all cities, towns and villages are *urbanizado,* as are some, but by no means all, housing estates (*urbanizaciónes*).

Rural Land
(also known as rústico or no urbanizable)

This is almost all land not included in the above. *Rural* land is essentially agricultural land and makes up the vast majority of land in Spain. However, at any time some part of it may be re-designated as *urbanizado*. This can happen anywhere, but is most likely to occur in areas with high development potential, such as those near the coast or, perhaps, near to a booming town or village.

If an area of land is redesignated as *urbanizado,* all the liabilities and benefits inherent in the redesignation of the land occur. This redesignation of the land can be fantastically advantageous, make little real difference or be disastrous – depending on the extent of your land, your finances, the cost and extent of the work required, and the execution of the infrastructure project.

> *Be extremely wary of buying property that is classified as Rural*

Existing properties located on *rural* land need to be treated with exceptional care. They may be legal, partly legal or completely illegal. Equally, at any time, they may be subject to a change of designation.

Subject to obtaining the correct planning permission and abiding by strict regulations (such as the size of the property allowed), you can build a new property on *rural* land. However, this normally requires you to have a significant plot of agricultural land – although the regulations on this depend very greatly upon the given Spanish region (*comunidad*). Furthermore, the law changes frequently, which means that you must always check carefully with a lawyer the precise regulations in force (in your particular region) before buying anything.

Currently, as an example (though there are various exceptions), you would need some 10,000 m² of land in the Comunidad de Valencian before you could build legally.

Land Grab and The Redesignation of Land

The impact of land being redesignated from *rural* to *urbanizado* can be drastic. So, any buyer or owner of property in Spain should be wary if there is a possibility that the land could be reclassified. He will face a certain and significant liability as he is required to contribute money towards the new infrastructure works – and he may lose some (occasionally a lot) of his land. This, in essence, is what land grab is all about!

These infrastructure works may involve the widening of roads and will certainly include the surfacing of roads – together with the installation of mains water, sewage, electricity and landline telephones. Pavements and street lighting will also be installed. Land may be compulsorily purchased ('land grabbed') should it be considered necessary to, for example, widen a road or to provide leisure or other community use facilities.

Be aware that any rural property can be reclassified, at any time, as urbanizado and will then be liable to significant costs and, possibly, tremendous disruptions

The cost of *urbanización* works can be considerable. The work is chargeable on the basis of how much land a person owns within the relevant area to be urbanised. In effect, the local authority will divide the total cost of the intended infrastructure works by the m^2 of the entire land to be urbanised. This will then provide a cost per m^2.

So, let's say the cost per m^2 of the infrastructure works is €40 per m^2. If you own 1,000 m^2 within the area to be urbanised, you will have to contribute €40,000 to the *urbanización* costs. Similarly, if you have 1,500 m^2 you will have to pay €60,000; if you have 5,000 m^2 then €200,000 ...

Unfortunately, the implications of *urbanización* do not necessarily end with this cost. If for example, a road on the boundary of your property is widened, part of your land will be taken by the local authority, even if this is where, say, your swimming pool. Though your *urbanización* cost will be reduced as a consequence of losing some of your land, the reduction is unlikely to compensate you for the loss of part, or all, of your swimming pool. Equally, the reduction may not cover the reconstruction of your boundary – perhaps an expensive stretch of walling.

If the roads around a property do not have pavements and street lighting, the area has almost certainly not been urbanised

41

Almost certainly, you will also have to incur further expense to be able to make use of the new infrastructure to your property. The local authority will ensure that the new mains water supply, mains drainage and electrical supply are brought to your boundary, but they will not connect these to your house. So, potentially you will be faced with the considerable expense of installing and connecting all the relevant pipe work. Should this need to go across an existing terrace or driveway (or maybe to another side of your property), the cost and disruption could be significant.

On the face of it, it seems grossly unfair for a property owner to have to pay for these infrastructural costs and the ancillary expenses. However, that can be too simplistic a way of looking at the matter. Often the original owners had built their houses illegally or on non-designated building land and therefore on agricultural land that was almost valueless. Accordingly, the actual cost of their property was only the *build* cost – rather than the build cost *and* the cost of a legal building plot. Of course, almost by definition, professional architect and licence fees were usually avoided too!

In UK terms, the original building of the property is equivalent to a landowner building a new house on, for example, his paddock area without planning permission – and despite it not being designated as a building plot. The offending property would be demolished quickly by the local authority and the owner liable for any associated costs. However, in Spain, for various reasons, a blind eye was (and sometimes still is!) turned.

Very roughly, the equation for an identical property (one built on *urbano* land and one on *rural* land) could be stated as follows:

Property built on 1,000m² of rural land:

Plot cost (possibly nothing), but say	€6,000
Build cost (approx)	€100,000
Total cost of property	**€106,000**

Property built on 1,000 m² of legal building (urbanizado) land:

Plot cost (approx)	€100,000
Build cost	€100,000
License and professional fees (approx)	€10,000
Total cost of property	**€210,000**

The percentage cost differential to anyone building in the UK may be somewhat similar. However, whichever way you look at it, the person who builds on non-designated land gains a property at about half the cost of someone who has had to pay for a legal building plot. He may not have all the accompanying infrastructure, but he has managed to build a home for much less than the market rate.

The Spanish government therefore takes the view that the owner of the illegally built property must pay for the effective 'legalisation' of his property. Needless to say, the original owner of the property may have sold his house to someone else (you!) before any *urbanización* project has taken place. In that case, the current owner pays for the *urbanización* costs!

Ironically, the owner of a property built on *rural* land can still benefit from being urbanised, despite the costs imposed upon him. So, following the example above:

Property built on 1,000m² of rural land:

Plot cost	€6,000
Build cost	€100,000
Urbanización cost (approx)	€40,000
Total cost of property	**€146,000**

Thus, the 'illegal' owner has still managed to save some €64,000 (despite paying €40,000 in *urbanización* costs) plus he has a property that has a full infrastructure and has been legalised. Better still, the property's value will have increased considerably together with its saleability.

Land Reclassification Benefits and Dangers

Understanding the classification of Spanish property prior to buying is of the utmost importance. If you know what you are buying, you should be under no illusions about the safety of the purchase. You (or preferably your lawyer) must always check the current designation of a property well before you buy it. Indeed, this is so vital that you should insist that your lawyer provides written confirmation of the designation of your intended property so that you have perfect clarification.

Unfortunately, one of the problems with *rural* properties is that it is impossible for anyone (a lawyer or otherwise) to know for sure if, or when, a *rural* area will have its designation changed to *urbanizado*. There may be an existing published urban plan (*plan parcial*), of course. However, even if it is the case that no obvious intention or indication of redesignation exists, this should not be taken to mean that, sometime in the future (tomorrow or in 10 years time!), an *urbanización* project will not occur. So, if you buy a property that is classified as *rural* you buy always into an element of uncertainty.

To some extent you can use logic and common sense to reduce the uncertainty factor. For example, if your proposed property is in the middle of the countryside (the *campo*) with nothing much around it, the chances of redesignation and any *urbanización* project are normally very slight. However, buy a property in the middle of a cluster of other properties or near a 'growth' area and the chances are probably high.

Appreciate that, in principle, any rural land could be redesignated at any time as urbanizado

As mentioned earlier, the redesignation of land from *rural* to *urbanizado* is by no means all bad news. Indeed, there is a reasonable chance that many people owning properties on *rural* land attend church several times a week to pray that their land will be urbanised. There are two reasons for this:

- **Modernisation of infrastructure:** Lack of mains electricity, mains water and a landline telephone with ADSL makes life difficult in the modern age. When this is combined with dirt tracks, septic tanks and unsafe and unlit surrounding areas improvement to the infrastructure is naturally desirable. As mentioned earlier, *urbanización* also increases the value of a property (generally well above the cost of the infrastructure works) and usually, its 'saleability'.

- **Development potential:** The redesignation of land from *rural* to *urbanizado* means that the land becomes 'building' land – subject, of course, to all normal planning constraints. So, if you have a plot of *rural* land that is less than the minimum size allowable to build upon (say 10,000 m² in Valencia), you will now be able to build legally upon it.

Of course, if you have a large plot then you may be allowed to build *several* properties on the land once it has been designated as *urbanizado*. In effect, your land now has an intrinsic value that far exceeds its previous worth – which may have been little more than the value of its agricultural production. If this is the case, the infrastructure costs will be (relatively) minor when compared with the potential profit you can earn from a development project – or from selling the land as building plots.

Imagine you own 6,000m^2 of *rural* land. The value of this as agricultural land may be (say) €6,000 per 1,000m^2 i.e. a total market worth of €36,000. However, this changes radically should the land be urbanised.

For example, if building plots in your general area are worth around €100,000 per 1,000m^2 and your land is urbanised then:

Your 6,000m^2 of land (6,000m^2 x €100,000) will become worth:	€600,000
You will have to pay *urbanización* fees Of (say) €40 per m^2 x 6,000m^2:	€240,000
New net value of land	€360,000
Less previous value	€36,000

Potential profit   €324,000

Clearly, the equation above is dependent upon many variables, including how much of the land is seized by the local authority. Also, much depends upon the saleability of building plots and the prices those achieve within a given area. This value may vary considerably, depending upon market conditions and other factors.

Equally, the value of *rural* land itself can vary greatly. This is particularly true if the owners of the land concerned are aware that their land may be urbanised. In this case they may value their land on the basis of an *urbanización* project occurring and therefore far in excess of any purely 'agricultural' value.

Nonetheless, the equation above shows the potential 'positive' impact of *urbanización* on an owner of *rural* land. However, it also shows, of course, why there has been so much corruption in Spain – and the huge stakes involved for landowners should an *urbanización* project involving their land take place!

Indeed, the figures above show only a profit on the sale of the new legal plots to those wanting to build. Imagine the potential profit should the landowner turn developer on his *own* land. This could turn him into a millionaire many times over – when only a short time before he was a poor farmer eking out a living from orange groves ...

Obviously, whatever the size of your *rural* plot, you have to be able to afford the infrastructure cost should a redesignation of your land occur. If you have stretched yourself to buy your property, and perhaps have a mortgage, the *urbanización* costs may be simply unaffordable. However, they must be paid (albeit normally in installments) and if you cannot pay them you will have to sell your property, or a part of it. This has been a problem for many North Europeans who hadn't expected or been advised that their property – right from the very start – had potentially significant liabilities.

> *The cost to you of an urbanización project, in principle, depends upon how much land you own – the more you have, the greater the cost*

In reality, the most dangerous situation is when you don't have enough land to sell on for development – or when you have paid too much for your property in the first place. You may, for example, have mistakenly paid an *urbanizado* price for a property that should have been bought for a much lower *rural* value. (Again, the latter would have taken into account the lack of infrastructure and the potential of an *urbanización* cost.)

For example, if you have 2,000m² or more of land, often the bank will provide a loan to pay for your *urbanización* costs on the basis of you being able to sell your excess land for building plots. However, if you have a property on your existing plot of only 1,000m², it is unlikely that you will have enough spare land to sell for development. In which case, a bank is unlikely to lend you the money.

Without doubt, you should be very wary of becoming involved in an *urbanización* project or buying somewhere that could be urbanised. This is not something to be taken lightly, even if it might be very profitable in the long run. The projects are run by the local authority, the tendering process is sometimes dubious, the costs high, and the execution of the works occasionally appalling. Indeed, sometimes the infrastructure works can take an astonishingly long time with poor communication between the different agencies involved, such as the electricity, water and telephone providers.

Often an *urbanización* project can seriously blight a property until completion. If, as often happens, the project takes a year or more, (I have known it take seven!) it can be extremely frustrating should you wish to sell or rent your property – or just enjoy your long dreamed of tranquil, Mediterranean life. Considerable mess is created as roads are widened and pipes are laid and the process, like any major construction, is both noisy and extremely disruptive.

The Coastal Law (Ley de Costas) and Beachfront Properties

The Coastal Law was passed in 1988 and is a 'Damocles sword' hanging over many coastal properties which have been built too close to the sea. In fact, in 1988, the Spanish government nationalised the first part of the coastline after the sea's edge. In theory, this was probably a good idea. It protected the immediate coastline for ecological reasons and provided an absolute right of access for the general public to the sea.

However, the Ley de Costas has been very erratically enforced since it was passed. As a consequence, thousands of properties (mostly blocks of apartments) have been built along the Spanish coasts that clearly breach the Coastal Law. In many cases, despite the transgression being blatantly obvious, no action by the relevant authorities has been taken. It is these potentially dangerous properties that you must avoid and that lie waiting for the unwary buyer.

The Spanish coastal law 'divides' the coastline into two areas of protection.

The first area is the public domain which is crudely the area between the sea and the furthest point at which the sea has touched the land in the worst known storm. This includes all areas of sand, shale and pebbles and is an area in which no building is allowed.

The second area of protection is divided into:

- The Protection Zone. This is the first hundred metres inland from the public domain (although this area can be extended a further hundred metres by the Spanish state, autonomous region or local town hall). No building of any nature whatsover is allowed within this area.

- The Zone of Influence. This area extends for 400 metres inland from the Protection Zone. Building is allowed – however restrictions are applied on a reducing scale of severity as you move inland from the sea.

Obviously, some properties in Spain were built within 100 metres of the sea prior to the Ley de Costas being passed. These can be subject to a 'concession' meaning that they can avoid demolision. However, any 'concession' must be treated with the very greatest possible care and should be subject to expert, independent, advice (in writing) from a specialist in Spanish land law.

Certainly, it would be an error to think that just because little action has been taken so far on properties subject to the Spanish coastal law – that no further action will be ever taken. Equally, just because a building happens to be a block of flats it does not mean that it does not transgress the Coastal Law. Indeed, as always with Spanish property, it does not follow that just because something is in existence and standing (however gig it may be) that it is legal!

In reality, so many properties breach the Coastal Law that any serious attempt to enforce the law would probably be politically unacceptable. Indeed, it would result in the ruin of Spain's reputation as somewhere safe in which to buy property and the Spanish themselves, who own tens of thousands of holiday flats, would make any enforcement virtually impossible.

However, the law exists and until it is revoked you need to know about it and to treat it as if it could be enforced. So, be extremely wary of buying a flat (or any other type of property) located very close to the sea shore.

Indeed, if you want to buy a front line beach property (they are always desirable) then make sure that your conveyancing lawyer specifically checks its legality with regard to the Coastal Law. Importantly, get any advice provided by your lawyer placed in writing and, if you have any doubts, then either obtain a second opinion or look for another property elsewhere.

Finally, many expatriates seem to believe that planning regulations and building controls do not exist in Spain or that, if they do, they can be ignored. This is a serious error – albeit one that is sometimes shared by the Spanish themselves, who, in the countryside, appear to do pretty much whatever they want. This includes not just altering and extending their properties, but also building new ones illegally.

In fact, Spain probably has as many planning constraints, regulations and controls as the UK. Keep this uppermost in your mind if you intend doing any work on a property or wish to buy a property that appears to have had significant alterations. You must always check with your local authority whether you can alter or build anything and whether any alterations have been correctly licensed. Almost invariably you will require an architect to alter the structure or distribution of your property or to extend it. A minor works license, at the very least, will be needed even for general improvements.

> *Always check with a lawyer, architect or*
> *surveyor whether you need a license for any*
> *proposed building work*

Often North Europeans think that, because they are in a Mediterranean country, they can behave differently from the way they would in their own countries. However, though the enforcement of regulations in Spain can be somewhat tardy, there is almost always a day of reckoning – often when a property owner tries to sell his property, as it is at this stage that any illegal works come to light. This can result in a fine, endanger a sale, and possibly, result in an order to reverse the work done.

The Nature of Spanish Housing

Spain can be a somewhat frustrating place in which to find your ideal property for long-term relocation. This is partly because the classic British dream is often a type of property that rarely exists in Mediterranean Spain.

For many, their perfect home would be a Spanish version of an English vicarage with a large garden, a swimming pool and perhaps a few acres of land. The sea would be accessible from the property and the house only a few minutes' gentle walk to a pretty, Andalusian type of village. Meanwhile, the house itself would be full of flowing arches, spacious rooms and an inner courtyard with trickling fountains. Unfortunately, this sort of property is extremely difficult to find – at any price.

Traditional Land Use

Traditionally, land use in Spain has been very different from that of the UK and has resulted in a property market quite different to that found in Northern Europe. There are few *quality* old properties, particularly in Mediterranean Spain. Indeed, most villas have been built within the past 30 years on relatively small plots. These villas tend to be fairly uniform in style and located on formal estates that are often situated on steep hillsides several kilometres from the nearest village.

Appreciate that, historically, land use in Mediterranean Spain has been very different from that of much of Northern Europe

Finding an individual, fully legal, dream property close to a village and beside some unspoilt coastline, or even within the countryside itself, is therefore nothing if not difficult. Indeed, it is quite hard not to find yourself buying a property that is a compromise on what you would really like. Much of this has to do with the way that Spain has developed over the ages. Accordingly, there is little point in trying to track down properties that never existed in the first place. That does not mean that there are not superb properties in Spain – merely that they might be different to what you expect.

To state the obvious, in the UK if we have land we have always tended to live on it. If we have a farm or smallholding, our home will be situated firmly on that land – and we would never consider living elsewhere. It is equally true to say that almost every house, even in major cities, has traditionally had a garden (often a small one in the front and a larger one to the rear).

In Spain, this has generally not been the case. Indeed, the Spanish have tended to live in their villages and *gone out* to their land to farm it. As we shall see, this has immense significance for land along and near the Mediterranean coastline.

Modern Development

Until around 30 years ago, there were very few lone properties in the Spanish countryside. A comparable area in the UK would have a profusion of properties – whether farmhouses, workers' cottages, smallholdings or great estates. But the Spanish countryside consists of acres of farmland in which islands of habitation (the villages and market towns) can be found. The only notable exceptions were some landowners' mansions (*masias*, *pazos*, *caserios* or *cortijos*), which stood outside villages and housed the local notable and his workers.

Within the villages there were (and often still are, in the centres) a 'rabbit warren' of townhouses, few of which had more than a tiny ground floor and a rear courtyard. To the householders of these small towns, lack of a garden mattered not at all, as they invariably owned land of some sort outside their village and could go to it should they so wish. Being a largely agricultural nation, most people worked on the land and considered a garden superfluous.

However, the population of Spain more than doubled between 1900 and 2000 and during this period, many people moved into the towns, where industrialisation provided employment and, for some, more income than agriculture ever had. In the towns, most of the 'new' housing comprised flats, which were cheap to build and, initially, an improvement on the old townhouses.

By the end of the Franco dictatorship in 1975, the majority of the Spanish population were based in the towns and cities with the remaining people living as they always had, in villages and old townhouses. There were still very few lone properties in the countryside. To some extent this suited the Spanish – who are a gregarious people by nature and whose countryside is often harsh.

However, after the death of Franco, Spain experienced a surge of wealth. EU money poured into the country and Spain's cheap rates of labour made it a compelling place for the manufacture of goods for the rest of Europe. At the same time, mass tourism was developing rapidly and bringing considerable income to the population in the coastal regions.

Illegal Building in the Countryside

One of the things the urban Spanish started to do as they accumulated spare money was to build summer houses (*casitas*) and some 'starter' homes. These were constructed on the plots of agricultural land, outside their towns and villages, that they or their family still owned. Initially, many of these buildings started off as little more than storerooms (*trasteros*) for tools, tractors, tables and chairs, and barbecue equipment. Gradually, bedrooms and a bathroom were added, together with a small kitchen, a reception area and a roofed, open-sided terrace (a *naya*).

Normally, these *casitas* were bungalows, though some mimicked more conventional two-storey homes. Of course, what the majority of these properties had in common was that they were built 'illegally'. As a consequence, they often lacked electricity, a telephone landline and mains drainage. A water supply was normally obtained from the agricultural irrigation system and much of the actual building was undertaken without the supervision of architects or any building control. Indeed, the construction work was often 'self-build' and thus properties were often devoid of damp-proofing, any logical internal distribution, insulation or central heating.

For the most part, it didn't matter to the owners that their *casitas* were poorly built. Nor did they mind that the *casitas* had to be accessed via rough dirt tracks. The properties, after all, were never meant to be anything other than family weekend residences or places to stay over the summer. Certainly, most were never intended nor designed as permanent homes or as properties to sell on the marketplace.

Over time, clusters of *casitas* developed on the outskirts of towns and villages. In many cases, these clusters became estates of sometimes a hundred properties or more – and most lacking infrastructure. There are many examples of these 'estates' today, although sometimes the properties have gained mains electricity and, occasionally, landline or satellite telephones. Nonetheless, the roads in the area tend to be unofficial (and often, single lane) and lack pavements, mains drainage and proper lighting.

For the first time, the Spanish Mediterranean countryside had a scattering of properties. These properties, to incoming North Europeans, appeared to be villas or country homes roughly similar to those in their own countries. Indeed, some of these properties even had swimming pools. This 'luxury' item (almost always illegal, or a converted water deposit) deceived many North Europeans into thinking they were looking at high-quality, fully legal properties..

Worse still, because many of these 'estates' had grown up illegally, they were, almost by definition, liable to be urbanised'. By doing this, local authorities recognised the cluster of houses as an 'estate', but required it to have a modern infrastructure. This is absolutely right.

Until they are urbanised, these properties are rarely suitable for long-term living. Most North Europeans expect at least mains electricity, mains water and a landline telephone capable of taking ADSL. The trouble is, these properties, during the glorious sunshine of summer, can appear like viable permanent homes to the unwitting. This perception has been frequently exploited by ruthless agents (and others involved in real estate), who have assured potential buyers that these houses were well-constructed, long-term homes.

Furthermore, potential buyers were often told that a telephone line was an easy thing to obtain or that mains electricity would be connected soon. Of course, little or nothing was said about the likelihood of the area being urbanised – let alone that the buyer would have to pay substantial costs and perhaps lose some of his land!

As a consequence, many North Europeans bought properties for far too high a price despite the possibility of an (often very necessary) *urbanización* project, as the sale price should have been discounted to allow for the potential *urbanización* costs and attendant disruption.

In some more notorious cases, properties have been constructed in protected areas and national parks. Agents have even boasted of the fact that the area around intended property could 'never be built upon'. Of course, the unwitting (and stupid) buyers often did not realise (until far too late) that they could never carry out any work on their *own* property, as it sat in parkland! Worse still, this was a property unlikely to ever obtain a modern infrastructure, however much the owner was prepared to pay.

To add insult to injury, many zones populated by illegal *rústico* properties are prone to seasonal flooding. This is of concern to the Spanish authorities as the properties are downright dangerous. Some properties have been built also on a low-quality substrate such as expandable clay – often ignoring the rather wise decision situate the nearby village over an area of stable bedrock.

New Estates

Meanwhile, the obvious lack of adequate detached housing (both in terms of quantity and quality) for relocating North Europeans kickstarted the development of modern (generally, fully *urbano* and *urbanizado)* estates along the Mediterranean coast of Spain. Some of these date back to the early 1980s but many are more recent and a direct result of the building boom between the late 1990s and 2007.

Many of these new housing estates (*urbanizaciónes)* were built almost exclusively for relocating North Europeans and were constructed close to the coast and/or near existing villages and towns. Almost invariably, the new estates were built on marginal land, many on hillsides overlooking the sea. The estates vary considerably, with some housing high-quality, luxury villas right through to single-storey, two bedroom villas and new townhouses; some estates have a mixture of all types of modern housing.

A classic Mediterranean estate will contain new villas (i.e. built within the past 20 years) that comprise three bedrooms and two bathrooms, a kitchen, lounge, *naya* and a swimming pool – all on a plot of around 850m². To some extent these properties deliver a version of the North European retirement dream, as often they possess fine views of the sea, are low maintenance and have clean, modern lines. Normally (but not always!), they have mains electricity, mains water, mains drainage, landline telephones and well-surfaced roads with pavements and street lighting. In other words, a modern infrastructure little different from that of any estate in the UK. At the entrance to the estate there is often a restaurant and perhaps a few shops and estate administration or sales office.

New estates have also been built primarily for holiday-makers and those wishing to have second homes. These developments are often based around a golf course and can comprise a combination of flats, maisonettes and townhouses with centralised swimming pools, restaurants and, sometimes, shops. Some of these developments are close to the coast, but a surprising number are half an hour's drive (or more) away.

The landscape surrounding some of these new estates can be desert-like, with little natural greenery, extreme heat during the summer and a clay substrate. Worse still, some recent developments remain without their promised communal facilities (like shops and restaurants) and the reality can be far from the impression given in original sales material. Although some developments are complete, occupied, and functioning as planned, others have been affected by the economic crisis – and any incomplete construction may remain thus for many years to come.

The main problem with many new estates is that they are devoid of native Spanish life and culture. Indeed, many estates are effectively high concentrations of North Europeans. Some estates are largely composed of just Germans, just Dutch, or just British and so on.

To some extent, these 'artificial' environments can work well in providing relocating nationals with an immediate and easily accessible community of their compatriots. Often a Spanish infrastructure used to dealing with foreigners has developed nearby. Indeed, a working knowledge of English among Spanish shopkeepers, tradesmen, professionals and banks is common and can help greatly during the first year or so of adjusting to living in Spain.

Native Spanish Market

During the past 10 years or so, the Spanish have also built property for themselves. Indeed, the flood of poor immigrants into the country provided a market into which the Spanish could sell their old flats. This they did with alacrity and with a view to upgrading to modern, well-equipped flats and new semi-detached houses (*adosados*). Both have been built in incredible numbers around virtually every village and town in Spain. This has been complemented by the development of brand-new shopping malls on the edges of most large towns and cities and (often very optimistically) extensive new industrial estates.

Coastal Properties

The Spanish have also built extensively along the Mediterranean coastline, both for themselves and for holidaying North Europeans. For many years there seemed to be a simply limitless demand for coastal flats. This demand came initially from North Europeans whose increased wealth over the late 1990s and beyond made the purchase of a holiday flat viable.

However, the Spanish are as keen on beach holidays as North Europeans and tend to share the dream of owning a holiday flat on the coast, and with similar fervour. The economic strength experienced by Spain over the preceding 15 years meant the Spanish had sufficient wealth to buy their own holiday apartments – which further stimulated the building of vast numbers of flats (some illegal!) along the coastal regions.

Summary

The property market in Spain is nothing if not complicated. It has been subject to massive change and astonishing growth over the past few years. This has resulted in a wide selection of properties becoming available. Some building has been illegal and some properties have a build quality that is very poor indeed. There are also properties that have potentially serious future liabilities – and others that are sound in every regard and completely safe to buy.

In short, the Spanish property market must be treated with great care – especially if you are to buy a property that will be not only suitable for long-term living, but also a secure investment. As always, the best test of the wisdom of buying a property is whether it is easily resaleable. However, as we've already seen, this is something that is not always obvious!

Types of Spanish Property

Adosado

Adosados are modern, terraced houses that can normally be found on the outskirts of Spanish cities, towns and villages. Usually, they have a ground floor area that acts as a garage/storage area. The main accommodation is generally on the first and second floors with the kitchen, a bathroom and living room (with a balcony/terrace) on the first floor and the bedrooms (three or more) and any extra bathrooms on the second floor. The properties are often light and attractive inside – however outside space is frequently limited to a roof terrace or small courtyard. Occasionally, a line of *adosados* will have a community swimming pool.

Note: This type of Spanish property is a great advance on old townhouses, though lack individual character and often have little usable outside space – making an al fresco lifestyle wellnigh impossible. *Adosados* also tend to appear soulless and uniform and many lack nearby shops, bars and restaurants.

Adosados are normally *urbanizado* and fully *urbanizado*.

Apartamento

This is a flat on the beachfront and should not be confused with a *piso* (see below), although the construction can be almost identical. *Apartamentos* can vary considerably, depending on when they were built, but most new ones will have three bedrooms, two bathrooms, a kitchen (sometimes American style), reception room, small hallway and a balcony.

Note: *Apartamentos* are meant for holidays and generally do not have central heating, although they often have air conditioning (hot and cold). Be aware that in winter, the surrounding amenities may close and some holiday blocks are almost completely deserted out of season. The most desirable *apartamentos* are those on the beachfront with uninterrupted sea views.

Apartamentos are normally *urbanizado* and fully *urbanizado*.

Casa de Pueblo

This is a townhouse, one of the most common forms of property in Spain. These are invariably very old (sometimes hundreds of years old), terraced houses with almost no outside space. *Casas de pueblo* vary from tiny, single- fronted properties to astonishingly large, double-fronted houses with interior garages and ground floor courtyards at the rear. Occasionally, *casas de pueblo* have gardens and, very rarely, a swimming pool.

Note: To reform a *casa de pueblo* can be a huge commitment and many builders 'demolish' the interior and effectively reconstruct the house that they are modernising. Generally, all the services within an older townhouse need replacing and sometimes light needs to be introduced into houses that are naturally dark. Parking can also be a major problem and you should be wary of buying a *casa de pueblo* unless it has a useable garage (or a dedicated parking place) and a decent-sized, ground floor courtyard.

Casas de pueblo are normally *urbanizado* and fully *urbanizado.*

Casita

This is often a single-storey property that was erected as a summer house by its Spanish owner. Most *casitas* are pretty basic and often were constructed without an architect. Sometimes they are DIY builds. They generally comprise a small kitchen, three or four small bedrooms and a bathroom – all leading off from the reception room. Normally, the front door leads straight into the reception room (i.e. there is no hallway) and outside of that is an open-sided *naya* with a roof. Gardens can vary greatly in size and may amount to several thousand metres squared land.

Note: Unless a *casita* has been substantially renovated, it will lack central heating, damp-proofing and thermal insulation of the walls. This type of property may also be illegal or subject to a future *urbanisación* project.

Furthermore, *casitas* may lack mains electricity and landline telephones – neither of which may be possible to obtain until an *urbanisación* project has been completed. Water may also not be on mains supply (*agua potable*). A *casita* may have a swimming pool – but make sure this is not just a reformed water *deposito,* which usually lacks a pump and filter system and may be illegal. Often *casitas* are accessed through unofficial roads without pavements and street lighting.

Another important consideration with regard to *casitas* (and *villas*) is that you must look very carefully at how the property is situated in relation to winter sun. If the *casita* is situated close to hills or within a mountainous area it may be in the shade during the winter – sometimes for long and sustained periods. This can be devastating because you lose the effects of the sun when most you need them.

Casitas are often neither *urbanizado* nor fully *urbanizado*.

Duplex

This is a flat on two floors, often on the top floors of a block of flats. The duplex can be a beach *apartamento* or *piso* but is normally intended for year-round living. Duplexes are generally very desirable and can be luxurious. Often they have a very large roof terrace.

Note: As ever, the location of the block of flats will be vital

– so look to buy where there is activity all year round.

Duplexes are *normally urbanizado* and fully *urbanizado*.

Finca

This is a farmhouse, normally with land attached. This type of property is usually very old and, unless it has been renovated, may need serious work to modernise it. Like most old buildings, *fincas* are a compromise between charm and constant maintenance. Good, reasonably priced *fincas* near coastal Spain are surprisingly hard to find and, once renovated, fetch excellent prices. Note that the term *finca* can also be used to denote a block of flats.

Note: Due to their age, *fincas* are normally legal, although you should check this, together with the legality of any new alterations or additions, carefully. Equally, just because your *finca* is in the middle of the countryside does not mean you can avoid obtaining permission to undertake alterations. These will obviously have to comply with area *normas* and regulations.

Fincas can sometimes prove awkward to buy from Spanish owners, as many members of a family may have rights to the property or a part of it. Be aware of the possibility of *urbanisación* projects – although these can sometimes be to your advantage financially.

Fincas are normally not *urbanizado* or fully *urbanizado.*

MASIA in Valencia or Cataluña, *PAZO* in Galicia, *CASERIO* in País Vasco, *CORTIJO* in Andalucía

Any of the above terms refers to country mansions, generally with many outbuildings. These were the homes of major landowners and often have landscaped grounds and impressive entrance driveways. This sort of property can be vast and sometimes has 30 to 40 rooms.

Note: Older *masias* in their original state will invariably require terrific amounts of renovation and will absorb huge amounts of money. However, they can be ideal for converting to hotels or residential centres.

Masias tend not to be *urbanizado* and fully *urbanizado*.

Parcela

This refers to any piece of land, whether built upon or not. So, your villa may stand on a *parcela* of 800m^2 or you may wish to see some 100,000 m^2 of *parcela* on which to farm.

Note: Always make sure you know the designation of any *parcela* you wish to buy. You may, for example, be considering a *parcela* for agricultural use and find subsequently that it is protected (*protegido*) and commercial usage forbidden. Equally, be careful to check the validity of any promised water rights.

Piso

A *piso* is a permanently lived-in flat (as opposed to a holiday flat). They come in all shapes and sizes, from tiny studio flats to 200m^2 luxury homes. They are found in all villages, towns and cities. Not all have lifts, and avoid the ones that don't, as they are difficult to resell.

Note: *Pisos* can be very noisy because the sound proofing of blocks of flats in Spain is often insufficient. Also, before buying a *piso*, check the maintenance/communal costs, as these can vary considerably. Equally, try only to buy one that is south facing, is on a quiet, wide road, and has both a large light well and dedicated parking (this is usually in the basement and is absolutely essential).

Pisos are normally *urbanizado* and fully *urbanizado*.

Solar

This is a term used for a plot of land (*parcela*) that has proper planning permission for building. This will be subject to all existing regulations and norms.

Note: If you intend to buy a *solar*, it is vital that you or your lawyer double-check exactly what you can build on the plot. There are many coefficients and regulations that restrict building and development – just as in the UK. So, whereas you might be thinking of constructing two three-storey houses, you may be restricted to one, or perhaps one that has a maximum of two floors and a limited habitable volume. Of course, some *parcelas* may not be big enough to permit the building of a dwelling at all.

Solar, by definition, is *urbanizado* and is always fully *urbanizado*.

Villa (Chalet)

A villa is a substantial property that has been built and designed for year-round living. It is a detached house, sometimes on three floors, and often has a swimming pool. Normally, it has been built within the past 30 years, although many were constructed over the past 10 years or so, during the Spanish property boom. The quality and size of villas varies considerably, although the basic specification tends to be: three bedrooms, two bathrooms, kitchen, reception room, covered terrace, garage (or dedicated parking) and 8m x 4m swimming pool. Many villas also have an under build area that can (subject to proper licensing) be developed into further accommodation.

Note: Wherever possible, make sure that you buy a villa that is *urbano* and fully *urbanizado* and always use a surveyor to check the property – particularly if it is on a hillside. Villas on steep plots need particular care to ensure that their foundations were correctly laid. Depending on local regulations, use of the under build as accommodation may be illegal so be sure to check that first.

Note: Many villas are already built up to the permissible limit of living (habitable) space – so that any further legal extension or conversion may be impossible. Do not take it for granted that you can enclose a terrace or convert an under build into accommodation.

It is also worth noting that some high-density developments utilise a loophole in the law, whereby each house owns a percentage share of a communal plot. This is effectively a twist on the '*ley horizontal*', a planning law intended to apply to flats (which are normally freehold in Spain). However, some developers use this law to build small villas (i.e. villas on 500m² plots) in zones where the minimum legal plot size may be (for example, often in the Valencian region) 850m². This way a developer can achieve perhaps four houses on 2000m² where normally he may have been able to build only two. This practice is somewhat questionable as it is, to some extent, an abuse of what the planning restrictions were designed to achieve. Many buyers of these properties actually have no idea that they only own a horizontal percentage share of their large communal plot – rather than the plot within what appears to be their own boundary.

It is a good idea to go for villas that stand on flat plots and are without stairs going up to the entrance. If, or when, you come to sell your villa, your market will likely expatriate – in which case your buyer is probably going to be of retirement age. Most elderly people are reluctant to buy properties that are on many different levels and that are in any way physically demanding.

See the notes above with regard to *casitas* and winter sun. As villas are often built on hillsides, lack of sun in the winter can be an unexpected drawback – one that you are unlikely either to recognise or think about when viewing properties during the summer.

Any swimming pool should be investigated carefully. It should have a pump and filtration system *in working order*. Pay particular attention to any pool that is not full (this almost invariably indicates a problem) or if there are any structural cracks in the pool or on the terrace surrounding it. A building survey will normally include a visual check of the pool structure – however you should instruct your surveyor expressly to check the swimming pool. Pools can be expensive to rectify if the problems are significant!

Villas are sometimes *urbanizado* and sometimes *urbano* and *fully urbanizado*.

Choosing Your Property

Choosing the right property is vital. However, in Spain, this is not just about ensuring that your future home has adequate accommodation and is 'pretty', your 'dream', or somewhere with which you have 'fallen in love'. These are important aspects, but far more important is whether your proposed property is:

- Legal
- Transparent (with regard to any potential liabilities)
- Easily resaleable

Legal

As mentioned earlier, there are many shades of legality in Spain with regard to property. Some properties are fully legal, others have gained 'rights' and yet others are completely illegal (or, at the very least, have an illegal element to them). At first sight, it can be difficult to tell where your proposed property lies on the scale.

For example, a villa may be *urbanizado* and *fully urbanizado* and yet still be illegal because, say, the under build has been developed into habitable accommodation and the property now exceeds the maximum living space allowed on the plot. Unfortunately, illegality does not rest just with villas and *casitas*. Townhouses (old and new) can be illegal, as can whole blocks of flats (for example, if they have been built too close to the shoreline).

> *Never, ever, buy an illegal property,*
> *no matter how tempting!*

Establishing legality is not a simple matter. It is not just about seeing or reading through the deeds (*escritura*) of a property or looking at the *catastro* – even if you are fluent in Spanish. Assessing the true status of a property – as in the UK – requires the attention of a first-class, independent and experienced lawyer who specialises in conveyancing. On no account should you avoid using a lawyer. This may seem obvious, but it is astonishing how many North Europeans do not use a lawyer – or when they do use a lawyer, choose one who is not:

- Independent
- A specialist in conveyancing
- Fluent in their language

Transparent

As we saw earlier, there are sometimes very good reasons for buying a property that may have future liabilities. You may make a fortune or you may find your property considerably improved at a cost that makes great sense. Equally, just because a property is classed as *rural* does not mean that you should not buy it. There are some excellent properties on *rural* land that will provide you with a wonderful life and also prove to be sound, long-term investments.

Importantly, however, the value of a property that is *rural* is normally considerably less than its *urbanizado* equivalent. As a rough rule of thumb, a *rural* property might realistically be worth only one half to two thirds the value of the same sized property that is *urbanizado*.

Never buy a property until you know every potential liability

However, you must know always what, if any, liabilities are attendant. Once you know the worst-case scenario, it is your call whether or not to go ahead with your purchase. But never, ever buy into a property or piece of land, however much you like it, unless you know every possible implication.

Nota Simple

One of the ways of quickly establishing reasonably reliable information on a given property is to obtain its *nota simple*. You can do this by going online and buying one for around €10 *(www.registradores.org/principal/indexx.jsp).*

Alternatively, you can ask your lawyer to obtain it and advise you of the contents. The latter option is best as *Notas Simples* are not always quite as conclusive as they seem.

A *nota simple* is a certificate issued by the Property Registry (*Registro de Propiedad*) and describes the specific property requested. The information provided will include:

- The name and identification number of the owner
- The boundaries of the property
- The total land mass (m²) of the property and, critically, any existing buildings
- The classification of the property (*urbanizado* or *rural)*
- Any information on charges and encumbrances on the property, such as mortgages (*hipotecas*), life interests (*usufructos*), rights of way and so on.

All of this is critical information. After all, you need to know that the person you *think* owns the property actually does (the *nota simple* is normally taken as conclusive proof of ownership). Equally, you need to know the extent of what you are buying and its exact classification (*urbanizado* or *rural*).

Obviously it is also important to know early on whether any buildings on your intended property have been properly registered. If they are not mentioned on the *nota simple*, they are almost certainly illegal! Finally, being forewarned about debts is important as some debts are fixed to the property rather than to the owner! In that case, you or your lawyer must not forget to have these debts cleared before signing an *escritura*.

You should note that every single property in Spain is registered with the Land Registry – irrespective of whether it is *rural* or *urbanizado*. Indeed, every property has an address, even if it only amounts to *parcela* 121 of X town. So, never let a property be palmed off to you by someone saying it is not on the registry! This is a warning that something is very wrong …

However, bear in mind that a *nota simple* is not always up to date – not least because it is not obligatory to register an *escritura* with the Land Registry. Equally, classification of land can be out of date – for example, if a property has been recently reclassified as *urbanizado* and the town hall concerned has not yet advised the Land Registry. Similarly, the Land Registry might not be aware yet of a court order regarding the property or current owner. So, do not dispense with your lawyer just because the *nota simple* appears to show a problem-free property. This would be looking at Spanish property legalities in far too simplistic a way.

That said, *Notas Simples* are important documents and by obtaining one quickly you can save a good deal of time that might otherwise have been wasted. Certainly, applying for a *nota simple* is the first action a Spanish buyer is likely to take once he has identified a property that interests him.

To apply for the *nota simple* of a property, some basic information is required. At the very least, you will need the name and identity number (*DNI* or *NIE*) of the owner and/or the full address of the property. It is also preferable to have the Land Registry code. This is always in the *escritura* (deeds) and provides the location of the property details in the Registry.

Resaleable

No one can guarantee your relocation will be successful. Moving is always a risk and never more so than when it is abroad. Despite all your careful preparation, life in Spain simply may not suit you. Alternatively, some other matter may arise that means you have no choice but to move – whether back to the UK or elsewhere. An unexpected grandchild may be born, you may have financial problems, fall out with your partner, or a serious illness may befall you or a member of your family.

It is therefore vital to buy a property with an exit strategy in mind. This must revolve principally around the potential for easy resale. Indeed, it is a cardinal rule that you must buy only a property that is easy to resell. Always compromise on what you want if it means the difference between being able to sell easily or not.

Only buy a property that is easily resaleable

Ensuring that a property is legal, and establishing any potential liabilities, are comparatively simple and can be achieved through an excellent conveyancing lawyer. However, establishing whether a property will be easily resaleable is a different matter altogether. Certainly, it is not a matter in which you can expect much help. When it comes to assessing resaleability, real estate agents are rarely impartial and lawyers are neither qualified nor generally willing to comment on this. So, any assessment will need to be done by you – and you alone.

Fortunately, there are guidelines that any industry insider or professional developer abides by, and that will help you become aware of the necessary elements almost instinctively. The problem is that, in the excitement of finding a potentially viable property, it is hard to be dispassionate. This is true particularly when you are in Spain. The great weather and lovely ambience have a tendency to distract even the most naturally analytical mind. Furthermore, the very idea of reselling is usually the last thing on your mind when you are about to buy a property!

However, if ever you need to be controlled and 'North European', it is when assessing a property for resaleability. It is this facet more than any other that will determine whether you have made a good investment or not.

Like any marketplace, the property market is driven by supply and demand. The more demand there is for a given type of property, the greater its saleability, value and potential for capital growth. If, however, you buy into a property where there is a restricted demand, or an over-supply, you are making a poor investment and one difficult to liquidate quickly. If, for some reason, the market deteriorates, you may find yourself stuck in limbo as your beloved property becomes almost impossible to sell and declines dramatically in value.

The key to buying property is therefore to establish, before you buy, what the general marketplace wants – and then to buy a property that will appeal to as many people as possible within that marketplace. Of course, there are different criteria for different properties. The criteria for buying a studio flat in the middle of a city have little to do with those of a luxury villa – albeit that the overall approach to the assessment is much the same.

Villas, justifiably, tend to be the most sought after type of property for relocating North Europeans. For this reason, we will use the villa as an example of the way to assess resaleability.

So, what does the market desire, irrespective of budget, when it comes to villas? In fact, there is no secret and the requirements of most people relocating are remarkably similar. They tend to want:

- A detached villa that is low maintenance (and therefore either new or in good order)
- Three bedrooms (minimum)
- Two bathrooms (including an en-suite)
- A swimming pool
- A reasonably sized (1,000m^2–2,000m^2), flat plot
- A decent view (preferably of the sea)

And sometimes, to live no further than 15 minutes from the sea and no more than an hour from an international airport.

Note that the above criteria do not include subjective preferences like the property being 'attractive', 'individual' or, perhaps, having a particular 'character'. These factors have not been included because one person's preferences are rarely those of another!

There are good reasons for all the above criteria – most of which are obvious. Three bedrooms tends to be the minimum required by most people, while an en-suite bathroom has become a common expectation over the past few years. A swimming pool, of course, is the dream of all North Europeans!

For the vast majority of people, Spain is all about the Mediterranean coastline. Indeed, mention 'Spain' and 'Mediterranean' is the first thing that will come to most people's minds – just as 'islands' are to Greece and 'gourmet food' to France. Being close to the sea in Spain is therefore a common requirement (and often, a specific demand) for the majority of North Europeans.

> *Know the marketplace and what*
> *the majority of buyers want*

A flat plot is considered desirable (and is surprisingly hard to find!) by many North Europeans of retirement age. Accordingly, they are either looking to the years ahead when they will be less fit or already suffer from bad backs or knees, or a disability. The last thing they want is to live on a steep plot with many steps and levels – let alone a property with many floors. Furthermore, older people often have young grandchildren who need a safe area in which to play. An area in which the swimming pool is easily visible, accessible and preferably also securely enclosed.

Most people also want a plot of a reasonable size that has some privacy, a decent garden and sufficient area in which to enjoy to the full the al fresco life of Spain.

Finally, proximity to an international airport (preferably one that offers cheap flights) is always important. It makes visits from family easy to manage and return visits to the UK convenient.

You would think that to buy a Spanish villa with the above criteria would be simple. The professionals within the market know what is wanted and therefore, surely, such villas will have been constructed?

The opposite is true. Poor planning, lack of thought and sheer greed on the part of many developers has resulted in villas that rarely combine all of the above components.

Yet, every missing criterion reduces the saleability of your intended villa – unless there is some other remarkable aspect to the place.

> *Only buy a property after you have visited it at night, during the day and at weekends*

One way of ensuring resaleability is to identify potential obstacles and benefits of a given property and give them values. From this you can gauge the potential impact these would have in the marketplace. This is a crude but surprisingly effective way of concentrating the mind. This is, of course, educated guesswork, but well worth undertaking.

Imagine that you are looking at a villa that is legal, *urbano* and *fully urbanizado*. It has two bedrooms, two bathrooms and a swimming pool. It has a decent-sized plot, but is on a steep hillside. The swimming pool and terrace are below the main structure of the villa. The villa has dedicated parking, but the front door is reached via half a dozen steps. The villa is reached by a road that winds its way up through the estate. The villa has terrific views of the sea. In short, it is a somewhat typical example of the small villas found on many estates.

If we presuppose that 100% of the marketplace (subject to budget and price) would buy our original then look what happens to the one described above:

The Negatives
- The existence of only **two bedrooms** is likely to be unattractive to many people and certainly to anyone with grandchildren (as there is no way of accommodating adult children and grandchildren at the same time).

  Possible minus of potential buyers: 40%

- **Steep plot** with steps down to the villa entrance. This would not be welcomed by anyone disabled, a bit 'creaky' or wary of old age approaching. Equally, not popular with grandparents who have young grandchildren.

Possible minus of potential buyers: 25%

- **A swimming pool** on a terrace at the base of the villa. Inconvenient – and a worry if small children are likely to be around.

  Possible minus of potential buyers: 10%

- **A winding road** up the estate to the villa will be unattractive to drivers who lack confidence (such as the elderly) and will prove inconvenient for daily life.

  Possible minus of potential buyers: 10%

A total of 85% of buyers may be put off this property on the basis of the above factors.

The Positives
- **A stunning sea view**

  Possible plus of potential buyers: 20%

So, 85% negatives less a 20% positive = **65% negatives**.

Therefore, 65% of the potential marketplace will be unlikely to buy this property. This means, at best, only a minority of all potential buyers within this property's price bracket.

Of course, if the villa was not *urbano* or *fully urbanizado*, lacked a landline telephone, or had no ADSL or mains electricity, the percentage of potential buyers would drop radically. In that case only a fool would buy the property from you. Obviously, fools exist but they are unfortunately often in short supply when you need them most!

Obviously, this is a rather clumsy and unscientific way of looking at 'risk management'. However, it has the benefit of common sense.

> *Look carefully at the property and ask yourself:*
> *what obstacles exist that would prevent other*
> *people from buying it?*

Let's take the same approach with a townhouse (*casa de pueblo*). Often these are bought by North Europeans who realise too late that fundamental flaws make the houses unsuitable for full-time living, despite their considerable charm and their being a superb base from which to integrate into a Spanish community.

Imagine a three-storey townhouse that has been well renovated and has three to four bedrooms and a couple of bathrooms. It has a large reception area and a fair-sized kitchen as well as a tiny patio to the rear of the house and a roof terrace. There is no garage or space in which a car could be parked easily. The road to the townhouse is a narrow one-way road. In other words, we have here a somewhat typical old village townhouse.

The Negatives

- **No parking**. This is a massive disadvantage and over a period of time can drive you to utter despair.

  Possible minus of potential buyers: 30%

- **No real outside space**. Roof terraces can be discounted, as they are inconvenient and feel a lot like a frying pan as soon as the sun shines. Conversely, a small ground floor patio rarely gets sun, particularly when it is overshadowed by neighbouring properties. This hardly presents the opportunity to live the al fresco life and thus will put off most North Europeans.

  Possible minus of potential buyers: 20%

- **Three floors**. This will not appeal to anyone elderly or with very young children.

Possible minus of potential buyers: 20%

- **A narrow, single lane street**. This will result in a house being almost perpetually dark and cold in the winter with access by car to the property often problematic.

Possible minus of potential buyers: 25%

- **Noisy**. Living in the middle of a Spanish village is nothing if not noisy both due to traffic (cars and motorbikes) and the late-night lifestyle.

Possible minus of 10%.

A total of 105% of buyers may be put off by the above factors. Indeed, this explains why the Spanish themselves have moved out of these properties and into *adosados*.

The Positives

- **Convenience** of living and accessibility to Spanish community life. The latter can be tremendously enriching. Not having to drive everywhere is user-friendly, cheaper and more pleasant.

Possible plus of 25%

- Good chance of **resaleability** to native Spanish or non-North Europeans who naturally choose (and often prefer) to be in a town or village. As a consequence, the native Spanish market is much bigger than any expatriate market and therefore a major re-sale advantage.

Possible plus of 25%

So, 105% negatives less 50% positives = **55% negatives**

Again, this is a rough figure (and I might have been over-generous!) Of course, what a transformation should the townhouse be situated on a wider road and have dedicated parking or a large, easily accessible garage! If this was combined with a decent courtyard, or garden, saleability is positively transformed. Indeed, townhouses like this are highly sought after by both native Spanish and North European buyers and, sadly, are therefore expensive and difficult to find.

Don't buy a property until you're expert enough to guess the price, give or take, to within 10%

Finally, it is always a sound idea to buy a property that will appeal to buyers from more than one target market. Generally speaking, when relocating a North European will buy a property (normally a villa of some kind) on an estate that is composed mainly of their compatriots and that has few, if any, Spanish residents. This means that a successful sale is reliant upon the health of a particular overseas market.

There have been two recent examples of the danger of relying on a specific foreign market. The first was in the early 2000s, when the German government launched a general tax investigation into German nationals with assets in Spain. This triggered a bout of selling on 'German' coastal estates in Spain by those who could no longer afford to own a second home or who tried to quickly liquidise their assets. This was a classic case of more supply than demand – and prices on these estates, as you can imagine, dropped radically.

The second example was when the value of sterling collapsed by around one third against the euro in 2008/9. British pensioners were particularly hard hit and suddenly found Spain expensive as the purchasing power of their pensions was greatly reduced.

As a result, many Britons (including non-pensioners)

decided they had no option but to sell their properties and return to the UK. This meant that the prices of property on 'British' estates collapsed (this was not helped by the world credit crunch).

Of course, the weaker sterling also affected incoming British buyers. In 2004, £200,000 (at £1,45 to the euro) bought a property worth €290,000. In 2009 (at £1.01 to the euro), the same amount of cash could buy you a property worth around €202,000 – a colossal difference of some €88,000!

Ironically, despite the drop in Spanish property prices, the weak sterling meant that British buyers still found properties in Spain expensive – so sellers on 'British' estates found that, despite dropping their prices radically, it was still difficult to sell to their compatriots. Effectively, this created a downward vortex as sellers drop their prices continually, in desperation, to tempt buyers from their narrow marketplace.

The point is that it is not a wise move to buy on an estate or in an area that is largely or exclusively populated by one foreign nationality. Doing so instantly limits potential buyers should you wish to sell – and you enter a dangerously artificial and volatile market.

Certainly, it is fair to say that few Britons will willingly buy on an estate that is, for example, almost exclusively Dutch or German any more than a Spaniard will buy on an estate that is mostly British. In a perfect world, of course, you should buy on an estate that is largely Spanish owned but has a healthy mix of different nationalities! But that can be very hard to find …

Finding Your Property

At some stage, you will have to get your hands dirty and look at individual properties in detail. For many people this is the exciting part of the relocating process. However, it can quickly dominate their every action and thought – and sometimes produce a dangerous momentum of its own.

Obviously few things will be more important to you than finding your dream house, but you must never lose your objectivity or become obsessed by a particular property to the exclusion of all else. This happens frequently and it is easy to lose perspective as to the purpose of your move. If ever there was a time to be careful and controlled, it is when you start looking seriously at individual properties. Relocating, after all, is about improving your quality of life – not just about buying a bigger or better property than you have now.

There are a number of tools available to you in your search for the right property:

- The Internet
- Estate agents
- Relocation agents
- *Urbanización* (estate) management agencies
- Banks
- Auctions
- *Se Vende* signs
- Advertisements
- Leafleting
- Networking

The Internet

Most people start to look for properties on the internet. A profusion of websites display Spanish properties for sale, while many Spanish lifestyle sites have links to property pages. Researching these sites can be invaluable in assessing what is on the market in your price range. The sites can also give you an idea of what particular areas are like and the type of lifestyle they offer.

Property websites tend to be divided broadly into four types:

Property web portals

These websites showcase a vast number of properties throughout Spain. The properties are listed by individuals, developers and estate agents, all of whom pay a fee to list their properties. Some websites, like Idealista.com, can have as many as 250,000–300,000 properties for sale at any given time. Other examples are Fotocasa.com, www.girasol.com and kyero.com. These types of websites are great if you want further information on a given property as they link you straight to the owner, agent or developer concerned.

Estate agents' and developers' websites

There are tens of thousands of individual websites, some with thousands of Spanish properties for sale and others with just a few hundred, or less. These tend to be specific in location though the detail of the content may vary widely. Any enquiries you make about a property will go directly to the agent or developer who has listed it.

These websites can be found through doing a search (for example on Google) using as specific keywords as possible, such as 'villas Villalonga La Safor Spain' or 'townhouses Fuengirola Costa de Sol'. A little practice and perseverance will result in many websites for the area that most interests you. It is then a case of narrowing down the websites to ones that provide you with the best possible information.

Information websites

These websites principally specialise in providing information on Spain and can be very useful. Sometimes the sites are professional: other times they are the pastime or hobby of the person concerned. They provide information regarding life in Spain as well as forthcoming events, established and new clubs and associations, details of various areas (sometimes very localised). Often these websites will have forums and blogs on a wide variety of topics – and most have a link to property for sale or a selection of their own properties for sale. Examples of some highly regarded sites are:

- www.thisisspain.com
- www.propertyinsightspain.com
- www.practicalspain.com
- www.eyeonspain.com
- www.olivepress.com
- www.costablancauncovered.com

Private websites

It is becoming more and more common for sellers to put up a website purely for their own property. This gives you direct contact with the owner and therefore you may by benefit from a sale price that is not inflated by an estate agent's commission. However, these websites are rarely well optimised by their creators and finding them can be difficult (often they are only found via some form of conventional advertisement or link that directs you to the website).

The Internet is great for property research, but far from perfect a means of accessing *reliable* information. Anything you read, particularly when it involves property, must be treated with considerable caution. The property industry is a 'big money' industry, with high stakes for all involved, whether real estate agents, developers, banks, currency transfer companies, or relocation agencies. As a consequence, much of the information online is far from impartial. Be sure to double-check every reference you come across, whether this concerns location descriptions or sale pricing. The latter can vary considerably for the same property from one website to the next!

Obviously owners, developers and agents try to make the very best of any property they have for sale. So, a property may be photographed beautifully (and with great care) and described in glowing terms when in reality it is utterly dismal. This is hard to tell from looking at a website.

The internet is often ineffective at showing the area immediately surrounding a property. The house concerned may appear spectacular but sit beside a rubbish dump, or be located in an ugly area, or in a community that is disruptive or unwelcoming. When using the Internet, bear in mind that only the best bits of the property are shown.

Information on websites, blogs and forums varies widely in quality and reliability, and there is rarely an effective way to filter it. So, be wary of taking any information, whether about a property or something else, as Gospel until you have checked it through several different sources.

Looking at properties on the internet can become something of an obsession. Don't let this cloud the more important research needed to ensure that the overall area is suitable.

Estate Agents

The estate agency industry in Spain can be, understandably, confusing to the North European. There are conventional estate agencies that have fixed locations and offices on urban high streets. Other agents work from home or combine estate agency with another job such as running a bed and breakfast, shop, bar or even, a newspaper. Meanwhile, there are 'runners' (*corredores*) who specialise in finding property for sale for agents, but at times act on their own account.

Some agents are qualified and registered (those shown as *API*) and others are not. Some provide a superb service and with high integrity (qualified or not); others cannot be trusted in any way at all and should be avoided at all costs. Some firms have a mix or multilingual staff, whether Spanish, British, German, Dutch, French, Russian or Chinese.

The only consistency is the bad name that the industry has among both the native Spanish and foreigners. This should not take away from the excellent work of some in the industry. However, most estate agents need to be approached with the greatest of caution if you are to avoid being ripped off.

> *Understand how estate agents in Spain operate before you start looking for property and doing business with them*

Spanish estate agency differs markedly from that of Northern Europe. For example, the relationship between the estate agent, seller and buyer is blurred. While the seller clearly pays the agent, it is with the buyer that an agent is most likely to form a close relationship. However, the complications of buying abroad and the extensive pre- and after-sales care that a foreign buyer expects have direct implications upon the commission charged by agents. This enormously time-consuming work justifies fees, within reason, that would be considered high in Northern Europe.

In Spain, furthermore, most sellers place their properties with as many agents as they can, without signing any agreement to safeguard the interests of an agent (not even for a short time period). Consequently, agents are left to market and sell properties on a multiple agency basis and face perhaps a dozen, or more, local competitors. This makes the marketing of a property a hazardous and potentially expensive process for the agent.

Sales commission for an agent tends to be worked out on the basis of one of three options:

Fixed-rate commission

The most common and least contentious way of charging commission is for an agent to agree with a seller on a fixed commission. Depending upon the area, this might be somewhere between 3% and 10% of the gross sale price of the property – though it can sometimes amount to as much as 18%.

Sold for above a set amount

Here a seller agrees to pay the agent anything over and above the agreed minimum sale price. So, a seller may state to his agent that he wants €200,000 for his property. An agent will then be at liberty to set a sale price at any figure above the €200,000 and that he feels he can achieve. He may market the property for €250,000. If he finds a buyer prepared to pay this, he will receive €50,000 as his sales commission. This option has caused a good deal of contention, particularly when buyers (that could be you!) have found out they (effectively) paid a significant amount of the property 'value' as an agent's commission.

In many ways, earning commission this way can be compared to any other business deal. The seller is happy because he obtains the price he wanted. The agent treats the transaction as a business deal in which he extracts the maximum profit possible. And you, as the buyer, must be content as you have willingly parted with your money! On the face of it, this option is fair. However there are problems that have made this practice notorious.

Firstly, sellers often rely on agents to act in good faith when providing property valuations. If an agent deliberately undervalues a property, he can earn an inflated commission, which is unfair to the seller. Secondly, the size of commission can artificially inflate the true value of a property. This leaves a sour taste in the mouth of the buyer, who may well have been relying upon 'his' friendly agent to act as an 'honest broker' –dispensing sound advice on the true merits and value of a given property. Thirdly, the same property may be on the market for wildly varying prices, depending on where you look.

Never confuse an estate agent's 'friendship' and what is a business relationship based upon profit. You are his client and he is the deal broker

Combination: Seller's commission and buyer's premium

Sometimes an agent will charge both a buyer *and* a seller a commission. For example, an agent may agree with a seller that he will receive a commission of 3% should he sell the house. However, at the same time, an agent makes an agreement with the buyer (maybe you!) that you will pay him 3% of the sale price of any property you buy through him. In this event, the agent will earn a commission of 6% on any property he sells to you.

Buyer's premiums are quite common and are accepted, to some extent, by the Spanish. In some of the big cities, locals are used to paying around 1.5% of the sale price to their agent and the seller paying a similar amount.

The trouble is that this system has been frequently abused by agents dealing with unwitting North Europeans. The latter are sometimes asked to sign a document (occasionally presented in poor English!) stating that, once shown a property by the agent, they will only buy the property through that agent. This is an uncontentious agreement.

However, often within the same document is a clause stating that if you buy a property shown to you by the agent, you must pay him or her a fee of x amount (effectively the buyer's premium) of the purchase price. As most people do not read this document through carefully (or have problems with the poor English), they do not realise the importance of what they have signed.

Never, under any circumstances whatsoever, sign a document without your lawyer present

Ruthless agents rarely advise a buyer of the full implications of this type of contract. Indeed, without exception, everyone that I have met who has paid a buyer's premium did not realise they had to pay the agent until *after* they had paid a non-returnable 10% deposit on the property they wished to buy! Only then did their agent point out that they also owed him a fee. This can be a horrific experience – particularly if you have been balancing budgets carefully and then find you must pay your agent thousands of euros!

Some types of properties consistently earn agents exceptional fees. These are generally new development properties, particularly those aimed strictly at overseas buyers. These are frequently places that are built on cheap land, creating an artificial environment far from towns and villages, and that may suffer from water shortages. A developer may, for example, construct a golf course and swimming pool complex in this sort of area and surround it with apartments.

By their very nature, properties within these developments can be difficult and expensive to sell – and indeed, very hard to resell. Estate agents use pressure salesmanship to earn commissions that can sometimes exceed 18% of the gross sale price – a property will have to appreciate substantially before you, as a buyer, have any hope of a return on your investment.

Sheer logic dictates that if properties are easy to sell, no owner or developer needs to offer huge commissions to ensure their sale! The more genuine demand there is for a product, the easier it is to sell and the more a seller will begrudge paying an unnecessarily high commission to any salesman. In short, it is worth always trying to find out the commission being paid by a seller to the agent, as this will give an indication of the desirability (and resaleability) of the property!

However, none of the above should take away from the value of estate agents. Indeed, a good agent can make a tremendous difference to the success of your move. Not only will an agent be able to competently show you properties and explain their benefits and detriments, he will be able to put them into perspective for a given area. He will also be able to advise you (to some degree) of the implications of buying a particular type of property and whether the valuation of that property is fair or not.

> *Make certain that a significant proportion of your purchase price is not an estate agent's commission*

Usually an experienced agent also has considerable local knowledge and contacts that can prove invaluable – both for your move and during your first, vulnerable months in Spain. Indeed, a good agent can be a linchpin in the process of relocating. Normally, they know reliable builders, removals companies, garages, tradesmen and professionals – along with how best to work through the local infrastructure.

Agents dealing with international clients often provide what amounts to a relocation service. Some will help you obtain your *NIE* (Spanish fiscal number) and *SIP* card (Spanish national health card) and assist you in placing your children at a school. Translating is frequently undertaken as part of their service together with acting as a factotum on a wide range of day to day problems.Of course, the level of service between agents varies widely. At their best, agents can be lifesavers and many provide an exceptional service in the hope that you will recommend them to friends and relatives thinking of moving to Spain. This may seem self-interested, but, if it costs nothing and results in valuable assistance, this is well worth having.

Certainly, most people need help. This is as true of the time before you buy as when you move into your new home. Unless you have a friend or some family already living in your chosen area then, one way or another, you will need someone to lean on – even if only for the first few months. The best of agencies provide this magnificently and some have dedicated staff to supply a complimentary after-care service to buyers.

Of course, and understandably, any agent is primarily motivated by making a sale. However, choosing an estate agent who will provide you with real assistance beyond that is critical. As critical, in fact, as not using an agent that is a self-serving, unreliable crook!

Without doubt, the best way of choosing an estate agent is through personal recommendation – preferably from several different people. This is easy to suggest, but hard for you to ensure when you are living a thousand miles away from your intended destination.

However, there are some indicators of an agent's worth.

Before you come to Spain:

- A clear, informative website
- Rapid and articulate responses to e-mail and telephone enquiries
- Helpful, accurate and authoritative ancillary information
- A good selection of different properties
- A willingness to listen to you and to develop a clear specification
- Transparency as to pre-purchase and after-care charges. Normally (but not always) help and support are free

In Spain:

- Good timekeeping and organisation
- Patience
- A sound knowledge of Spanish land law
- Transparency about sales commissions
- Obvious in-depth knowledge of the relevant area
- A good knowledge of his properties and the details of those he shows
- No set agenda that could indicate commission-led prejudices
- No hard sell techniques
- Reasonable Spanish (if not a Spanish native)

There are also some guidelines with regard to agents that should be broken only at your peril:

- Never sign *anything* unless you have shown the document to a lawyer.
- Be wary of buyers' premiums or anything that purports to make you (as a buyer) liable to your estate agent for purchase fees.
- Never finalise any form of purchase agreement without your lawyer present.

- Never be rushed or pressurised – it is better to lose an excellent property than to buy a disaster.
- Always, always double-check, with an independent source, whatever you are told.
- Never confuse your relationship with your agent during the buying process. This is not about friendship, just work – however well you seem to get on.
- If you discover your agent being deliberately inaccurate or evasive, walk away and never return to him.
- Be especially wary of any agent who tries to discourage you from having a structural survey or from consulting your own independent lawyer.

Finally, do not forget to use native Spanish agents and to visit their offices and showrooms. Normally, these are scattered around any town or city with Spanish agents operating largely the same way as North European agents. They can deliver a thoroughly professional level of service. Indeed, many Spanish agents in coastal areas employ North Europeans or have English, Dutch or German speakers who are used to dealing with relocating foreigners.

Relocation Agents

Relocation agents are different from estate agents in that helping to purchase a property is only part of their overall service. Relocation agents normally do not list properties nor have them for sale themselves – although often these lines are blurred in reality.

As a rule, a relocation agent will charge you an advance fee. The agent will then provide advice as to how and where to relocate, as well as assist you with the process. The agent will assist in the negotiation of the purchase, any liaison with and choice of lawyers and surveyors, and any associated financial requirements.

Without doubt, competent and effective relocation agents

can be invaluable. They can be useful particularly for people who are inexperienced in moving, relocating or operating in foreign countries. Equally, if your own time is short, a relocating agent can maximise the free time you *do* have available. At best, relocation agents in Spain are time-served professionals who know the country intimately. This means they can help to translate your desires into reality and find you somewhere that is both suitable and safe. This, when it works well, is a wonderful service and can cut short a good deal of time, energy and cost.

However, relocation agents are not always quite as objective as they seem. They often collaborate with real estate agents, making a deal whereby they earn a proportion (sometimes 50%) of the sales commission earned by the estate agent. This is normal. However, bear in mind that commissions vary throughout the country and depending on the type of property.

For example, in the northern Costa Blanca, sales commissions can average around 3% while commissions further south average 5% or more. As seen above, some developers offer up to 18% commission on some new development properties. So, there is an obvious danger that your relocation agent may have a vested interest and direct you to a property that will provide a higher commission to him than others on the market.

Certainly, it takes little to manipulate a potential buyer away from a certain property or area. A few well-placed doubts (an area is 'unfriendly' or has 'a reputation for poor building') are enough to put anyone off. Your agent may well be right – but always be a little suspicious if he is reluctant, or obstructive, when it comes to taking you to a property or area that you are keen to see.

It is therefore always best to combine independent professional advice with that provided by your relocation agent. Truly impartial in-house service is rare, particularly given the high sales commissions available on some properties in Spain. Certainly, there is no replacement for a reputable and independent surveyor or lawyer, who will not have a vested interest.

As with any business arrangement, it is vital to ensure that you know all the implications of an agreement before you sign it. So, make sure that you read carefully any contract with your relocation agent. Indeed, it is wise to show a copy to your lawyer before signing it so that he can confirm that the execution of the agreement will deliver what you want and that there are no hidden charges.

Urbanización (estate) management

Many new estates (*urbanizaciónes*) have a management office that is responsible for the administration of the estate. Often these are the offices of the principal developer of the estate and used to be (and sometimes still are) their sales office. These are normally manned by an administrator or supervisor (*conserje*) who, on international estates, often speaks English. His office is usually at the entrance to the *urbanización* and close to where there is often a bar or a few shops.

Estate administrators tend to have an astute knowledge of what is for sale on their estate. Apart from dealing with administrative matters, the estate office often has an ancillary maintenance department (garden and pool maintenance, changeovers and cleaning and so on) and sometimes a home security team. Invariably, the estate office has a network of contacts among the residents of the *urbanización*.

Not surprisingly, many sellers on estates automatically place their properties for sale with their local estate office. This is particularly true when the property concerned is a holiday home and one where any rentals are frequently administered by the estate office itself. The office, therefore, often has keys and can provide access to any property of interest to you.

Of course, estate offices work on a sales commission basis too. So, do not, for one moment, think that they are showing you a property out of the goodness of their hearts, as this would be very unlikely. Indeed, the sales commission charged by an estate office to the seller may be the same (and sometimes greater) than that of formal estate agents.

However, if you are seeking a property on a particular u*rbanización,* the administrator's office is worth visiting. Certainly, you are likely to be welcomed warmly – as you will represent a potential sales commission!

Se Vende Signs

In Spain, it is common for sellers to place their own *Se Vende* (For Sale) signs on their properties. These signs will normally display the owner's contact numbers and occasionally the number of an estate agent.

In fact, it is only when their own attempts fail that Spanish sellers are likely to approach an estate agent. Even then, they rarely agree to any sole agency agreement and will retain their own *Se Vende* sign in the hope of making a private sale and saving on an estate agent's commission. Increasingly, expatriate sellers now also often place their own *Se Vende* boards, sometimes with a note indicating that English or German is spoken.

Certainly, when the Spanish look for property they tend to drive around the area to which they want to move and contact directly any owners of properties for sale. This is a relatively efficient way of finding property and also has the added benefit of providing a buyer with immediate and direct contact with the seller himself. This can mean that, as a buyer, you may obtain an immediate discount on the property sale price as there will be no estate agent's sales commission.

There is nothing to stop you doing the same and contacting the owners of properties with *Se Vende* signs. Invariably sellers will show you their homes and make an effort to overcome any language difficulties. That said, life is made much easier if you employ someone as a translator – even if it is only for the time that you are looking around a given area.

Of course, there can be problems with going directly to the seller:

- Any language barrier can lead to mis-understandings and not all translators are effective or reliable.
- There may be a security issue if you are, for example, a woman on your own.
- You may lack the benefit of a professional agent able to advise you on the true merits of the property.
- It is not unknown for Spanish sellers to raise their price markedly when approached by a North European, who they often perceive to be both wealthy and naive.

Negotiating a sale without an agent can be extremely difficult, particularly if you do not speak the seller's language. This can be overcome by deferring to your lawyer, a friend (who is fluent or native) or a surveyor – but most will either charge you for this service or may not be very effective negotiators.

Finally, by no means do all properties for sale have a *Se Vende* board. So, you must never gauge what is for sale in a given area purely by the presence of *Se Vende* boards. If you do this, you may miss out on a raft of other properties for sale.

Advertisements

Of course, you can find countless properties through advertisements in newspapers, magazines and *guias* (small Spanish magazines). Both agents and owners place advertisements in a range of publications and these are well worth browsing through. Most areas throughout Spain also have an English-language newspaper (often free) and usually these are crammed with properties – as well as every other conceivable object, service and product – for sale.

Equally, there are normally a range of free Spanish magazines and *guias* (guides) that can be found in bars and outside shops and estate agencies. These are worth looking at, albeit the text will be invariably in Spanish. However, the critical parts to any property advertisement are normally easy to understand!

Of course, you can place an advertisement, stating that you are a buyer and explaining your preferences, in a newspaper or magazine local to the area that interests you. This can be very effective and can elicit a lot of response. In fact, you should avoid placing your telephone number on the advertisement and use just your e-mail address. This will allow you to filter the replies – many of which may come from estate agents (for better or worse) or from sellers offering properties that are inappropriate.

If you place an advertisement into a magazine or paper, be as specific as possible about what you want. State clearly the minimum number of bedrooms and bathrooms (an en-suite?), the reception rooms you want (a conservatory or office as well?), a garage (enclosed?), a swimming pool (what size?) and the type and size of plot (flat, mature, views of the sea, over 1,000m^2?). Also, ask the seller to state the exact location of the property together with its designation (*rustico, urbano, urbanizable,* fully *urbanizado)* and whether it has services such as fast internet access – if this is important to you. Finally, always state your maximum budget.

Leafleting

Leafleting can be both very effective and a lot less work than it might appear to be. It is useful particularly if you have found a specific area, such as an estate, where you want to live and yet find that you are struggling to obtain a suitable property there. Almost invariably at the entrance to any estate there will be a bar or restaurant with a notice board. Placing a leaflet on this (using the same guidelines as when placing an advertisement) can attract people who are thinking of selling but have yet to take the final decision. It can also bring into the open sellers who you or even local agents may have missed.

Networking

Networking can be invaluable – though it depends upon having some contacts within the area of interest. This is often more promising than it may seem, given the number of people who have moved from Northern Europe to Spain and the desire of many people to move near to friends or family.

There is normally a good reason for a property being underpriced. Establish why – before buying it

Most communities of foreigners in Spain tend to have a 'community' website or an e-mail contact list of people in their area. Information is often regularly circulated to the local expatriates on a range of subjects, whether a property for sale, a social or cultural event, potential work or a new service or product.

If you have a friend or contact in the area, it is an excellent idea to ask them to circulate an e-mail on your behalf to the local expatriate community. You may be surprised by the extent of the response and genuine help and advice that you receive.

Banks

One of the consequences of the 2008 property crash has been the inevitable repossession of properties by banks. Indeed, the depth of the economic crisis has meant that banks are effectively huge estate agents, albeit they own the properties they have for sale. This, of course, is not a business model that suits banks and it is common knowledge that they have to clear their stock of properties to restore their liquidity.

In Spain, many of the banks have their own estate agents. Other banks release repossessed properties directly onto the marketplace, sometimes in considerable numbers. For example, in early 2009 the Cam Bank was releasing some 500 properties onto the marketplace on a monthly basis. This was undertaken by supplying registered estate agents with these properties.

Obviously, the primary interest of the banks when they have repossessed a property is to get back the money owed to them. So, the prices of the repossessed properties may be low, even valued just at the outstanding debt, with perhaps an administrative fee.

However, a 'repossession' does not always indicate a bargain. If, for example, a 100% mortgage had been granted on a property during the boom, its redeemable value to the bank may be higher than that for other, similar properties on the market. Indeed, if similar properties have reduced in value since the boom (by say 20–30%), the repossessed property may have a debt that is higher than its current market value!

So, be careful not to become obsessed with bank repossession properties and be ruthless about negotiating any bank sale price. You should do this irrespective of claims that the price is really low because it is based 'only' on the bank's debt.

To get a genuine bargain for a repossessed property, you need to be able to move quickly. This is because often you will be competing against professional investors (corporate or otherwise) whose decision to buy will be on set investment criteria or formulae and allows investors to make decisions rapidly – at a time precisely when you should be at your most cautious.

> *It does not always follow that because a property is underpriced it is a good buy*

One of the potential advantages of buying a repossession property from a bank lies in the bank already having the property legalities and paperwork in place. This does not always follow though and you should still use an independent lawyer for any conveyancing.

Indeed, Spanish banks lent on property with dubious legality during the boom years and some of the most cavalier banks lent on deeply flawed properties. So, any purchase still needs exceptionally close investigation despite its appearance or claims to the contrary. Of course, most of the time these properties will be legal and have the added advantage of being easy to re-mortgage. However, take nothing for granted – irrespective of whether the seller is a bank or an individual!

The main problem, of course, will always be the temptation and pressure to act quickly and this is not something that you should ever do if you are moving to Spain for the first time. So, treat your own excitement at seeing a cheaply priced property with caution – otherwise you may buy a property for a marvellously low figure that is entirely wrong for you in the long term. Worse still, it may be something incredibly hard to resell …

Finally, these properties can be obtained by approaching the banks directly or through their estate agencies. Properties are also available through mainline estate agents who have been granted the right to sell the properties by given banks.

Auction Houses

Auction houses that sell properties exist in Spain but not to the same extent as in the UK, where every town tends to have an auction house. Furthermore, auctions are rarely used by the Spanish and therefore have not developed extensively. Attendance tends to be low and buyers are generally professionals. As a consequence, public auctions (particularly those run by the Spanish state ministries) are not for the inexperienced, let alone the first-time buyer of a property in Spain. Indeed, you must be very careful when buying at public auctions in Spain. Specifically, take care when dealing with auction staff as they have a reputation that is less than favourable!

There are some private auction houses scattered around Spain, although increasingly these are internet based. However, because auction attendance is poor, the properties for sale can be a a very limited cross-section of those for sale within the overall market. Equally, the sale prices of the properties are not always as low as would be expected.

Obviously, if you chose to use auctions, ensure that you have professional support at all times. This means employing both a first-class lawyer and surveyor to guide you through every stage of the process, whether in assessing the property or its legalities. Even then, as with any auction, you need to apply iron-like personal discipline to ensure you do not overbid on a given property.

Part Exchange

A result of the 2008 property crash has been the development of businesses offering part exchange properties: someone will offer their property, for example in Almeria, in exchange for a property in Marbella (or perhaps back in the UK). If there is a differential in price between the properties, the person with the higher priced property will be paid the difference by the other.

Part exchange can work. However, the sensitivity of location and the differentials in individual properties (let alone the subjectivity of people's tastes) can make this a cumbersome process. It is one way, of course, of relocating if you are unable to sell your property conventionally, but can be a bit like finding a needle in a haystack. The likelihood of finding a part exchange that really suits you is low. Indeed, the sheer sensitivity of finding the right long-term location means that for part exchange to work you will need to rely greatly upon luck.

The Property Professionals

Buying a property in Spain can be safe or dangerous. It is as simple as that. It all depends on how you go about buying your property. If you are careless and gullible, or uncontrolled, or operate in ignorance, the chances of encountering problems are high. However, if you are knowledgeable and use excellent industry professionals, purchasing a property should be safe and trouble free.

Three professionals lie at the core of buying property safely. To try to save money by not employing them is foolhardy in the extreme. Despite what anyone may say to the contrary, always, always use:

- A specialist conveyancing lawyer
- A building surveyor
- A notary

There is also a further line of protection that is worth considering, albeit ancillary:

- A reputable bank

Specialist Conveyancing Lawyer

It is essential that your lawyer fulfils *all* the following criteria and is:

- **A specialist in conveyancing**
  On no account should you use a lawyer who specialises in anything but conveyancing. Criminal law, litigation, commercial law or any other type of law are not appropriate. Your lawyer must be up to date and thoroughly conversant with property conveyancing and undertake this as his primary daily work.

Only use a professional fluent in your language when it concerns legal, medical or accountancy matters

- **Fluent in your language**

  It is essential that both you and your lawyer fully understand each other so that miscommunication – whether written, face to face, or on the telephone – cannot occur.

- **Independent**

  This is vital. On no account should you use a lawyer who is linked to your seller or estate agent. Equally, never fall into the trap of agreeing with a seller (sometimes a developer) who offers to get his conveyancing lawyer or legal department to also do your conveyancing, even if this is offered for free. If you suspect your lawyer has the slightest conflict of interest, walk away!

- **Fully registered and insured**

  Always make sure your potential lawyer has an insurance policy that is up to date and valid. It may feel embarrassing to ask for proof of this, but is nothing compared to the foolishness you will feel if your 'lawyer' proves to be either unqualified or uninsured.

- **Working from a formal office**

  All professional, full-time conveyancing lawyers will have an office. Be suspicious of any that do not or who work from temporary or inadequate premises.

Make certain that your lawyer understands that on no account will you allow him to act for both yourself and any seller

Make sure there is a coherent 'paper trail' showing what your lawyer has done and the advice he has provided. If his advice and actions are always in writing, this will ensure your lawyer is far more cautious about what he does and says. So:

- Obtain all quotes for work in writing. In fairness, the uncertain nature of conveyancing means that your lawyer will probably only provide a cost estimate. However, you should know beforehand what his hourly charges are and ensure that you are advised when any bill reaches an agreed initial limit.

- Get all important advice in writing. Make sure this is either on paper or in the form of an e-mail – and retain a copy.

- Always make sure that you receive from your lawyer a proper invoice that is correctly stamped, dated, numbered with an *NIE* or *CIF* number present. The invoice should state clearly what work it covers. Never pay your lawyer cash unless it is backed up by a written invoice – and make sure you keep a copy.

> *Never try to save money by opting out of using a lawyer for your conveyancing needs*

Without doubt, choosing your lawyer is important and justifies considerable time, effort and research. At the end of the day, it is your lawyer who will ensure that you know what you are buying and that all the legalities are in place. In short, the duty of a conveyancing lawyer in Spain is much the same as anywhere else in Europe. It is to ensure that you, as his client:

- Know exactly what you are buying
- Understand the implications of buying your particular property
- Obtain a clean and clear title to your property

The title of the property will need to be verified together with the right of the former owner to transfer it. Critically, the extent of the property buildings and boundaries will need to be carefully checked against the *catastro* and any rights or encumbrances will need to be investigated together with any outstanding or pending liabilities. A new deed (*escritura*) will need to be drawn up and the contents of this document agreed upon with the seller.

Unfortunately, the reputation of Spanish lawyers varies. Though there are some superb conveyancing lawyers who sparkle with integrity, competence and efficiency, others are careless, inexperienced and inefficient at best – and corrupt at worst.

Certainly, some agents have tended to recommend particular lawyers to clients depending upon the degree of legality or problems inherent in a given property. A lawyer with integrity is sometimes recommended to a buyer when a property is completely legal and problem free – while less 'objective' lawyers are recommended occasionally when properties have inherent problems.

> *Only use a lawyer who is registered and independent, speaks your language fluently and specialises in conveyancing*

Obviously, the best way of finding a quality lawyer is through the recommendation of others. However, avoid acting on the advice of a single person; rather use a lawyer held in high regard by a number of people. Recommendations can sometimes be found by visiting expatriate websites, blogs and forums or even expatriate bars in your intended area. Quite often, you will find the same lawyers spoken of time and again – whether those to avoid or those who have provided a consistently good service.

Finally, it is wise to sign a power of attorney (*poder notarial*). This is particularly important if you are living outside of Spain. Many actions require your signature and if you cannot provide this promptly, the process (for example, the contractual stages of buying a property) can be paralysed.

Obviously, it is always best to be personally present to authorise and sign any contract or deed. However, this is not always possible and can be obstructed by unexpected flight cancellations or illness. In this event, you may be unable to meet contractual commitments and may lose your property (and with it, any deposit). Accordingly, it is worth having a plan B in place.

Power of Attorney

Any power of attorney agreement has to be signed by you in front of a *notario* and, obviously, can empower (with some exceptions) any adult you choose to act for you. So, rather than your lawyer, you could appoint a trusted friend.

Obviously, you must be extremely careful about granting a power of attorney to anyone. These are extremely powerful documents and many actions taken under power of attorney cannot be undone. As a consequence, it is wise to ensure that:

- The person you appoint can only act upon receipt of written instructions from you. A good lawyer will insist on this as it prevents misunderstandings.

- You have the text of your power of attorney in both Spanish and English. This ensures you know exactly what you are signing before you go before a notary.

- The power of attorney expires after a certain time period.

A power of attorney is a very powerful document and you must only grant this to a totally trustworthy person

Power of attorney can be:

- General *or*

- Limited to a specific function (for example, the signing on your behalf of the *escritura* to your intended property)

Of course, working out the extent of the power that you grant is always something of a balancing act. Though limiting power to a specific function is often wise, it can sometimes be too restrictive.

Finally, note that you can revoke a power of attorney at any time by attending any notary's office in Spain with the original power of attorney document or a certified copy. There is also a procedure to revoke your power of attorney available at Spanish embassies and consulates around the world.

A Building Surveyor (perito de obras or experto en construcción)

In the UK, buyers always use a qualified building surveyor or structural engineer to undertake a detailed report on the condition of a property before buying it. Indeed, it is almost unheard of to do otherwise.

Incredibly, many people buy property in Spain without doing this. All too often they heed the advice from people (including self-serving industry professionals) who say a survey is 'not necessary' or 'not normally done in Spain'. Though the latter has some truth to it when applied to the Spanish, the former could not be further from the truth!

The quality of construction in Spain has been erratic. Some of it has been excellent, some acceptable, and a reasonable amount atrocious. The problem is that, for the non-professional, it can be very difficult, if not impossible, to recognise the difference between good and poor work. This is hard enough in one's own country, never mind abroad, where construction techniques are often different and the properties unlike those you have inhabited previously.

Equally, when it comes to new properties it is vital to realise fully the shortcomings of the *seguro decenal* (or 'builder's guarantee'). This is not comprehensive and does not protect you sufficiently from many of the common defects found in Spanish new builds. Some sellers and agents may use the existence of a 10-year 'guarantee' to try to deter you from commissioning an independent survey – but for a safe purchase, a survey is *vital*. Ideally, get your lawyer to prepare contracts 'subject to survey', whatever the age or type of the property.

> *Before you buy, always use a fully qualified*
> *and insured building surveyor*

A consequence of the amount of poor new building is that a proper survey of your intended property is always necessary. Certainly, not to have a survey performed – particularly on some types of property (such as villas on hillsides) – can only be described as sheer madness. Frankly, if you avoid having a survey undertaken, you deserve all the trouble that will almost certainly come your way!

The trouble is that, in Spain, there is no distinct profession comparable to that of a qualified UK building surveyor – someone whose primary specialisation is to assess the construction and condition of an already built property. Indeed, the closest is an *aparejador*. This is someone who has trained and qualified as a building engineer and who normally oversees and implements building work as designed and specified by an architect.

Without doubt, many a*parejadores* are highly skilled and properly qualified building industry professionals. However, surveying an existing building is a specialisation that involves interpreting cracks, spotting potential construction faults, and investigating the general workability of an existing property and its services. This is not something for which *aparejadores* have been specifically trained. Indeed, few will know how to undertake a truly comprehensive survey – let alone communicate the results effectively in your language and in the type of detailed, written report expected from a UK building surveyor.

> *Always ensure that your surveyor provides you with a comprehensive, written report on the condition of your proposed property*

Interestingly, it is increasingly common for experienced building surveyors to provide expert witness evidence in cases of *aparejador* and architect negligence. Sadly, the property boom years did little to enhance the overall reputation of some of the Spanish *aparejadores* and architects who became linked with wealthy and powerful developers and, as a consequence, all too frequently turned a blind eye to defective works. Sometimes these were signed off – even though they were clearly inadequate.

Certainly, an experienced and independent building surveyor should be able to provide you also with some idea of the value of your intended property. If he is busy and successful, he will have first-hand knowledge of the sale prices of property in your area. So, he should be able to indicate whether your proposed property is over-priced or a bargain.

Obviously, fluency in both Spanish and English is important if your surveyor is to be able to communicate effectively to your seller (who may be Spanish) and any associated professionals. This is particularly important should your surveyor have to make any enquiries or investigations with the local town hall. In many cases, the town hall will not have English speakers or anyone sufficiently fluent to communicate about more detailed matters accurately.

Fortunately, there are qualified British building surveyors who have relocated to Spain and who offer their services in much the same way they would in the UK. It is worth seeking out these surveyors and employing them to conduct your survey. The only major problem is that some insufficiently qualified 'surveyors' do not hold insurance to indemnify themselves against an incompetent survey. This means that suing them in the event of an incompetent survey is likely to be a waste of both time and money.

Check that your surveyor holds professional indemnity insurance and is experienced specifically in Spanish building techniques, planning law and regulations

If you try to locate a British surveyor, you must check that he is properly qualified and obtain proof of this. An appropriate qualification would be a degree in building surveying and membership of a relevant chartered body (which requires professional indemnity insurance to be held by all members). Indeed, unless a surveyor is a properly qualified member of an appropriate professional body, he will usually be unable to secure indemnity insurance.

Obviously, as with lawyers, you cannot beat a personal recommendation when choosing your surveyor, albeit this should not come from anyone with a vested interest!

Alternatives to a qualified building surveyor are architects (*arquitectos*) and *aparejadores*. Some members of other surveying disciplines such as 'quantity surveyors' or 'auctioneers' may also offer 'structural survey' services. However, be wary of using them as they may not be qualified to undertake structural surveys. In fact, they may be operating, by definition, outside of their specific training and qualifications.

Building surveyors are, as the title suggests, best qualified for carrying out surveys on buildings. However, always check with your surveyor that his discipline is relevant to the service he is offering. There are many different surveying disciplines and not all will be appropriate or sufficiently specific to provide you with an authoritative structural report.

Always make sure that any survey results in a written report and a formal and legal invoice for the work performed. This will concentrate the mind of the surveyor and will provide you with a useful record. The report will stand also as a helpful document from which you can instruct any builders.

Of course, all surveyors work under disclaimers and none can sell guarantees on buildings. This is primarily because they cannot see various hidden elements of a structure or inspect exactly what a building sits upon.

However, a professional building surveyor's inspection and advice will typically give you a much better idea of what you are buying. They will be able to identify any defects or potential problems and the implications for any remedial works. They will also advise on whether further investigations are necessary. Their advice on defects may justify a lower offer, or they may steer you clear of a property that could be a terrible liability.

Finally, note that you should take care with the term *perito* (expert). Unless a person is specifically a building surveyor (*perito de obras* – also translated as *experto en construcio*n by the College of Architects in Spain), he will not be specifically qualified to deal with your building problems. Indeed, he may be an expert in a completely different field.

A Notario

In Spain, you should never transfer the title of real estate without the deeds (*escritura*) being notarised. This is when a *notario* formally checks the *escritura* and associated documents and certifies them as correct and valid. If this is not undertaken, there is no conclusive proof of the legal transfer of the property. This is an important point to understand.

If you buy a property, you and the seller (or any lawyers duly empowered by a power of attorney) should always sign the *escritura* in front of a *notario*. To do otherwise (whatever anyone says) is foolish.

If the escritura to your proposed property has not been notarised and registered at the Land Registry, there is no conclusive proof that you own your property

Notarios, from a British standpoint, are something of an anomaly. In Spain it is extremely difficult to become a *notario* and they rank as some of the most highly qualified (and well-paid) professionals in the country. However, they have a limited role within the transaction and are highly unlikely to provide you with any advice on the day of signing the *escritura*.

At the time of your signing, their remit is primarily to ensure that:

- The parties to the signing of the *escritura* are clearly identified
- The signatories are legally capable
- All parties know precisely what they are signing

Critically, a *notario* has no responsibility to you regarding the deal you have made. It is of no interest to him whether you have been wise or not, or whether what you are buying is good or bad, ridiculously priced or otherwise. His interest lies only in ensuring that you know exactly what you are buying (in purely *objective* terms) and that you and the seller are legally capable of signing and are who you purport to be.

Be aware that a notario is no substitute whatsoever for a lawyer

118

Among many Britons there tends to be some confusion about *notarios* and their precise role. Indeed, some people equate a *notario* to an impartial judge employed by the Spanish state. This is not at all accurate.

Notarios have a distinct profession, just like surgeons, accountants and engineers. Their businesses are privately run and profit driven (they are not state employees) and they are not 'judges'.

> *Do not expect a notario to provide you with any advice on the day of signing your escritura*

So, be very careful should another party to a sale assure you that you do not need a lawyer for your conveyancing and that the *notario* will be sufficient. Indeed, if the other party happens to be a developer or agent (who perhaps provides the *notario* with a lot of transactions), their advice may be anything but objective.

This is not to say that you cannot turn to a *notario* for property advice. You can do this and some *notarios* can be helpful. However, by definition you will be mistaking the quite different roles of a conveyancing lawyer and *notario* and this can be very unwise indeed!

Finally, you should note that while the *notario* reads through the contents of an *escritura* on the day of signing, it is the registrar (*registrador*) of the Land Registry (*Registro de la Propiedad*) who can object if there are inconsistencies or errors. However, avoiding this depends upon you properly registering your *escritura* at the Land Registry (see *Loose Ends*).

A Reputable Bank

Banks tend to check rigorously a property, for their own protection, if they intend using it as security for a mortgage or loan. This is particularly true after the credit crunch, which has acted to restrict the worst of the wild lending of some of the Spanish banks during the property boom.

No longer do the banks want to hold as security properties with innate problems. This is good news for buyers and can be a reason (albeit one to consider with care) for applying for a mortgage (even a small one). As a mortgage provider, banks will increasingly act (out of pure self-interest) to double-check the work of your lawyer – although they must never be considered a substitute.

Banks insist on a full valuation (*tasación*) of any property on which they are going to lend money. This is undertaken by a bank-appointed valuer (*tasador*), who will often measure and note down every part of your intended property, from the boundaries to the exact size of every room. He will then check for any inconsistencies against the existing legal documentation. Finally, he will assess the value of the property and provide a valuation worked out on a strict mathematical basis combined with knowledge of the prices of comparable properties. Subject to the results of his report, you should be provided with a firm mortgage offer.

The valuation report, of course, must never be confused with a survey. A survey is primarily concerned with the physical state and condition of a property. A bank valuation, however, is about ensuring that the existing property (including the boundaries) is legal and consistent with the *catastro* and *escritura*. It is also about ensuring that the value of the property as a whole is sufficient to cover the loan requested.

> *Use a bank valuation report as a further safety*
> *check – even if it means agreeing, in principle,*
> *to a small mortgage*

The difference between surveys and valuations are often misunderstood by buyers, especially as some banks refer to their valuer as 'the surveyor'. However, a bank may lend you money on a property despite their valuer advising of any buildings about to collapse. To the bank this does not matter as long as their loan is covered by, for example, the value of the land – irrespective of the condition of the buildings!

However, importantly, a bank valuation potentially will pick up problems that would not be spotted necessarily by either your surveyor or a less than diligent lawyer. For example, the extent of the existing property and its boundaries need to be measured carefully and assessed against the relevant existing paperwork. This is not normally something that a surveyor will undertake unless specifically requested to do so. Equally (and obviously) this is something well beyond the remit of a lawyer, who will rarely inspect a property to see if the paperwork reflects the reality of the existing buildings and boundaries.

As a consequence, a danger lies in relying on a survey report stating that a given building is in good structural condition, when unbeknown to the surveyor, the building may not have been built legally nor properly registered on any documentation. Equally, you cannot rely on your lawyer, who is restricted to looking at documentation – which may be perfectly correct in theory, but inaccurate in reality. This may be the case, for example, if a garage has been built but is not shown on any documentation. If your lawyer has not visited the property or been told about this, there is no way that he will notice this inconsistency.

Obviously, you will have to pay a fee to your bank for a valuation report. However, this is relatively modest, particularly in the light of the overall cost (and potential risk) of buying a property with innate problems. Meanwhile, you will benefit from a report that is objective, written with corporate rigour and that should be actionable if inaccurate. For these reasons, using a bank to double-check your property is compelling. Of course, you do not need to take up any mortgage offer subsequent to the valuation report, so there is little to be lost pursuing this route.

To Summarise

Certainly, you must be careful, when buying property in Spain, to employ only the best possible professionals. These need to be people who operate according to the very highest standards of probity and efficiency. On no account should you attempt to cut costs by skimping on professional fees.

Of course, you must check out any professional you intend using. Take time to do this and, wherever possible, double-check any previous work undertaken.

Spain has numerous examples of property transactions that have gone terribly wrong and therefore you must be, if anything, over-careful at all times. The sheer quantity of existing property that is illegal or has serious and costly liabilities is proof of the danger of buying in Spain.

> *Always use a professional and make sure he is the best your money can buy*

Amazingly, many foreign owners of defective properties (legal or otherwise) in Spain did not employ professionals before buying their properties. On the other hand, some did – only to find the level of service, advice and protection provided to be dreadful. Be alert to the fact that even among professionals, collusion, corruption and incompetence sometimes exist. Be wary at all times and never, ever tolerate any conflict of interest on the part of your professional advisors.

If you employ a professional, always check his professional indemnity insurance cover. Some professionals lack proper insurance liability cover and others have cover so low that it may not fully indemnify the value of any claim.

Finally, make certain when buying property that you:

- Always use a qualified professional
- Employ the right professional for the work you require
- Check – before hiring – that the professional has a high insurance indemnity cover

Property Finance and Enabling

There are four prerequisites for buying property in Spain:

1. Obtain your Spanish *NIE* number (*Numero de Identificatión de Extranjero*)

2. Calculate the potential overall costs of relocation

3. Understand the specific and unavoidable costs of buying a Spanish property

4. Arrange your financial situation accordingly

All of the above are essential either to understand or have in place before you make any attempt to buy a property in Spain. Without an *NIE* number, for example, you will be unable to sign any *escritura* ('complete') on a Spanish property. Meanwhile, if you do not appreciate the significant costs of buying a Spanish property, you may unwittingly overstretch your resources or look right from the start at properties beyond your budget.

Of course, any purchase of a property involves getting your finances in order and this is even more complicated when it involves a foreign country, particularly when it comes to choosing a new bank, applying for a mortgage, transferring money or exchanging currencies i.e. sterling to euros.

Spanish NIE Number

You cannot sign an *escritura* (in UK terms 'complete') on any real estate in Spain unless you have an *NIE* number. This number is an individual fiscal identity number that is issued by the Spanish authorities (the *Policia Nacional*) and that is granted as of right to an EU citizen. However, it needs to be applied for in person, which can make it inconvenient to obtain.

> *Obtaining an NIE number is an absolute*
> *necessity if you want to buy property in Spain*
> *and it must be applied for in person*

To apply for your *NIE* number you need to obtain the relevant form from a *Policia Nacional* office or *Oficina de Extranjeros*, which can be found in all major towns and cities. The one-page application form is free and relatively easy to complete – albeit the instructions are in Spanish. Once you have completed the form you will need to return to the application office with the form and a copy of the back page of your passport (the one page with your photograph). Your application form will be checked then against your passport and sent for processing.

Normally, when you apply for an *NIE* the clerks processing the application will advise you of roughly when it will be ready for collection. This can take some weeks and depends on how busy the particular office is. Once issued, your *NIE* number will remain at the application office until you collect it, so it matters not if you are unable to return for some months.

Your *NIE* number is typed on a disappointingly modest single sheet of headed paper. However, this should not mask its importance. Indeed, you should make many copies of the original, file some away carefully and always carry a copy with you. Your *NIE* number is certainly crucial for the signing of any *escritura* and day to day you will be asked for it, whether you are trying to buy goods or as a form of identity for almost every document of importance.

Applying for and receiving your *NIE* number in no way prejudices your UK situation whether for tax or residency purposes. There is therefore nothing to be lost by applying for it – even if subsequently you never use it. As a consequence, it is always worth applying for your *NIE* number even if you are thinking only vaguely of buying a property or moving to Spain.

It is a simple process to apply for your *NIE* number. However, in practice, finding the right office, choosing the right queues and filling out the form correctly can be exasperating and take up considerable time. It can be useful therefore to obtain help. This is available normally from your lawyer or most real estate agents, both of whom generally have blank *NIE* application forms (thus saving one bout of queuing!). Equally, there are businesses that specifically offer a service to help you obtain your *NIE*. Some of these even promise a same day service so that you can apply and obtain your number straight away.

Certainly, if time is short or if facing bureaucracy alone makes you nervous, it is worth seeking assistance. This may cost you a few euros, but removes the worry of fighting your way through a system that can appear baffling.

Note: At the same time as applying for your *NIE* number you can apply for registration to the National Foreigners Registry *(Registro Central de Extranjeros)*. This is obligatory if you stay in Spain for longer than three months (See *Residency*).

Costs of Relocation

Always try to calculate your overall relocation costs before you set a budget or decide on a particular price band of property in Spain. These costs can mount up and you should include a decent amount for contingencies.

Examples of potential relocation costs are:

- Investigation trips (perhaps 2–3 trips to a given area with a minimum of (say) a week's stay each time)
- Flights

- Car rental
- Accommodation
- General expenses

Your relocation costs will always be more than you think – so be realistic with your calculations

Relocation

- Removal costs (and perhaps specific insurance for valuables)
- Air fares (or fuel and motorway tolls if you drive to Spain)
- Accommodation (until you move into your new home)
- Car hire (perhaps until purchase of a right-hand drive vehicle)
- Car purchase
- Veterinary costs (such as inoculations and pet passport)

General property-related costs

- *NIE* fee (if you require professional help with the application)
- Surveyor's fee
- Estate agent's fee (if there is a buyer's premium)
- Lawyer's fee for new wills (essential)
- Specific property buying costs (*see below*)
- Potential building/renovation costs

    These costs will, of course, be impossible to work out until you have chosen a property! However, it is worth making an allowance for renovation works. Invariably, any property will need some form of adaptation or improvement even if it is just to take into account your own taste.

- Contingency

- Unfortunately, any move (even in the UK) always ends up more expensive than anticipated. So, allow a sum for unexpected costs. This should be a generous amount!

Specific Property Buying Costs

Buying property in Spain is an expensive matter. Indeed, the rule of thumb is to allow 10% on top of any sale price. Note that the following costs exclude obtaining a mortgage, fees payable for a surveyor's report, removals costs, relocation costs, and any short-term rentals.

Standard buying costs are as follows:

- **Purchase tax:** This is payable to the Spanish state by the buyer of a property and is calculated at 7% (8% if a new build) of the declared purchase price of the property. So, for example, the purchase tax on a €200,000 property will be €14,000.

- *Notario* **fees:** These are payable at the time of the signing of the *escritura* and depend on the price of the property. Sometimes the costs are shared by the seller and occasionally paid entirely by him, though this depends on the agreement made. Allow for €400–500.

Always allow 10% on top of any sale price to account for the unavoidable costs associated with buying a Spanish property

- **Registration of title deeds:** An essential action for any buyer. The fee depends on the price of the property. Allow for around €400.

- **Lawyer's fees:** These depend greatly upon the type of property that you are buying and the complexity of any conveyancing. Allow for between €1,000–2,000.

Normally, the costs above will amount to just below 10% of an average purchase price – but allowing for 10% provides a reliable contingency figure. If your calculations show that you are likely to pay more than a total of 10%, you should be alert to some possibly unwelcome problem and investigate it immediately.

Finance

Finance can be broken down into four important components:

- A bank in Spain
- Currency transfers from one country to another
- Mortgages
- Tax avoidance

Banks in Spain

There are two main types of bank (other than commercial and investment banks). These are:

- **Savings banks:** These are roughly similar to the UK building societies of the past and are 'non-profit'. They vary in size considerably – some (like *Caja Murcia*) have only a few dozen branches, while others (like *La Caixa*) have thousands of branches. They are often referred to as *cajas or caixes.*

- **'Private' banks:** These are shareholder-owned banks (such as Lloyds, Santander, BBVA, and Banesto) and are operated for profit. Again, they vary considerably in size and in the extent of their branches across Spain.

For day to day banking, either type of bank will be suitable for you and deliver a service not dissimilar to elsewhere in Northern Europe. Spanish banks tend to provide a high level of easily accessible personal service, which can be charming and greatly aid efficiency. Additionally, their staff are open often to negotiation on charges and you should try always, on any matter, to see if you can make a better deal than that being offered initially. Some firm but elegant arguments can produce surprising results!

> *Choose your Spanish bank with great care and ensure your branch has an efficient, permanently appointed member of staff who speaks your language fluently and will be dedicated to your account*

At a minimum, you are likely to need a current account, debit card, credit card, deposit account and probably a sterling (or other currency) account. None of these facilities are hard to find. However, for the long term, your proposed bank should have also:

- A branch close to you that has a dedicated and permanent member of staff who speaks your language fluently and with whom you feel comfortable. This is absolutely essential as banking miscommunications can lead easily to horrifically stressful problems.

- A bank that has many branches throughout Spain. This is important particularly if you intend travelling a lot within Spain.

- Internet banking and bank statements in your own language.

- Reasonable charges. These tend to vary considerably. Ensure that you know what you will be charged for a variety of actions before you join a given bank. Some banks are surprisingly expensive and charges can vary between different banks far more than they do in the UK.

Currency Transfer and Exchange Rates

One of the best ways of losing money quickly (and often unnecessarily!) is to exchange money from one currency to another and then to transfer that money from one country to another. If you do this carelessly then it can be a very costly experience. As a consequence, you should be very careful and plan ahead to ensure that you do not experience a particularly unwelcome shock.

Indeed, often people negotiate very hard for the price they are prepared to pay for a Spanish property – only to find that the price drop they achieve is immediately cancelled out by the loss they make on exchanging their sterling to euros and transfering their money from the UK to Spain. This is a bitter pill to swallow and should be avoided at all costs!

Equally, if money is tight, then you may be buying a property where every £ counts and where your finances simply cannot take any major variation downwards in what you believe you have to spend. If you find yourself charged £1,500 for the transfer of your money from the UK to Spain then this may destabalise your finances terribly. Meanwhile, get the exchange rate wrong and you may find yourself short of, quite literally, tens of thousands of pounds!

So, what can you do?

Firstly, you must understand how you can act to limit any loss on currency transfers and the actual exchange of money from one currency to another. This can sound complicated and 'high' finance – but it is easier to understand (and action) than you may think.

Furthermore, the tools exist (such as currency transfer companies) that can help you to maximise any exchange of money and minimise the costs of so doing. This is the dedicated service that currency transfer companies offer with Foreign Currency Direct an example of highly regarded specialists in this area. Indeed, Foreign Currencies Direct, Currencies Direct and Moneycorps tend to offer a personalised service from staff who are well used to people not fully understanding (or trusting!) the process!

There are two aspects to currency transfers and exchange rates that you should appreciate:

Currency Exchange

Obtaining a favourable exchange rate from Sterling to Euros is vital. The difference, for example, of obtaining 1.25 Euros to the £, instead of 1.15 Euros to the £ on a capital transfer of £300,000 is a very significant €30,000! That is the cost of two swimming pools, a couple of new cars or maybe a better property, not touching your pension for a year or so or flights to your Spanish property for the rest of your life ...

Obviously, it is difficult to calculate the movements of international currencies, which are volatile at the best of times and stretch the patience of even the most experienced of currency traders. Not least, the latter battle against the stabilty of economies, political uncertainty, terrorist actions and acts of God – all of which can raise or drop a currency (and your careful plans) with shocking speed!

In short, the future movement of currencies is extremely difficult to predict – and yet their impact on your plans can be truly dramatic.

So, if you are thinking of buying a property in Spain then, obviously, it is important to be certain of the value of your money – particularly if you are relying on your money matching the calculations you have made for its purchasing power. Needless to say, the purchasing action (the signing of the *Escriture* and full payment for your property) may be weeks or even months away.

The question, of course, is how to obtain 'certainty' when the value of currencies is so constantly in a state of flux?

Well, this is where currency transfer companies like Foreign Currency Direct, Currencies Direct and so on come into their own. They allow you to buy what is called a *forward contract* where you can secure a rate of exchange on a given currency for anything up to two years in advance – thus removing the risk of currency fluctuations denting your pocket.

A *forward contract* sounds pretty confusing. However, quite simply, what it means is that you can decide to buy a given amount of currency (say €200,000) at an agreed (with the currency transfer company) *guaranteed* rate that will remain the same for two years – *whatever* happens to the currency market in the meantime.

So, if your agreement with the currency transfer company was to buy €200,000 euros at €1.20 to the £ then this is what you would get – whether the euro to £ rate went up, down or had stayed the same when you came to use the money. You would have secured certainty over the period of the agreement with the currencies company and this is a very precious commodity.

Of course, whilst you would not lose money if the £ weakened neither would you gain if the £ strengthened between the time you signed the contract with the currencies company and used the money. That can be frustrating but the point, of course, is to buy into certainty – not to 'play' the markets!

So, how do you decide what rate is the best one to buy into for your *forward contract*?

This is a knotty problem – unless you are a professional currency trader because judging the 'right' price to fix upon is extremely difficult. However, currency transfer companies normally provide help and advice to complement your own instincts. Indeed, the best currencies companies, once they have your details, can dedicate a trader to help you decide – and provide you with constantly up-dated information as to what is anticipated with regard to the currency markets.

Of course, you can use your bank to undertake currency transfers but, increasingly, the banks have been outflanked by the currency transfer companies. These tend to provide a better, quicker and more responsive service. Invariably they are also significantly cheaper ...

Needless to say, you can also use currency transfer companies for not just large capital amounts but also smaller transfers whether pension payments or small lump sum movements of money.

Currency Transfer

Amazingly, you can be charged for the actual transfer of money from the UK to Spain or vice versa. Indeed, unless you are very careful you can be charged a significant amount for this service – even by the bank in (say) Spain that is *receiving* your money!

Indeed, it is not at all unknown for a Spanish bank to receive the money and then charge you anything up to and including 1.5% of the amount sent. So, if you are sending £100,000, for example, the charge could amount to £1,500!

Frankly, to pay anything is unacceptable and completely unnecessary – if you know what you are doing!

In any event, there are three types of standard currency transfer charge (unless you take action to avoid them!):

- **Shared:** Your sending bank (say, in the UK) and the receiving bank (for example, in Spain) agree to share the charge levied upon you for the transfer.

- **Own:** All the charges are levied by one bank – the sending bank.

- **Beneficiary:** The receiving bank charges for the transfer.

So, how can you avoid paying any charges?

The first thing is to ensure is that you never send any money from the UK to Spain or vice versa without knowing what the bank charges will be are beforehand! If you do not do this then you may be in for a real (and very unwelcome) shock.

If, you find that there will be bank charges then try to negotiate these charges to the absolute minimum. Some Spanish banks, for example, will not charge for some incoming transfers particularly if they are in large amounts. However, make sure that any agreement on the part of either (or both) the receiving and sending bank is evidenced in writing!

Fortunately, most currency transfer companies charge nothing for transfering money from one country to another. This is because they invariably have a euro account in Spain, so any transfer acts (effectively) as an internal Spanish transfer and therefore usually removes the danger of any bank receiving charges. Obviously, this is the case in reverse – with regard to their sending your money from Spain to the UK.

So, on the whole, using dedicated transfer companies like Foreign Currency Direct or Currencies Direct and so on, can act like a one-stop shop that will enable you to exchange your money efficiently, buy into a fixed rate and then transfer that money at minimal or zero cost.

Mortgages (hipotecas)

Obviously, mortgages and loans exist in Spain and are as widely used as in the UK – and the marketplace just as confusing, with a wide range of options. However, it is important to recognise that the amount that you can borrow on a property differs depending on whether or not you are fiscally resident in Spain.

To be fiscally resident you must be paying Spanish tax as well as be formally resident. If this is the case, you can invariably borrow a higher percentage on the value of your property than you can as a non-resident.

At the best of times, choosing the right mortgage package is difficult. However, it has become even more problematic since the world credit crunch, which has made finding the best long-term financial package difficult within the volatile marketplace.

Certainly, in Spain, matters are complicated also by the different designation of properties. So, for example, it can be more difficult to obtain a mortgage on a property located on *rústico* land than on one that is classed as *urbano*. There is obvious logic to this (albeit this was not always displayed by bank lending during the property boom years). Equally, bank valuations on *rústico* properties can be significantly lower than those on *urbano* ones – despite sale prices for the same size and type of property occasionally being similar.

Some banks are cautious about lending to non-residents on properties far from the coast (as this can make resaleability difficult). This can follow also for properties on large new estates where a proportion of the properties have not been built or sold. Bank finance for commercial properties can be also difficult and expensive to obtain. All of these factors may change as the economy in Spain recovers.

Typical loans available:

- **Interest-only mortgages:** As the name implies, you pay only the interest on your mortgage until the end of the mortgage term, at which time you must pay off the original loan. The terms may vary between five and 40 years depending on your circumstances and the bank concerned.

- **Repayment mortgages:** You pay off both the interest and the debt over the term of the mortgage. As for interest-only mortgages, the terms will vary.

- **Lifetime mortgages:** These are mortgages on which you will make no monthly payments. However, upon your death (or perhaps removal to a retirement home) your property will be sold and any loan and interest then repaid to the bank. To take advantage of this type of mortgage you need to be 65 or older.

- **Offshore mortgages:** Offshore mortgages allow you to pay off your mortgage in a currency of your choice. So, for example, if your income comes from the UK then you can pay off the mortgage in sterling. This avoids the expense and uncertainty of currency fluctuations when transferring your money into euros to make your payments.

- **Equity release:** This allows you to obtain a loan by using the equity you have within your property as security. However, increasingly, money borrowed this way is being limited to a specific renovation project or to buying a second property. The expenditure may be checked by your lender, who may also inspect the completion of the works for which you have borrowed the money.

- **Unsecured loans:** These are increasingly difficult to obtain due to the impact of the world credit crunch.

At the time of writing, the extent of borrowing that banks are prepared to do varies considerably. Equally, the computation of what exactly they will lend with regard to a given mortgage is difficult to determine.

> *Obtaining the best possible mortgage deal is complicated. Use a professional mortgage broker and also go to several banks directly*

The preferred method for banks to establish the viability of providing a mortgage is to check the ability of the person concerned to make regular mortgage payments. This is called the debt-to-income ratio (DTI). Lenders normally assess net monthly income after deducting worldwide debts and then come up with a maximum possible monthly payment. This then defines the size of mortgage they will grant, together with its term (5, 10, 25, 30 or 40 years and so on). Normally the DTI is between 30%–50%

You may, for example, earn €2,000 a month net. However, you may have a car loan and an HP agreement amounting to €200 a month. If this is the case, then the following computations could be made:

40% DTI

Income of €2,000 a month multiplied by *40%*	€800
Less loan and HP debts	- €200
Maximum potential monthly payment	**€600**

This would allow you to have a mortgage of €100,000 for 25 years at a 4% interest rate. The monthly premiums would be €527 a month – a little less than you can actually afford.

50% DTI

Income of €2,000 a month multiplied by *50%*	€1,000
Less loan and HP debts	- €200
Maximum potential monthly payment	**€800**

This would allow you to have a mortgage of €140,000 for 25 years at a 4% interest rate. The monthly premiums would be €738 a month.

Obviously, the maximum amount that your lender decides you can pay – and the size of mortgage granted – depends on the interest rate at the time and the length of the mortgage term. Accordingly, the computations above could change significantly, though they are a useful guideline.

Finding the right mortgage is always difficult and there is much to be gained from taking independent professional advice. This is provided by a range of mortgage brokers, both native Spanish and North European. The latter are frequently professionals who have settled in Spain, and within these are British brokers with relevant UK qualifications and previous mortgage broking experience.

Check that your broker is fully qualified, insured, and transparent about his charges

The primary advantage of a mortgage broker when compared to an individual bank is the variety and scope of mortgages the broker can offer. For obvious reasons, an individual bank can only offer its own in-house mortgages and loans, which may, of course, be as good (or possibly better) than anything found by a mortgage broker. However, often a professional mortgage broker can be effective in:

- Advising you about the loans and mortgages available within the marketplace and as offered by a vast spectrum of banks and finance houses. A broker can also explain clearly the implications of differing conditions and any benefits or detriments of the financial packages available.

- Suggesting the most appropriate loan or mortgage for your requirements and situation.

- Obtaining a better than normal deal. This a broker can sometimes achieve because of the volume of business he may be placing with a particular finance house.

- Completing all the paperwork necessary to obtain acceptance of a loan or mortgage while liaising with your lawyer.

Obviously, brokers make their money from selling loans and mortgages – through charging you a brokerage fee and by receiving a commission from a finance house should you agree to take up a mortgage or loan arranged by them.

Brokerage fees vary considerably, from around €500 to over €3,000. Meanwhile, the commission brokers receive from a bank is around 1% of the value of the mortgage or loan sold. Some brokers do not charge a brokerage fee and rely on commission only.

Of course, the danger in using a broker lies in being advised to take a loan or mortgage that provides them with the biggest possible commission, irrespective of whether it is appropriate for you. Certainly, unscrupulous brokers may do this – making any brokerage fee largely irrelevant to them. So, if you go to a broker for a mortgage or loan ensure your broker is:

- **Qualified:** In the case of a British broker this would mean being MAQ/CERT C11 (MP) certified.

- **Transparent:** Check there are no hidden charges

within any agreement. An example would be inflating the cost of a banker's draft – perhaps from a normal €10–20 to €300!

A creditable **professional British broker working in Spain** will normally:

- Provide a money back guarantee of his fee – if your mortgage is not approved prior to the valuation.
- Follow the UK national mortgage code of conduct. Though this is not actionable by the UK authorities, it does provide a widely accepted service guideline.
- Be SL registered (Spanish limited company). This is important because many banks will not work with brokers who are not registered as limited companies – thus reducing the variety of finance products they may have available for you.

Generally, mortgages in Spain can be activated quickly – so long as you are able to provide all the relevant paperwork to the finance house. Invariably, you will need to give them:

- Proof of identity. This will be a copy of your passport and a copy of your *NIE* number.
- P60 and pay slips (if you are employed) or your previous year's certified accounts and/or tax returns if you are self-employed.
- Bank statements for three months providing proof of your income and outgoings.
- A credit report, normally from Experia or Equifax (although sometimes your bank will apply for this directly).
- The name and contact details of your lawyer.
- Details of the property you wish to buy or use as security for the loan or mortgage.
- Payment of fee for a valuation report. This will be

conducted by a specialist valuer (but do not confuse his report with a full structural survey performed by a qualified surveyor).

- Access to your property (or the one you wish to buy) so that the valuer can assess it. This will involve an inspection visit, during which the valuer is likely to measure each and every room of the property together with its exact boundaries. All of this will be compared against the existing legal paperwork, before valuation for the purposes of your intended loan or mortgage is made. Typically, the calculation will be based on database records of other properties that have recently sold within the zone.

Most mortgage applications are often held up by incorrect paperwork from the applicant – so ensure that you have ready all the possible paperwork a lender needs

You should note that valuations can vary widely given what you have paid or are about to pay for your property. There are two reasons for this:

- The Spanish property market has a number of genuine 'distress' sale properties within the marketplace. These (yours may be one) often have purchase prices that are well below their real market value. If this is the case then the valuation placed upon your property may be higher than what you paid. In this case you may find your lender will allow you higher borrowing than you thought. This is not usual, but can happen.

So, for example, your lender may have a policy whereby it lends only up to 60% of the valuation price – but up to a maximum of 90% of the purchase price.

If your purchase price was €200,000 and your valuation comes in at €280,000 then you could borrow €168,000 or 84% of the purchase price.

- The banks are now conservative with valuations of properties after their consistent overvaluation of properties during the property boom. So, you may find your property valued lower than the price that you are about to pay. This does not mean that your property is overpriced. Indeed, the price may be correct but the valuation artificially low (but not negotiable!) due to a lender's caution.

Finally, if you take out a mortgage on your property, it will be registered at the Land Registry as a charge on your property and the lender will retain your original *escritura*. If you are buying your property and it will be mortgaged, a representative of the lender will attend the signing of the *escritura*. Only at the actual signing of the *escritura* will he release the mortgage money to you.

Tax Avoidance

Obviously, you will want to avoid as much tax as possible when you come to Spain. This is an area fraught with difficulty at the best of times and dependent on ever-changing laws as governments seek to close loopholes.

Currently, one way of potentially saving tax is by buying your Spanish property through a UK limited company that is set up specifically for this purpose. In this way, you can potentially make considerable savings on any Spanish inheritance tax should you or your partner die. Any attempt at tax avoidance needs to be treated with immense care and should only be undertaken with the aid of up-to-date advice from qualified professionals of the highest integrity.

Negotiating The Deal

The negotiating process, whether it is with someone of your own nationality or with a Spaniard, is much the same anywhere in the world. As always, the key is to negotiate directly and face to face with the seller. You should do this always whether or not you have an agent – and if you do use an agent, he should always be with you when you negotiate.

Nothing is ever as effective as sitting down with a seller and speaking to him directly – even if through an interpreter. It is only then that you can see the eyes of the person and read his reactions. Most buyers are reluctant to negotiate personally, but by not doing so they abrogate the very essence of effective negotiation. This is always about seeing the reaction of your 'opponent' and is something impossible for anyone else to convey accurately to you.

Never, under any circumstance, sign anything without first showing the document to your lawyer for his approval

Oddly enough, people ask frequently whether it is possible to make offers for property in Spain. Of course, it is! In fact, you would have to be crazy not to do so. How else are you supposed to find out the true limits of a seller?

Any negotiation is about finding out the lowest possible price for the maximum benefit. You will never establish this unless you make an offer. However, you should do so dispassionately. All too often buyers make an offer and then take it as a personal insult when this is refused. This is no way to negotiate and simply shows that you are approaching the negotiations as an amateur.

Don't forget to add 10% for buying costs on top of the sale price when working out what you can afford

The only way to find out the best deal available is by making an offer. If refused, you follow with a slightly better offer or one structured in a different way. Gradually, ramp up your offers (after refusals) until you reach the point at which any further refusal by the seller is beyond what you are prepared to tolerate.

Treat negotiation as a sophisticated game, albeit one with a finite end. This will be, of course, your personal limit, beyond which you will not cross under any circumstances. By doing this, you will be able to establish unemotionally the boundaries of any potential deal. Be calm, enjoy the process and never take a refusal personally. Instead, analyse the reaction of your seller and see if he is showing signs of weakness or loss of nerve. As soon as you see this, you will know that you are close to finding his limits and thereby the maximum benefit possible for yourself.

Of course, to read a buyer you must become an intrinsic part of the process. Leave the negotiation to your agent or lawyer and you are unlikely to be able to correctly interpret your seller. So, whenever possible, if you are going to make an offer or counter-offer, meet up with the seller and make the offer personally. Often, this is best done on neutral ground. It is therefore a good idea to make the meeting place a cafe or bar local to the property in which you have an interest.

Always negotiate face to face with your seller and never leave this to a third party

If you are using an agent, realise that, at the end of the day, he works for the seller. It is the latter who will pay him and his duty is not to you – despite the most earnest protestations to the contrary. Furthermore, if he is being paid on a straight commission basis, it is in his interest to ensure the sale price agreed is the highest possible! So, be wary of trusting 'your' agent during the negotiation phase and be extremely cautious if, for some reason, your agent attempts to stop you speaking directly to your seller. If there is nothing to hide then your agent will have no objection with you speaking to the seller face to face.

Remember that the actual structural condition of the property should influence any offer you make. Indeed, all negotiations and contracts ideally should be made post survey or at least 'subject to survey'.

Many buyers regret having made offers before knowing the full structural condition of the property. This can be a severe negotiating error, as it is difficult to ask for more money off when a deal has already been agreed. Nonetheless, having a survey is always worthwhile – even if you have already agreed a price and paid a 10% deposit. If the property has grievous flaws then you may be better off sacrificing your 10% deposit rather than going ahead and signing the *escritura* on a nightmare of a property. In any event, always inform your lawyer that the whole purchase process must be contracted 'subject to survey' and this should become a term of any deal.

Before the legal process can be started in earnest you need to make sure that you have an agreement 'in principle' with the seller. Normally, this will revolve around:

- The sale price of the property
- The items to be included in the sale price of the property
- The intended date of signing the *escritura* ('completion')

- The date for signing the private contract (similar to 'exchange')
- The date of the main (normally 10%) deposit

The Sale Price of the Property

Unfortunately, this is not always a simple matter as there can be two sale 'prices':

- **The declared price:** This is the sale price that will be placed upon the *escritura* and the price on which you will pay purchase tax (7%) and on which the seller will pay any capital gains tax (18%).

- **The real price:** This may be different from the declared price and include a proportion of 'black' money. For example, you may agree to buy the property for €300,000, but only declare the sale price as €275,000. In this case, the *escritura* will state €275,000 and you will pay 7% purchase tax (and the seller any CGT at 18%) on €275,000 – rather than €300,000. The €25,000 difference will be paid by you to the seller in undeclared cash. Clearly, both you and he will have saved money by not being taxed at the correct amount.

Obviously, it is illegal to under-declare the price paid for a property. The Spanish state loses tax and you may be investigated by the tax authorities. This will happen if the Spanish tax office (the *Hacienda*) concludes that there is a discrepancy between the value of the property and the sale price placed on the *escritura*. In this event, the tax authorities can (and will) penalise you with a heavy fine.

Do not pay any 'black' money and make sure the sale price shown on the escritura is the real sale price

Many properties are sold with an element of 'black' money involved. This is often important particularly to Spanish sellers, who may have owned a property for many years (perhaps pre-property boom) and have a very low original *escritura* value. This means that when they sell their property they can face a considerable potential CGT liability.

Every *escritura* shows the actual amount paid by a buyer for that property. So, any tax assessment will be made (in principle) on the difference between the price shown on the seller's original *escritura* and that of the new *escritura* evidencing your purchase of the property.

The under-declaration of sale prices is common and known to everyone in Spain, whether tax authorities, real estate agents, banks, lawyers or *notarios*. However, because it is illegal you will see little in writing about it and, of course, no references to it in legal documents. Indeed, if you agree to under-declare your sale price then the whole of your legal process will be done without any mention of the real sale price.

Only at the very time of the signing of the *escritura* will you be expected to hand over any cash differential (say the €25,000 as in the example above) to the seller and of course under conditions you must control carefully. Indeed, any provision of cash to a seller must be done only as you sign the *escritura* – never before.

One of the problems of having a system with two 'sale prices' is the difficulty of agreeing on a sale price! For example, both you and the seller may agree a sale price of €300,000. However, you may not be able to come to an agreement as to the 'black' money element (the price to be declared on the new *escritura*). Your seller may want (say) €100,000 in 'black' money. You may refuse to pay this as it is a considerable proportion of the property's market value of €300,000. A discrepancy of a third will more than likely alert the tax authorities and result in a subsequent fine – which you (not the seller) will have to pay!

Alternatively, you may refuse (rightly) to pay any 'black' money at all or simply be unable to do so because you have a high mortgage requirement. In the latter case, paying any 'black' money may be academic. Your mortgage provider, for example, will, obviously, only bring a cheque or banker's draft for the seller at the signing of the *escritura*. So, if your mortgage is very high then you may not have any extra cash to pay a seller.

Of course, your seller is well within his rights to refuse to sell you his property if you refuse to pay a certain amount of 'black' money. Indeed, to your chagrin, you may find the seller agrees with another buyer to reduce his 'real' sale price if that buyer offers him a substantial amount of 'black' money!

In reality, the Spanish authorities and the ever tighter European regulations concerning money laundering are making 'black' money deals ever more difficult. Indeed, I would strongly advise you to avoid any 'black' money deal and make sure that the declared value on any *escritura* is the 'proper' sale price.

Certainly, you should bear in mind that if ever you resell, your buyer may be someone who needs a large mortgage – and may be unable to pay you any 'black' money. In this case, the declared value will have to represent the proper sale price of the property. As your (original) *escritura* will be artificially low, you will then have to bear a potentially far greater CGT burden than ever you intended!

Finally, if a 'black' element to your purchase price is unavoidable, be extremely wary of paying too much. Crudely, within the property 'industry', 10%–15% of the 'real' purchase price is considered the maximum you should pay.

However *always* try to avoid any 'black' deal, regardless of the amount involved. It is dishonest, invariably troublesome, and can lead to a very unwelcome fine – and significant complications when you come to resell your property.

Items To Be Included in the Sale Price of the Property

Obviously, you will need to agree what is included with the property. This should always be written down as a schedule including the contents specifically agreed on by you and the seller. Often Spanish sellers will leave all the contents of their property, except for personal items and particular objects of personal worth. You may, of course, not want this, in which case you will need to agree that the property is sold clean and cleared. Items to consider discussing are:

- Furniture and fittings (lights, curtains ...)
- White goods (dishwasher, fridge, freezer)
- Garden tools and machinery
- Car, dog, building materials (such as spare house tiles), and so on

Be specific about what is to be included in the sale price and always get your lawyer to draw up a full and precise schedule describing the details

The Intended Date of Signing the Escritura ('completion')

You obtain possession of the property when you have signed the *escritura* and fully paid the seller. This is an important date to fix in principle and can be the cause of considerable negotiation depending on the intentions of both you and the seller. You may wish or need, for example, to set a longer target date than the seller wants or vice versa.

Never allow yourself to be rushed nor place your lawyer under too much pressure

In fact, it is worth setting a date further away than you might want, as matters invariably take longer than anticipated. This can be particularly the case when financing is required. Though this can usually be done quickly it takes little to disrupt its progress.

The Date for Signing the Private Contract ('exchange')

Signing the private contract (*contrato privado*) is a priority because until you have done so, or until your seller receives some money (even a token deposit), your intended property will not be taken off the market.

Obviously, the last thing you should do (however much you want a property) is give a seller money that is not evidenced by a proper, legally binding contract drawn up by your lawyer. So, be realistic about the timing required to complete this work.

Normally, a good conveyancing lawyer can draw up a private contract for the purchase of a property within a few days. This contract can state that a small initial deposit (dependent on agreement with the seller) will be provided. Meanwhile, your lawyer (and surveyor) can undertake their full investigations into the property (See *The Legal Process*). The deposit is often relatively small (around €500–€3,000) but sufficient for the seller to agree to stop trying to sell his property to anyone else.

> *Never, regardless of any pressure, pay any money whatsoever to a seller or agent until your lawyer has drawn up a proper legal contract*

Before agreeing in principle to the date of the main deposit, it is vital that you speak to your lawyer to ensure he is able to make the applicable deadlines.

The Date of the Main Deposit

A critical part of any agreement is the payment (if there is to be one) of a deposit. This is normally, but not necessarily, 10% of the agreed purchase price. Obviously, this is important to any seller because it indicates the point of no return for a buyer. Though not strictly true, few buyers part with a 10% deposit unless they are serious about buying a property and signing the *escritura.*

Of course, fixing 'in principle' a deadline for the 10% deposit should be done only after consultation with your lawyer and under no account should you set this too tight, as you may underestimate the amount of work that your lawyer needs to undertake to ensure the property warrants the payment of the deposit. Certainly, establishing that the extent of your intended property is what it appears to be – and that it is legal and devoid of problems – is never the work of five minutes!

Services

Finally, in your negotiations, make sure that you can take over the existing supplier contracts for services such as mains water, electricity and the telephone line. Avoid having these contracts terminated by the seller as reconnection can be expensive and exasperatingly slow.

Normally, the seller will agree to pay you any outstanding debt on his services bills on the day of the signing of the *escritura*. The approximate amount is worked out by looking at previous bills and assessing what would be owed if the given services bill was delivered on the day of signing.

So, for example, if the previous water bill was €50 for a month and the signing is halfway through the next billing period, the seller will give you €25. The same follows for the electricity and telephone bills.

After the signing of the *escritura* you should go immediately to your bank and ask them to place all service contracts in your name and on direct debit. You will then be responsible for all subsequent bills (including any remainder owed by the seller).

The Legal Process

Buying in Spain can be very quick if you have found the property you want and can agree terms with a seller. It is possible and frequently done by the Spanish (when no mortgage is involved) to see a property, pay a small initial deposit, and go to the notary to complete the *escritura*, all within a couple of days. The buyer can then take immediate possession.

However, in practice, this is not a safe way of proceeding if you are a foreigner buying property in Spain for the first time. It is better to follow a more measured buying process. Certainly, given the stakes, it is never worth rushing a purchase. This can place both your lawyer and yourself under immense stress – and is usually when mistakes are made that may have terrible long-term implications. Your priority should be always to buy safely – even if it means losing out on a property.

There are several routes through which the signing of the *escritura* can be reached:

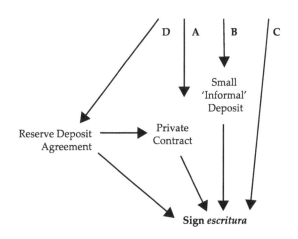

Outline Verbal Agreement to Buy

The best way of reaching the point of signing the *escritura* is Route A and this should be followed unless there are compelling reasons for doing otherwise. Route B is workable, but you risk losing your deposit with no recompense. Route C is workable, but provides you with little protection should your seller wish to 'gazump' you. Meanwhile, route D needs to be undertaken with considerable caution.

Route A

1. *Agreement 'in principle'*
2. *Private contract with (normally) 10% deposit*
3. *Sign* escritura

Agreement in principle

Once you have reached an agreement with a seller 'in principle', you should go to your lawyer and take his express advice on what has been discussed. Subject to his comments, you can then ask him to draw up a legally binding private contract. You must, obviously, provide him with details of your seller, the seller's estate agent (if there is one) and the seller's lawyer (if he intends using one). It is always a good idea to ask your lawyer to communicate immediately with the seller or his lawyer to ensure that your understanding of the agreement 'in principle' matches that of the seller.

As with any legal matter, make sure that you provide your lawyer with written instructions. These should set out clearly the deal that you believe is acceptable to you and the seller. It is important to place this is in writing as this starts a formal paper trail and prevents miscommunication or misunderstandings. Certainly, oral instructions are rarely precise and, when they involve dates and numbers, can be confused easily.

Private contract *(contrato privado)* with main deposit

Normally, it is the buyer's lawyer who draws up a private contract (similar to a UK 'exchange'). This, as well as other investigations, will be done after your lawyer has applied for and received the *nota simple* of your intended property.

The private contract terms normally encompass:

1. The sale price of the property
2. Details of what is included in the sale price (this should be clarified by a formal schedule of precise details)
3. Fixtures and fittings
4. Furniture, tools, car, dog, and so on
5. The date to sign the *escritura*. If possible, allow yourself a date for signing the *escritura* that is further away than you would like. Invariably, some problem arises and it is vital that you do not allow yourself to be tied to a deadline that becomes too tight and adds unnecessary stress. Though you can bring forward the date for the signing of the *escritura* (with the consent of the seller) with relative ease, to delay can be extremely difficult and endanger your main deposit. Certainly, for understandable reasons, most sellers will want the signing of the *escritura* scheduled as soon as possible!
6. The date for receipt of the main deposit. There is no legal requirement for the main deposit to be 10%; thus it can be any amount.
7. The date and amount of any reserve deposit (normally payable immediately). This reserve deposit will usually be small – around 1% of the purchase price. Its primary function is to ensure that your seller removes his property from the marketplace until the date for the main deposit. This gives your lawyer time to undertake his legal enquiries and provides you with some protection against being swindled. Equally, if your lawyer finds problems with the

property or you decide not to go ahead with its purchase, you will lose only your reserve deposit.

Gradually escalate your risk during the buying process. Never rush – or be rushed

It is wise also to insist that the terms below are inserted in the private contract. They are not obligatory but are commonly used and rarely contentious:

- That the seller must pay you twice the amount of the reserve deposit should he renege on his agreement to sell you his property. So, for example, if the reserve deposit is €3,000, he would have to pay you €6,000 if he refuses subsequently to sell the property to you.

- The seller will return to you any reserve deposit should certain defined matters not be in order, such as an inherent flaw in the seller's title or right to sell you the property.

- You agree to allow the seller to keep the reserve deposit you have paid if you change your mind and decide not to go ahead with the purchase.

Note: Do not confuse a reserve deposit (normally a small sum of between €500–€3,000) and its terms with those of the main deposit. The latter (usually 10% of the purchase price) is invariably non-returnable!

Once your lawyer has drawn up the private contract, he will show it to the seller for the latter's agreement and a date for the signing will be arranged. Your lawyer should translate the private contract for you and provide a copy in your own language. Certainly, you must understand and agree to each and every clause.

The signing of the private contract normally takes place at your lawyer's office and takes the form of a relaxed and informal meeting. Both you and the seller must be present to sign unless powers of attorney are in place. At this time you will hand over to the seller any reserve deposit (if there is to be one) or the main deposit if it is to be received at this stage.

Signing the *escritura*

The signing of the *escritura* is always done in front of a *notario* at *notarios'* offices. These are normally busy offices with a series of rooms containing conference-style tables at which all parties involved sit. The offices also have an accounts section which deals with payment of fees to the *notario*. Normally, there are huddles of buyers and sellers talking to their lawyers in the foyer area adding to the general bustle as people pass to and fro.

You must have your original passport and original NIE number with you when you go to the notario to sign the escritura

You should always attend the *notario* with your lawyer. Usually your lawyer will find somewhere for you to sit down while he makes sure that the seller or his lawyer are present and ready and that there are no last-minute glitches. In particular, your lawyer will:

- Make sure the existing service (electricity, water and telephone) contracts will be continued. He will ensure also that the seller hands to you any outstanding amounts due between the last billing date and that of the date for signing the *escritura*. Normally, you will receive this money in cash.

- Check that you have the correct money with which to pay the seller. This is usually in the form of a banker's draft but can, of course, be cash. If the seller is liable for CGT on the sale of his property then 3% CGT will be deducted by your lawyer from the full sale price. This will be retained by you (the buyer) and must be paid by you to the Spanish tax office (*hacienda*) within 30 days of signing the *escritura.*

- Double-check there have been no further encumbrances on the property. Your lawyer will, at the *notario*'s office, undertake a final check to ensure the title of the property is still clear and that the seller has not placed some form of charge on the property over the previous few hours. He will do this by applying for a *nota simple* on the property, normally by telephone. This is a certificate issued by the Central Registry of Properties that shows if there are any charges or encumbrances on a property, such as mortgages and rights of way. This will be attached to the *escritura.*

- Pay the *notario* his fees.

As soon as your lawyer is satisfied that everything is correct, he will lead you into the *notario*'s office together with the seller and his lawyer (if he has one). The *notario* will then:

- Check the identity of all those signing the *escritura* by looking at their identity cards or passports and *NIE* numbers. These details he will double-check against those written in the *escritura.*

- Read out loud the contents of the new *escritura* from cover to cover. This provides:

    - A full description of the buyers and sellers by way of passport/identity card details and *NIE* numbers
    - A complete description of the property – the area (m²) of any buildings and the area (m²) of the land
    - A description of the boundaries
    - The sale price of the property
    - Details of any encumbrances or rights of way
    - A check of the details of the *escritura* against those of the *nota simple*

If either the buyer or seller is not Spanish, or fluent in Spanish, then the words of the *notario* will be translated. This is often done by your lawyer (who should always speak your language fluently!).

- The *notario* will then ask if you and the seller agree to the contents of the *escritura*. If you both consent, he will ask both of you to sign the document. At this time, the seller will pass the keys of your property to you and you will give to the seller the remaining purchase money (the sale price less any reserve deposit and main deposit already paid).

Now you own your property and have the right to immediate access! Normally, you will go straight to your bank to make sure that all the service contracts are changed to your name and placed upon direct debit. This is usually followed by a trip to the nearest bar ...

The signing of the *escritura* can happen quite quickly. Much depends upon how busy the *notario*'s office is on the day of signing and if any last-minute problems have transpired. Certainly, it would not be unusual for the actual signing process to be finished within 20-30 minutes.

Alternative Routes to Signing the Escritura

Route B
1. *Agreement 'in principle'*
2. *Informal deposit*
3. *Sign* escritura

This way of reaching the *escritura* is undertaken often by the Spanish (and particularly Spanish professionals) when they are buying property. In essence, a buyer will see a property that he likes and negotiate terms with the seller. If an agreement is achieved, then the buyer or seller may draw up a rough memorandum of their agreement or just shake hands on the deal. The buyer will give the seller a deposit (perhaps €500) and agree to make an appointment with the *notario* within an agreed (and normally very short) time period to sign the *escritura*.

The signing of the *escritura* will take place in exactly the same manner as in route A – but at no time will there be a formal private contract and often lawyers will not be involved.

This route is fraught with problems for a new buyer in Spain. Firstly, you may lose your deposit if you've given it to someone who turns out not to have the right (or all the rights) to the property title. Equally, there is a serious danger that the property will not be investigated thoroughly in the rush to sign the *escritura*. Though this may not matter to an experienced Spanish property buyer, it could be disastrous for you.

Route C

1. *Agreement 'in principle'*
2. *Sign* escritura

Again, this route tends to be taken by the Spanish and particularly by developers who are familiar with a given type of property and all its benefits and detriments. Normally, this route involves a seller who wants to act fast. If he sees a (new) property he wants, he will make an agreement in principle with the buyer and then sign the *escritura* (as in route A) as soon as a *notario* is available.

Obviously, if you place no deposit down on a property – even a small one – then no seller will take his property off the market. So, you may undertake extensive investigations only to find that your seller has sold the property to the first person to provide him with some hard cash.

Of course, in theory you can take as long as you like to reach the signing of the *escritura*. However, both routes B and C tend, in practice, to be used by the parties concerned to speed up the process before signing the *escritura*. Though this can be a significant benefit, it can also create a momentum that better suits the interests of sellers and agents.

Route D

1. *Agreement 'in principle'*
2. *Reserve deposit agreement*
3. *Possible private contract*
4. *Sign* escritura

This route to the *escritura* is usually undertaken when the seller is not available to sign a private contract. For example, the seller may be out of the country. In this case, an agreement in principle may be achieved between you and the seller's estate agent. It may be that you have telephone or e-mail contact with the seller, but an agreement in principle can also occur without any direct contact.

For example, the seller's agent may draw up a memorandum of the agreement whereby you will consent to providing a deposit to secure the property and thereby have it removed from sale. The terms of the memorandum are similar to those of a private contract. However, unless the seller's agent has a power of attorney for the seller, the agreement is unlikely to be legally binding or enforceable.

Nonetheless, you may pay a deposit (normally about 1% of the purchase price of the property) on the basis that, on the return of the seller, a proper, legally binding private contract will be drawn up and signed. Alternatively, you and the seller may decide to go straight to the signing of the *escritura*.

The problem with this type of agreement is:

- You are giving money (your deposit) to someone who has little or no legal right to it.

- You are making an agreement concerning someone else's property (the seller's) without his signature or presence.

- The agent may be only one of many of the seller's agents and therefore not have the authorisation to take the property off the market.

- Sometimes seller's agents increase their commission levels substantially and mask this from a buyer (and sometimes a seller) through this operation.

Without doubt, the safest way to proceed is route A if you have not bought property in Spain before. Even if you have, the other routes, though speedy, need to be carefully monitored.

Certainly, one of the greatest dangers you face when buying property in Spain is being rushed. It is almost too easy to buy quickly and to be impressed by a system that, on the face of it, is wonderfully simple (for example, route C). However, in reality, buying property is rarely trouble free. If it seems so, then you have either been very lucky or, more probably, you are unaware of inherent problems.

The secret of buying property in Spain is to make sure you are never pressurised and that, in turn, you never unduly pressurise your lawyer. Make sure your legal process is unhurried and methodical. In short, escalate your risk gradually. This may infuriate your agent and madden your seller, but it is the only safe way to proceed.

Of course, a cautious approach may lead to the loss of the property on which you have set your heart. However, inevitably, there will be something comparable elsewhere and you may have avoided the disaster of a lifetime ...

Loose Ends

Upon signing the *escritura,* you take immediate and full possession of your property and therefore any liability for it. So, you need to:

- Obtain buildings and contents insurance
- Ensure that all services are in your name
- Register with your local town hall
- Ensure your *escritura* is registered at the Land Registry

Buildings and Contents Insurance

Obviously, you must insure your property and possessions straight away. This is something you can arrange before the signing of the *escritura* and activate immediately afterwards. Certainly, it is not something to either forget or delay once you have taken possession of your property.

The situation with regard to insurance is very similar to that in the UK. The two elements of your insurance are separated into the value of the building concerned and the value of its contents. The building's replacement cost will be assessed on its size and thereby the cost of reconstruction. This is normally worked out according to a formula based on the cost of construction per m^2 relevant to your type of property.

Never forget to insure your new property and do not under-insure your possessions!

Your contents insurance premium will be based on your assessment of the value of your contents. Of these, particularly valuable items such as jewellery will have to be itemised with their specific values.

Buildings and contents insurance can be obtained from an array of companies. Most banks provide insurance, as do major companies such as Mapfre and Linea Directa (the Spanish version of Direct Line).

As always, it is worth obtaining a number of quotations as well as making sure that you do not fall into the trap of undervaluing your possessions for the sake of a slightly lower premium.

Finally, it is a sound idea to take photographs (preferably digital) of your property, all its rooms and the possessions you have there. These photographs will stand as a reliable record should you have a major fire or burglary. Often, after any such trauma, it is difficult to remember exactly what you possessed and describing accurately the condition of your property can be difficult. Obviously, make sure that your photographs are not kept in your property and are left with a friend or are accessible on the internet.

Ensure That All Services Are in Your Name

As already stated, make sure that no service (electricity, water, telephone and gas) contracts are terminated by your seller. This can lead to considerable delays in reconnecting them, as well as unnecessary costs. So, always make sure that your lawyer agrees with your seller to maintain the existing service contracts until the signing of the *escritura*. Thereafter, the details will be changed into your name. This is often undertaken for free by your bank and activated immediately. However, you will need to provide:

- Your specific instructions to change the names on the contracts
- A copy of the relevant service bills (with, for example, account details)
- A copy of the *escritura* (as proof of ownership of the property)

As in the UK, it is wise to place your service contracts on direct debit. Water, electricity and telephone bills are normally delivered monthly.

Register With Your Local Town Hall

It is essential that you register yourself as the owner of your new property with your local town hall. Your local town hall receives central funding dependent, to a great extent, on the number of people registered as living within the area. So, if you do not register, you will have a negative effect on the amount of funding your area receives. However, you need to register also to ensure that you can:

- Pay the rates (*IBI or Impuestos de Bienes Inmuebles*) on your property and any separate rubbish clearance charge. As the owner of a property (whether a flat, villa or *finca*) it is obligatory to pay these annually. To register, you will need to take with you:
  - A copy of your *escritura*
  - A copy of your *NIE*
  - Your passport

> *Do not forget to register with your local town hall – doing so has important consequences for local funding. Furthermore, you will frequently be required to show proof of address*

Again, it is worth paying your *IBI* by direct debit.

One of the most striking differences between the UK and Spain is how low the annual *IBI* charge is – often a fraction of UK council rates. This means the obligatory overheads of a property in Spain are amazingly low, particularly for *casas de pueblo* and flats.

Rubbish clearance is undertaken by your local authority from communal bins situated along every street within urban areas. There are also eco-parks outside most villages and towns where relevant waste can be disposed of.

- **Obtain a *certificado de empadronamiento***
  A *certificado de empadronamiento* is a document signed by the mayor of your local town hall certifying you as a resident of the area. The *certificado de empadronamiento* displays your *NIE* number and address and is a document you will be asked for frequently when dealing with bureaucratic matters. Normally, it costs around €1–€2 and can be obtained within a couple of days of making a request. Generally, it expires after six months, at which time you will have to apply for another one if it is needed for a specific function. It is not obligatory to have a valid *certificado de empadronamiento* but it is something for which you will be frequently asked!

On your first visit to your town hall for a *certificado de empadronamiento* you should take with you:

- A copy of your *escritura*
- Your *NIE* number
- Your passport

Ensure Your Escritura is Registered at the Land Registry

Make sure that your *escritura* is registered formally with the Spanish Land Registry, as this provides conclusive (and easy to show) proof that you own your property. At worst, not having this may lead to someone trying to place a charge on the property! Oddly enough, it is not compulsory to register an *escritura*, although any diligent Spanish lawyer should do this as a matter of course.

Always instruct your lawyer to register your escritura with the Spanish Land Registry

There is a fee for registration that varies according to the value of the property declared in the *escritura*. Normally, registration is completed within 4–6 weeks, at which time you or your lawyer will receive an original version of the *escritura*. This you should keep safely.

Finally, make sure that you keep your original *escritura*. Even if you have a mortgage, it is unusual in Spain for a bank to keep the *escritura*. So, ask for yours to be returned if your bank has retained it.

Construction Problems

The words 'construction' and 'problems' seem inextricably linked, irrespective of the country! Spain certainly has an indifferent record when it comes to the construction of new properties and it would be a grave mistake to associate a new house with safe and sound building. Indeed, considerable caution needs to be exercised when buying any property in Spain, whether old or new, flat or townhouse, *finca* or villa.

Some properties in Spain have been constructed extremely well, but others have been built very badly. Yet others may combine both good and bad building – for example, an excellent superstructure standing on inadequate foundations. The Spanish building boom of early to mid-2000 was nothing if not a time of poor building control, unskilled workers and rushed jobs.

Of course, telling the difference between a sound and an unsound property is the work of a qualified professional (see *The Property Professionals*). Certainly, you must never believe that just because a property looks good, or is of high value, that it is sound. The reverse may be true, with any faults masked by an exemplary finish. This is relatively easy to achieve given that most buildings in Spain are heavily tiled and have a rendered finish.

Certainly, few laymen can tell authoritatively whether roof design is appropriate, foundations adequate, proper damp proofing in place or if a hairline crack indicates a serious structural fault. This is the job of a qualified professional and you should not avoid using a top-class building surveyor to inspect your property before you buy it.

> *Never try to save money by not employing a*
> *qualified building surveyor to inspect your*
> *property – whether it is old or newly built*

Be aware also that Spain's weather can be quite extreme and can test the integrity of a building. This is the case even along the normally benign Mediterranean coastline, which can experience ferocious rainstorms (the *Gota Frìa* in particular) that last several days.

Meanwhile, winters can be chilly, particularly in buildings devoid of central heating and quality insulation. On the other hand, the blazing Spanish summer sun can be the test of the design of a property, whether in terms of the materials used or the quality of shade provided.

Of course, climate extremes, earth tremors and localised freak weather conditions (often affecting ground moisture content) can have adverse effects even on well-designed and well-built structures. Indeed, any building can be subject to structural defects at any time in its life cycle.

Building problems can be divided broadly into two types of property (although the problems of each can overlap):

- New builds (any property built within the past 10 years)
- Older properties

New Builds

Since 6 May 2000, by law (specifically, *'La Ley de Ordenación de la Edificación'*), any new build must have an insurance-backed, 10-year guarantee (this is similar to the NHBC scheme in the UK). In Spain, this scheme is called the *seguro decenal* and is often referred to as 'the builder's guarantee' or just the *decenal*.

Unfortunately, the *decenal* is by no means as comprehensive as its UK (NHBC) equivalent (although the NHBC has been criticised for some of its 'get out' clauses! However, you must be especially wary of relying on the Spanish *decenal* to resolve all your new building problems. Indeed, the very term 'builder's guarantee' is misleading. The *decenal* essentially only covers issues related to structural stability and resistance. This leaves many other potential issues unprotected, such as leaking roofs or damp.

Nonetheless, the *decenal* is important and does provide some protection for those buying new builds, albeit court action is sometimes necessary to get insurers to accept liability. Certainly, if a property has been built since May 2000 and does not have a *decenal* then the chances are that it was not, by definition, legally constructed – and you should be extremely wary of buying it.

An exception to this rule is if the owner is (or was) an *auto promoto'* (self builder). This is when a person builds his own house to live in rather than for onward sale. *Auto promotors* can avoid the obligatory *decenal* insurance; however they are restricted from selling their house for 10 years.

> *Be extremely wary of any new build agreement that purports to makes you responsible for the building of your new property*

Unfortunately, some builders have duped 'off-plan' buyers into signing up as *auto promotors* so the builder can avoid the costs and regulations imposed by the *decenal*. So, for example, the builder may avoid the cost of doing an obligatory geo-technical study of the substrate and not pay for the works to be supervised by an approved technical control organisation (often referred to locally as an '*OCT'*).

You must be very cautious of being persuaded to become an *'auto promotor'*. Unwittingly, you may end up with a new property that:

- Has no *decenal* and therefore no protection against structural faults
- You are not allowed to sell for 10 years

The *decenal* is intended to provide the following protection to the owner of a property until expiry of the 10-year period:

- Insurance covering issues that affect the structural stability of the insured elements
- Damages up to the cost of rebuilding the property – irrespective of responsibility

Problems With the Implementation of the Decenal

In theory, *decenal* insurers are legally obliged to pay out to the owner of a new build if there is a proven structural stability issue that needs correction. This is irrespective of whether the fault is due to the builder or architect and whether the problem is because of negligence, faulty materials or processes.

However, typically *decenal* insurers are extremely tardy about honouring their obligations. Indeed, usually they refuse to accept a claim unless negligence is proven in court. This is because they know full well that if, for example, an architect is proved negligent, then any remedial costs will be covered by the architect's own professional indemnity insurance.

Do not equate the protection afforded by a UK NHBC scheme with that of the Spanish decenal system. The latter is far weaker

So, although *decenal* insurers are legally obliged to act, they rarely act until forced to. This is despite the fact that they can potentially recover their costs from the builder or architect responsible for the defective or negligent work.

Certainly, the failure of *decenal* insurers to act promptly is a shock for many new build owners who have cause to make a claim. Unfortunately, most owners find the 'builder's guarantee' is not a quick rescue package. Furthermore, the *decenal* does not cover many of the more common building faults and therefore provides a disappointingly low level of protection.

Indeed, it is not uncommon for the future plans of owners of defective properties with 'guarantees' to be so disrupted that they are forced to return to the UK. This often involves considerable financial loss and can impose real stress on any relationship.

Certainly, there is little similarity between the UK NHBC scheme and the Spanish *decenal*. The really big difference is that the UK NHBC is backed up by a very good building control system. By comparison, the *decenal* system has proven to be unsatisfactory and a slow and ineffective backup for an extremely poor system of building control.

Certainly, the building control system in Spain is riddled with inexperienced and, sometimes, corrupt officials and professionals, which can lead to many claims for structural problems on new builds. There are grounds for suggesting that, as a consequence, *decenal* insurers are wary of honouring claims.

It is worth noting that a system of architect and builder responsibility existed for some time before the introduction of the *decenal*. Indeed, builders and architects had been always liable to some extent for the structural integrity of the buildings they constructed in Spain. However, sadly, the legal obligations of a builder with a *decenal* policy have not always impelled him to do good work.

> *Remember that a decenal ('builder's guarantee') on a new build provides little protection for lengthy, stressful and costly court action*

In fact, since the imposition of the *decenal*, some less-than-conscientious builders have skimped on the structural aspect of new buildings. This has been done possibly on the thinking that the client is covered anyway by the *decenal* policy should anything go wrong. As a consequence, it is quite common for a new build to feature less substantial foundations than a property that may be over 20 years old.

General Short-term Builder Liability

Fortunately, builders do have general responsibilities imposed on them by law. *Ley 38/1999 de 5 de Noviembre ('Ordenación de la Edificación')* states that a builder has an obligation to:

- Correct identified snagging points (normally assessed 15–30 days prior to signing the escritura)

- Correct just about any defect (other than normal wear and tear) during the first 12 months following completion

- Rectify functional issues that affect the enjoyment or habitability of a property for the following two years (i.e. a builder's responsibilities run for the first three years after completion)

Unfortunately, the devastating fall in the property market in 2008 has meant that many builders simply fail to respond to requests to correct issues. Alternatively, sometimes they buy time by purposefully botching repairs in a somewhat naive effort to get past the three-year deadline. Accordingly, you should avoid ever paying all that you owe to a builder until each and every defect on new building work has been remedied. Some of these may not be obvious or easy to identify. So, a wise buyer always will employ an independent building surveyor to conduct a pre-completion survey of a new build. This will result in an authoritative, rigorous and professional 'snagging list' and catch any problems at an appropriately early stage.

> *No matter what a builder or agent promises, always hold back on paying final money on a new build 'subject to survey'*

Without doubt, in a property market downturn it is the building industry that suffers grievously. This means that many builders go bankrupt or are left struggling with reduced manpower and a lack of skilled workers. As a consequence, trying to get defects rectified can be extremely difficult or, at worst, impossible. To state the obvious, if a builder goes out of business then no amount of badgering will work – and if he has no assets, then any court action is likely to be a waste of time and money.

Your builder may have had all-risks insurance to cover defects outside the strict scope of the *decenal*. However, this is rare and any enforcement likely only after a court hearing. That said, it is worth noting that early presentation of a court *demanda* should prevent a builder from closing down his company.

If a new property does not meet its specification or is uninhabitable, then this may merit the reversal of your agreement to buy. However, doing so is far from risk free and invariably it will involve a court action. This can be slow and costly and may even go to appeal.

You must be careful when buying an off-plan new build to check that any caveat within the plans or agreement to build is acceptable to you. Many developers reserve their right to make changes unilaterally to a specification via clauses in their promotional material and subsequent contracts. So, you may find that they are within their rights to change your new property, despite the alterations being contrary to any original intention.

If you are going to buy a new build you should:

- Ensure that your new property will have *decenal* cover upon completion
- Choose a builder who has an all-risks building insurance policy
- Employ a qualified and experienced building surveyor to inspect your property before paying all money due

Examples of New Build Problems

First Occupation License

It is essential that your new build is granted a *Licencia de Primera Ocupación* (sometimes referred to as a *Certificado de Habitacion* or '*Cedula*') before you pay fully for the property. This certificate is granted by the local town hall planning department on completion of a new build and declares the legality of the property. Also, it acts (in theory) as confirmation that the property meets all necessary local and national planning regulations.

However, the corrupt practice of some town hall officials has meant that some illegal properties have been unlawfully granted their license papers. A consequence of this is that some officials in Spain are now in serious trouble – and others already imprisoned. The government is compensating some owners of such properties and even allowing their properties to be fully legalised. However, this should not be taken as given, as other owners face the possibility of seeing their homes demolished. Their loss, to put it mildly, could be devastating.

If your property, when completed, does not have a *Licencia de Primera Ocupación* (sometimes referred to in English as a First Occupation License or FOC) then alarm bells should ring! One sign that this is the case is when a property is not connected to mains utilities (water, electrics and telephone). This is known sometimes as being on 'builder's electrics and water' – which is an accurate phrase! Indeed, your property's services may be connected to your builder rather than the services suppliers. This is usually obvious, but can be proven by the fact that you will not receive or be able to obtain any formal services bills.

Today, by Spanish law, utility companies cannot connect their services to illegal properties. If they do, they can be fined heavily. So, services suppliers tend not to connect to illegal properties, though in the past some turned a blind eye.

So, if your new property lacks a mains supply of electricity and water and a landline telephone, take this as a potential sign of illegality. At best, it may indicate there are delays with regard to legalisation or final completion of your project.

Note: Sometimes personal registry on the local *'empadronamiento'* can also be affected by lack of a First Occupancy License.

> **Do not pay your builder the full amount
> or move into your property unless it has a
> Licencia de Primera Ocupación**

Being 'on builder's electrics and water' used to be laughed off and was tolerated by many buyers of new builds, who were frequently told this was 'quite normal' and would be 'sorted out soon'. However, some found out later, to their great cost, that the underlying reason for this seemingly innocent delay was related to the far more serious and worrying issue of illegality.

Note: Failure to supply a *Licencia de Primera Ocupación* constitutes a breach of contract on the part of the seller. Indeed:

- You are not obliged to sign the *escritura* until the *Licencia de Primera Ocupación* is presented

- Your seller cannot cancel the contract on the grounds that you refuse to sign the *escritura* without the *Licencia de Primera Ocupación*

If your property does not have a *Licencia de Primera Ocupación* upon completion of the building works, you can cancel the contract and claim a refund of your purchase money with interest and related damages, irrespective of whether or not you have signed an *escritura*.

Obviously, it is best not to occupy your new property until everything is finalised and you have a *Licencia de Primera Ocupación*. However, some knowingly take the risk of buying a property on the basis that 'everything will turn out all right in the end'. This is unwise.

There are occasionally genuine factors for a delay in obtaining a *Licencia de Primera Ocupación*, but generally, any delay must be assessed carefully. Indeed, if your lawyer is in any way flippant about the lack of *Licencia de Primera Ocupación* for your property, you should obtain a second opinion immediately. Certainly, you should never, ever take any risks when there is an issue with a property's *Licencia de Primera Ocupación*.

Damp

Damp problems are common to:

- Sub-ground areas – often called underbuilds or *sotanos*. These often lack effective tanking. This is particularly true of illegal underbuilds.

- Terrace door surround areas and roof terraces. These are often poorly sealed and lack a waterproof membrane.

- Over-sealing of the living space. This causes condensation-related mould and is more common in new double-glazed properties than in older, poorly insulated houses.

Subsidence

Shockingly, some new properties are built on lesser foundations than even older properties might have. This was done by disreputable builders to save money during the rampant construction of the property boom. Indeed, poor building control (sometimes even involving false 'geo-technical ground surveys') has resulted occasionally in serious under-specification of foundations. This can cause movement to occur early in the life of a building and is very expensive to correct.

Just because a property is well finished does not mean the foundations are sound

The practice of building on 'leftover' sites (often comprising poor ground conditions) has meant that some properties are located on very steep, unstable ground, on backfill, or in flood plains. In some extreme cases, properties block natural flash flood water courses!

Retaining Wall – Movement and Failure

Many properties are dependent on retaining wall stability. Unfortunately, most retaining walls in Spain are not built properly and are rarely treated by either builders or buyers with the seriousness they deserve.

A retaining wall vulnerable to movement or collapse will often affect the built elements on a plot – such as the house itself and the swimming pool. Correcting a retaining wall is difficult and rebuilding it properly very expensive.

At first sight, what appears to be just a cracked 'garden' wall may seem of little relevance – but failing retaining walls can turn a dream into a nightmare. Certainly, they are far more relevant to the main house and pool than many people realise.

In some cases, retaining walls have been omitted and new properties sit either above or below cut slopes that are highly prone to collapse or landslides. This can risk lives. Unfortunately, some unscrupulous developers are prepared to sell properties with these issues to innocent buyers despite the dangers. This is because the construction of a proper load-bearing retaining wall significantly adds costs to a building project, while providing no obvious benefit to the layman.

Rot and Insect Attack

Termites and wood-boring beetles are prevalent in Spain and nearly all wood needs to be properly injected with the appropriate treatment if attack is to be deterred.

Although advanced attack is most common in older properties, some new properties also suffer.

Damp-related rot is very common in underbuild areas when timbers have not been treated properly.

Note: As many building plots were previously woodland or orchards, the ground typically harbours many types of insect and fungus that affect buildings. Town areas also have active attack in many older buildings, and airborne spores and insects in flight (termites have both a flight stage and ground networks) will soon access any vulnerable timbers.

Steel Reinforced Concrete Steel Decay

Although new builds rarely show signs of reinforcement corrosion, ventilation or surface protection may well have been omitted. In this case some new properties can be at high risk of decay in the future.

In much Spanish building, standard practice precautions to protect steel were commonly ignored during the property boom. This was combined, all too often, with poor building control and sometimes, inadequate knowledge on the part of those actually constructing properties. So, even new builds should be inspected professionally to ensure that reinforced steel work has been correctly installed and protected for the long-term security of a building.

Swimming Pool Defects

Surprisingly, even new swimming pools can have serious structural issues and in recent years many pools have been built defectively or over insufficient foundations (normally to save money). Equally, on very rare occasions pools have been 'faked': tiled with steps, dolphin mosaic and so on, but laid over a basic block lining with no reinforced structure. This has resulted in the walls and base failing once the pool is filled and the full weight of the water imposed on the structure.

Defective Services

A rush to complete a project and poor building control means that some new properties suffer from leaks in supply and waste drainage pipes. Although gas and electrical installations are generally subject to strict controls, defects can exist nonetheless. Any structural movement may also lead to gas and water leaks, increasing the risk of electrical fire.

Older Properties

Many established properties actually represent a better option. In the past, builders generally had a local reputation to uphold and were often time-served professional tradesman or experienced in good practice techniques.

However, poorly constructed self-build weekend homes (*casitas*) are common in Spain. Some of these can be seriously defective and typically were never designed for year-round use. Generally properties on formal urbanisations are more likely to have been built subject to architect control. However you still need to assess these carefully, particularly if an estate has been recently urbanised.

Exercise considerable caution with Rural properties as they may have been constructed without building control or planning permission

Examples of Older Property Build Problems

Subsidence

Older builds can also be affected by subsidence. Though a house may show few signs of movement in its early years, long-term ground erosion, seasonal shrinkage or heave (often amplified in a very wet or very dry year) can reveal problems suddenly. The attempted cover-up of such issues is quite common. Often it will take an experienced building surveyor to identify any telltale signs of past or ongoing structural movement.

Retaining Wall – Movement and Failure

Many older properties are as reliant on the stability of retaining walls as new builds, particularly if the slope on which the property is situated was cut out of a hillside. Certainly, the attractive stone walls seen in many coastal areas are not normally proper retaining walls, but simply decorative facing, when in fact the hillside is highly prone to movement.

Rot and Insect Attack

Advanced attack is common in older properties. Buyers of older townhouses and country properties often do not realise the timbers are made of softwood (and not oak, as we commonly expect in very old UK properties). These timbers are often infested with woodworm, termites and other wood-boring insects.

Structural failure of very old properties is actually quite common in Spain and must be taken seriously as some accidents have been fatal. This has meant that laws have been introduced more recently with 'repair or demolish' orders increasingly common.

Without doubt, the property boom saw a multitude of fake 'renovations' often carried out by North Europeans with the aim of selling on their properties for a profit. As it is very difficult to renovate properly and make money, skimping on repairs to important structural elements has been rife.

Risk of Decay in Reinforced Concrete Steel

The process of steel reinforcement decay can be slow and is therefore always more prevalent and advanced in older properties. Steel decay can result eventually in structural failure in floors – and even whole apartment blocks have been known to fail. Normally, professional inspection will identify initial signs of decay so that repairs can be made. However, these repairs are invariably expensive and complicated, and advanced decay can mean that substantial rebuilding is required. In some cases, the concrete itself may be sub-standard or even mixed with salt water and beach sand in coastal locations (albeit in rare cases).

Swimming Pool Defects

Older pools can, on occasion, be very well built and are sometimes based on converted water deposits. Nonetheless, many suffer structural issues in the long term, which can be expensive to resolve. A typical problem is expired galvanised iron pipe work. This eventually decays and leaks, which can cause erosion of the supporting substrates.

Defective Services

Old drains can be broken and septic tanks insufficient for year-round use. Equally, iron pipe work can be corroded; even some supposedly 'replumbed' properties may be connected to hidden iron elements. Rewiring is sometimes needed and some gas installations can be very dangerous.

Note: Legally, if you find any significant defects that have been deliberately hidden by your seller within six months of purchase then you may have a case for compensation against your seller. However, this can be very difficult to prove and it is always better to try and identify any issues prior to purchase by consulting a building surveyor.

Finally, note that the problems discussed above, of both new and old properties, are far from conclusive or comprehensive. Indeed, each and every property is individual and must be treated always as such!

Never be tempted to carry out a DIY survey – even taking a friendly builder on site is no substitute for hiring an experienced building surveyor

Planning Permission and Licenses

Do not, under any circumstances, fall into the trap of thinking Spain lacks planning and building controls and that you therefore do not have to comply. Although controls are not always obvious (and have been often abused), they do exist, and apply to new building, renovations and any additions to an existing building.

In fact, just like in the UK, there are stringent controls on what you can and cannot do. Indeed, be under no illusions! If you transgress planning regulations and building controls, you will be liable for serious penalties and, potentially, an order for demolition of your property.

So, before you start any work, always make sure that what you intend doing complies with the law and that you obtain (before work starts!) the correct licenses and permissions.

Certainly, it has become even more important to obtain correct licencing since the end of the property boom. During the boom, town halls had significant income from licence fees and little time or need to search for additional income from small works projects. That has changed with the drastic halt in the Spanish construction industry. This has meant that town halls have more time to ensure that all projects are subject to licences and pay the appropriate fees.

The drop in general construction activity after the property boom and the lack of income from licence fees has also made the enforcement of regulations more rigorous. This has been followed by the imposition of fines or even demolition orders. In some cases, bribes (previously aimed at encouraging officials to turn a blind eye) are now being paid to encourage officials to ensure *compliance!*

For example a builder trying to sell 50 legal, properly built properties may try to disrupt the completion (or even encourage the demolition) of a competitor's properties if he knows these breach the regulations. Certainly, the majority of notifications of breaches result from aggrieved neighbours reporting unlicensed works. So, on no account think that you can get away with illegal works. Equally, be wary of buying a property that has had any unlicensed additions or improvements.

> *Always check if your building work needs planning permission, however minor the works may appear*

If you are unsure about whether or not you need a licence or permission to do building work, enquire first at your local town hall with the technical officer *(aparejador)*. In principle, take the view that a licence will be required for any improvement or alteration of your property unless you are specifically advised otherwise. Certainly, be extremely cautious when builders claim you do not need a licence (for example, for works within the line of the existing walls). Be suspicious of anyone who states anything like 'anyway, no one ever gets one for this type of project ...'

Technically, all works (however minor!) require some form of licence. Certainly, this is the case for any extension of the living (habitable) volume of a property or for changes to the internal distribution of a house. Normally, the conversion of an underbuild, building on an existing terrace, and even enclosing or glazing a covered terrace will require a formal project presentation to your town hall – or at the very least a licence for '*obras menor*' (minor works).

Time and again, foreigners have found themselves in trouble with local authority planning departments in Spain. Often problems only become apparent when owners try to resell their property. It is then that any transgressions invariably come to light as a buyer, lawyer or bank valuer investigates the property. If there is no supporting legal paperwork for any work done, it can result in not just losing a sale but serious sanctions.

Often people do not check that their builders have obtained the correct licence before allowing work to start on their property. This is exacerbated by failing to insist on obtaining a formal town hall certificate of completion of work before paying off their builder or architect fully once the project has been finished.

Project documents mean nothing unless they are signed by an architect and stamped by the College of Architects (*Colegio de Arquitectos*) and comply with the local *normas* (planning guidelines for the zone). The licence for 'project of execution' is that held by the town hall and is worth double-checking. All too often property owners agree with builders to do the work, when only a part of the project has been granted approval.

So, for example, a plan for an underbuild 'apartment' (possibly presented to you by your builder in an effort to secure more work) is not legal unless the project has been expressly and legally approved by your local town hall. You must check this is the case – or you may agree to and pay for work that was never licensed. This can be a very serious error if the work results in an illegal increase in your 'habitable volume' and transgresses area *normas*.

Be aware that numerous builders fail to gain permission for 'optional' extensions to a property's living space without property owners being aware of this. Equally, numerous town halls are under investigation for passing projects that breach area *normas*. Indeed, some town hall officials are serving prison terms for issuing licences that contravened the *normas*, often having taken bribes to do so. Accordingly, it does not follow that just because the town hall has given 'permission' that this was granted legally.

As well as town halls, some 'in-house' lawyers collude with illegal activity. So, always make sure that you employ independent professionals to present and oversee a project i.e. those independent of the builder, developer or estate agent.

The authorities have a number of tools to aid them in controlling illegal building work, including satellite and aerial imagery. These are being used increasingly and the government is now also demanding that all town halls submit a list of known infringements. The net, it would appear, is finally closing in on illegal building activity!

Building and Renovation (reform) Projects

Without doubt, building works are the source of innumerable problems and similar to those experienced in the UK. There are good builders as well as reliable, highly skilled tradesman, but there are also those whose work is disgraceful. Cost overruns are common and time-management can be poor, with minor works faring no better than major ones.

Meanwhile, it is often only halfway through a job that you find either that you have chosen the wrong workmen or that you have mismanaged the project as a whole. Sometimes it is a combination of the two. However, the result is invariably the same: your first few months in Spain blighted by stress and unnecessarily wasted money.

Never underestimate building work – it is far more complex and problematic than it looks

If you intend undertaking any building work, then allow from the start for a process that is likely to test your limits. If you are not prepared to go through this, then you should buy a property that needs the bare minimum of work. As in the UK, even if you receive a fixed quote it is worth preparing yourself for an overrun of at least 30% and for the work to take twice the time intended. By mentally preparing yourself in this way, you may avoid some of the stress brought on by unrealistic expectations!

This is not to say that the workers within the building industry in Spain are worse than those in the UK. In fact, overall it is much the same, and irrespective of whether the builders are native Spanish, South American, East European or expatriate.

Always seek builder recommendations and references, go and see other work done by the builder, and speak to previous clients

Of course, if you speak no Spanish then matters can be exacerbated significantly as your builders and suppliers struggle to understand or interpret exactly what you want.

Many relocating Britons automatically avoid Spanish builders and employ expatriates, who they can understand. Though this is logical in part, bear in mind that British builders in Spain have a habit of charging UK rates to expatriates. So, it is worth always obtaining quotations from both nationalities – not least because builders new to Spain can suffer also from poor knowledge of local construction and materials.

One of the most justifiable criticisms made by builders (whether Spanish or British) is that rarely do they receive clear and precise instructions from their clients. This is invariably the root cause of many construction and reform problems. Indeed, unless a builder has a written schedule of works accompanied by a clear specification there will be always trouble – irrespective of how skilled and conscientious the builder is.

> *If the builder has no work to show you*
> *and no references, look elsewhere*

The problem is that most people are unwilling to spend money and time on developing a clear schedule of works, and few people know what a specification is. So, work usually starts on the basis of oral instructions or with only a few scraps of paper to illustrate roughly what is required. Supervision of a project is then invariably unprofessional and is matched by erratic or over-generous stage payments – culminating in full payment for a job far from complete.

Certainly, the involvement of an architect can help considerably. In any event, an extension, internal redistribution and structural works normally require an architect's involvement and supervision. For other works, a simple preliminary site meeting involving you, the builder and an experienced, bilingual building surveyor can usually clarify most key issues.

*Never try to save money by not employing a
qualified architect, aparejador or surveyor to
prepare a written schedule of works*

If you intend doing reformation or building work then
you must follow some basic rules ...

Before work starts:

1. Develop a clear **schedule of works** (*memoria de
    trabajo*)

    This is a highly detailed document that breaks down
    into defined sections the work that you require to be
    done. It should be accompanied (always) by drawings
    and, if possible, pictures or photographs demonstrating
    what you wish to achieve. Each section of the work
    should be priced (by the builder) independently.

2. Write out or obtain a detailed **specification** (*memoria
    de dalidades*)

    A specification is a series of documents that specify
    all the materials (their standard, quality and
    application) to be used. Sometimes a specification can
    be obtained from surveyors and architects – although
    normally you will have to pay a modest fee for a
    specification pertinent to your proposed work.

3. Translate both the schedule of works and
    specification into Spanish, if you intend using Spanish
    builders or asking them for a quotation.

4. Obtain quotations from three builders (no less!). Make
    sure that each has an identical copy of both the
    schedule of works and specification.

5. Make sure that any quotations state clearly that they
    are based on the schedule of work and specification. If

there are any suggested variations (that make sense to you!), pass these details on to the other builders so that all three can provide figures for exactly the same work.

6. Do not necessarily take the lowest of the three quotations. Assess the prices provided within each section of the schedule of works and see if there are any major inconsistencies that illustrate ignorance on the part of a builder about a particular aspect.

7. If you choose a particular builder:

- Check that he is properly registered (at the town hall) and insured.

- Draw up a contract (this is best done by your lawyer) and append it to the schedule of works and specification. The contract should itemise:

  - Start and finish dates for the contract.
  - Penalty clauses for time overrun.
  - A schedule of payments based on the stages of completion – including a minimum of 10% retention until after three months of completion.
  - A clause stating that no additional work ('extras') will be payable unless itemised, costed and given a time, evidenced in writing, and signed by the builder and yourself.

Of course, the best person to undertake all the above is a professional surveyor or architect. However, if you decide to manage the work yourself, the above is the *minimum* you should do (irrespective of the size of the job) to have any chance of a successful project.

Always check your builder has a properly issued licence for your building works before you allow him to start work

During the work:

1. Do not micromanage tradesman; rather inspect their work at logical intervals. Generally, if the working area is kept clean and tidy and the work itself is neat, straight and level, then your builder probably knows what he is doing. This will follow also if the work is continued with obvious momentum and the builder works regular, consistent times, without disappearing for days at a time!

2. Double-check the layout and that any fundamental measurements correspond to those you have specified. Leave something too long and redoing the work can be traumatic – and might result (possibly justifiable) in accusations from your builder that you saw what was being done and must have been happy with the way he was doing it ...

Ensure that a qualified architect, aparejador or building surveyor inspects your building project at given stages

3. Treat your builders with respect. Make them feel wanted, incentivise them and let your enthusiasm for the project infect them. Be as quick to praise good work as you are critical of sub-standard work.

   Bring in a professional surveyor or *aparejador* straightaway if you are unsure about the quality of the work or the way in which it is being conducted. The visit fee might serve only to allay your fears – but it could well save you thousands of euros and a great deal of time and heartache.

Note: Experienced building industry professionals are worth using early on to resolve disputes with builders. Invariably, they are used for mediation in construction disputes and frequently they can help prevent disagreements from escalating into court action. Where disputes are not resolved, consulting professionals prior to taking court action will often help to establish whether you have a strong case or not.

4. Pay in stages and in arrears (i.e. only at the end of each stage – and subject to work being satisfactorily completed). Equally, always hold back at least 25% of the project fee until final completion. In some instances, it is worth consulting a surveyor or architect beforehand to assess the standard of work and detailing to see what is normal and at what precise stages payments should be made.

   Typically, a building surveyor may identify an issue that, as a layman, you had no idea existed. Remember that while 'snagging' surveys are useful, unless the 'snagger' is a qualified building surveyor, his snagging list does not qualify as an authoritative full structural survey.

5. Certainly, a snagging list alone (especially if it is of lesser issues) may not be substantial enough to provide grounds for delaying completion (at least not legally) of any payment requested by a builder. On the other hand, authoritative identification of more serious structural issues may justify holding back final payments. It is advisable therefore to instruct an independent building surveyor to assess both structural and snagging issues in their report. In Spain, you must allow the builder access to put things

right, but this obviously has its limitations if the builder proves to be incompetent or unwilling to correct issues properly.

6. Never pay for all the work until you are satisfied (or your professional adviser is satisfied) that it has been carried out to an acceptable standard.

Never pay your builder for a completed project until you have received your certificate of completion from the town hall

Without doubt, overall persona supervision of any work is strongly advisable – particularly if the works are substantial or require ongoing decision-making. In this case, being close to your property is essential (even if you have to rent alternative accommodation throughout the works period). Normally, just the fact that you are not trying to live in the property will allow a builder to get on with the works more efficiently. Meanwhile, your 'constant' presence can ensure faster completion and greater attention to detail.

Of course, building work is a dusty business, so move, remove or cover all furniture prior to the works and never rely on a builder to do this as efficiently as you would do it. If possible, delay moving your possessions into your property until the works have been fully completed. Critically, do not arrange any incoming removals with too optimistic a date in mind. Building invariably takes longer than expected!

Your idea of 'clean' may also differ from that of a builder (unless you opt for an all-female work force!). So, ensure that your builder's quotation accounts for a final cleaning (preferably by a proper cleaning company). If this is not possible then make an allowance to get cleaners in.

Finally, do not invite friends and family to stay until several weeks after the planned completion date. Most new owners in Spain are itching to show off their new home with completed improvements and invite their friends and family over far too soon. This can prove disastrous should the building work completion be delayed (as it often is!).

Cif: z....
Fecha: 26/11/20..
Hora: 14:37

AIR TICKET

Usuario:	24-0230..
Contraseña	199z

Lhe ...

CUSTOMER S...
930 404 054
...@hactaia

Working in Spain

One of the great advantages of coming to Spain from another EU country is that, as of right, you can work in Spain (just as a Spaniard is entitled to work in, say, the UK or Germany). Obviously, you must register properly and abide by all appropriate business, health and safety, industry and tax regulations. While these are similar to the UK, there are, however, enough differences to make life seem complicated initially. Indeed, good professional business start-up advice is essential, as are the ongoing services of a first-class *gestor* and financial advisor and the backing of your lawyer.

Your main problem will be to find work that provides a secure and profitable income. This is not easy, particularly if you do not speak Spanish fluently. Of course, on the open market in Spain you will be competing against the Spanish themselves, so usually you will be at a significant disadvantage. This situation is compounded by the low salaries on offer in Spain. These bear little resemblance to salaries for comparable jobs in the UK, unless the work concerned is very specific or technical.

Furthermore, in Spain there is great reluctance by employers to place staff on permanent contracts. This is because of the cost of employing someone (including high employer's social security contributions) and the difficulty for an employer of terminating an employment contract. Accordingly, wherever possible, Spanish employers favour temporary contracts of employment. These, of course, do not provide the long-term security so desirable for someone who is relocating.

Finding viable work is not easy in Spain – so do not assume you can earn an income quickly and easily

You will find inevitably that the chance of obtaining work in the public sector is highly unlikely. So, you may be unable to find work where it would be available relatively easily in normal circumstances in your own country.

Certainly, you need to be realistic before coming to Spain about what you have to offer or your ideas for earning an income. Indeed, you should be extremely cautious about considering yourself exceptional just because you are from Northern Europe and therefore supposedly more sophisticated, organised or capable. Spain has a fine educational system and produces highly qualified professionals for every possible industry, whether highly technological or otherwise. It is not a backward country and its workers provide almost identical skill sets to those found in any advanced North European state.

In essence, you may find yourself restricted to:

- **Offering a specialist skill:** This is an excellent way of gaining an income. However, check very carefully that the skill that you consider 'specialist' and exceptional is as such and that it is applicable to Spain. Sometimes there are very good reasons why something that works in Northern Europe is not present in Spain. There may cultural reasons or, perhaps, a more commonly acceptable alternative.

- **Continuing or developing an internet-based business:** Obviously, a business based on the internet is ideal for anyone considering relocation. However, ensure that wherever you intend working has internet access suitable for your business needs – be rigorous in checking this particularly in the countryside (*campo*), where internet access may be either non-existent or not fast enough for practical business use. Equally, you should be wary of the Spanish postal service, which (curiously) is excellent for international post but sometimes unreliable for inland post.

- **Starting a business aimed primarily at the international community:** The most obvious market for someone not fluent in Spanish is the international market already in existence in Spain. The vast majority of North Europeans who relocate to Spain do not learn Spanish, despite often living here for years. They are therefore heavily reliant on English speakers to satisfy their needs. So, the British abroad tend to favour British builders, dentists, maintenance workers, lawyers, surveyors, web designers, SEO professionals, restaurants, bars, estate agents and activity holidays, as well as some products from the UK.

- **Working abroad and living in Spain:** It is possible, of course, to work in the UK (for example) and live in Spain. A number of people commute weekly, or regularly during the course of a month, to work or manage existing businesses. Although this is far from ideal, it can be workable, subject to your Spanish home being close to an international airport and airfares remaining cheap. Certainly, quite a few people base their family life in Spain while undertaking contract work on oil rigs or on Middle Eastern construction projects.

Just as in the UK, employment law and the administrative aspects of setting up and running a business in Spain are complicated. The decision to be registered as self-employed (*autonomo*) or set up a limited company (*sociedad limitada* or *sociedad limitada unipersonal*), a partnership (*comunidad de bienes*) or a public company (*sociedad anonima*) is also complicated. For any of these matters you will require the services of a specialist corporate lawyer or *gestor*. The latter will not only advise you of your options but also will set up the necessary paperwork to enable you to operate legally. *Gestores* will run your accounts and ensure, among other things, that you make any tax returns and VAT (*IVA*) returns correctly.

> *Ensure you have an excellent gestor to help you with the set-up and running of your Spanish business administration*

Work Options

In outline, the working options available to you are to:

- Seek employment
- Become self-employed (*autonomo*)
- Operate a partnership (*CB*)
- Form a limited company (normally an *SL* or *SLU*)
- Set up an *SA* (public company)

Employment

There are essentially two contracts of employment in Spain:

- **Temporary contract** *(contrato temporal)*
  Many people employed in Spain are on temporary contracts because of the expense of employer's social security contributions and the restrictions placed on employers when they want to terminate an employee's contract. There are restrictions on how many temporary employment contracts an employer can issue an individual before being forced to offer them a permanent contract. However, big companies tend to get around this by using a network of affiliated entities.

- **Permanent contract (*contrato indefinido*)**
  Most Spanish people consider a permanent employment contract very desirable. It provides significant security and compensation of 45 days work for every year they have worked for their employer.

Avoid offering permanent employment contracts to staff until you are absolutely certain of your employee's long-term worth

Self-Employment (autonomo)

If you want to operate as self-employed then you must:

- Register your business activity.

- Pay a monthly social security contribution (*cuotas seguridad social trabajadores autonomos*) by direct debit to the Spanish social security office. This is a minimum of around €250–300 a month and covers your immediate family for free state healthcare and education and, after 15 years of work, will entitle you to a pension. The higher your social security contributions, the greater the pension to which you will be entitled – so do not necessarily opt to pay the lowest amount possible!

- Deliver a VAT (*IVA*) return every three months.

- Issue accounts annually.

Make certain that you are properly registered to work. Working illegally can incur heavy sanctions

Operate a Partnership (CB)

You may wish to run a business in partnership with someone else. In this case you will need to set up a partnership (*CB*). You should note that, as in the UK, you will be responsible for all the liabilities and the debts of the business and for those of your partner if he defaults and is unable to pay. You will need to:

- Draw up a legally binding agreement between yourself and your partner(s)
- Arrange your personal situation as *autonomo*

Form a Limited Company (SL or SLU)

There are two commonly used types of limited company (among many variations):

- *SL* – a standard limited company that can have as many directors, administrators and shareholders as required
- *SLU* – a limited company which has a *single* shareholder, though there may be several directors and administrators

The most common form of company is an *SL*. Similar to a private limited company in the UK, this is a separate legal entity that provides you with a considerable degree of personal security. Should you have any business problems then, in essence, you will not be held liable for any debts beyond the value of your shareholding (though there are some exceptions). You should note that 1% stamp duty is payable on the share capital of a company.

If you want to protect your personal assets, set up a limited company

To set up an *SL* you will need to:

- Obtain an *NIE* number.

- Lodge €3,006 in a nominated bank account. Once the company has been formed properly you will regain access to this money.

- Appoint an administrator for the company who is tax resident in Spain. This person is legally responsible for the accounts of the company (as well as opening and closing them) and the appointment of staff (among other matters). This can be you and can be combined with the position of director of the company. However, if you are not yet tax resident then you may have to appoint someone else in your place temporarily. If you do this, exercise great care in choosing someone of impeccable integrity!

  You will need a lawyer or *gestor* to help you to set up the company and to ensure that all the necessary registration and procedures are followed. This may cost somewhere in the region of €2,000, depending upon who you use and the complexity of your requirements. It may take up to two months to complete the necessary steps.

To Set Up a Public Company

This is beyond the scope of this book and requires considerable professional attention.

Whether you are *autonomo* or running a company or partnership, note that:

- The Spanish financial year runs from the 1 January–31 December

- *IVA* (VAT) is chargeable irrespective of turnover and must be declared either quarterly or monthly

The Working Environment

For foreigners, the working environment in Spain is something of a paradox: as much as it is the same as that of Northern Europe, it is different! Not understanding this before you start working can lead to intense frustration and confusion.

Certainly, many people come to Spain believing that the business regulations, licensing, and procedures so prevalent in Northern Europe do not exist here, or are not enforced. This can lead foreigners to start businesses that are illegal or not properly registered. Sometimes, licensing is not undertaken or tax returns and accounts not filed – all of which can lead to severe sanctions.

> *Be aware that, in recessions, the Spanish authorities will be looking actively for those working illegally*

If you are going to embark on your own business then realise that whatever applies in the UK almost certainly applies *with the same stringency* in Spain. If you want to run a bar, for example, you will need a specific license. Also, you will be subject to health and safety *(seguridad y salud)* inspections and require a fire certificate. If you wish to change the use of a given building, this will require formal consent. Your business will also need to have public liability indemnity insurance and employed staff must have proper written contracts with defined terms. You must make proper tax returns, present accounts in the correct order, charge *IVA*, and file returns on time – and so on.

Spain, despite outward appearances, is organised and regulated, has enforcement officers, and has procedures that are obligatory. If you are found to be operating illegally, the state will take action against you. Furthermore, Spain (like the UK) will not accept any defence based on ignorance. Claiming that you are a foreigner and that matters are conducted in a different way elsewhere will not hold any weight.

Be extremely careful before starting a business to ensure you have excellent professional advice. This is absolutely essential and you must exercise far greater caution than you would in your own country. Check and double-check every aspect of your intended business and conduct the toughest possible due diligence. Look for proof of what you are told and seek advice from a specialist who knows the working reality of your particular industry in Spain.

If you are buying an existing business, be aware: the fact that it is operating does not mean necessarily that it is legal or that you will be able to obtain an operating license. Even if you do obtain a license, you may find the business needs to 'catch up' with current regulations that may be enforced only upon a change of ownership. You may suddenly find yourself committed to expensive alterations and delays. So, be very cynical about what business sellers or agents tell you.

Spain tends to operate at two levels: a legal one that is not dissimilar to the UK and a 'grey' area that is quite individual to the country. The latter is complicated, often a cultural matter, and can be difficult for a North European to fathom. However, you cannot 'fight' it nor dismiss its existence. This grey area is an integral part of economic life in Spain and you will need to find a strategy that allows you to operate effectively within it.

Always obtain permissions in writing. Never rely only on verbal promises

Certainly, as a foreign businessman you must err on the side of caution when it comes to the legality of your business activity. Spain retains a close-knit nuclear type of community – this is true particularly of the smaller towns and villages, which have deep-rooted and ancient family and commercial networks. Here corruption tends to be rife.

Sometimes corruption simply takes the form of local authorities turning a blind eye. Though this is often endearing, it can produce a false sense of security. After all, it only takes a political change in local government or a formal investigation to endanger what you thought was secure and permissible. So, always check the legality of your business activity or premises and never rely on verbal promises or agreements – even if they come from the local authority itself. If something is legal, then no one should have any problems placing this in writing, or providing you with a valid, written certificate.

It is common knowledge that Spain has a large black economy. Indeed, during the boom there were reportedly more €500 notes in Spain than anywhere else in Europe – which indicates how big the black economy is! Most businesses are family owned and many are rumoured to run two sets of accounts – one for the tax office and the other for cash that is earned and never declared.

Even salaries are sometimes paid partly in cash and partly by formal, declared payment. Indeed, it is the strength of the black economy that has probably made employer's national insurance contributions so high. Less income declared has meant less revenue and therefore higher taxation to make up for the deficit.

When assessing a business, do not rely only on what you are told or on the validity of any accounts

One of the problems of buying an existing business in Spain is the difficulty of finding out its real financial position. Accounts tend to be drawn up only for the taxman and are therefore in the pre-set format acceptable to the tax office (*hacienda*). This data is, of course, of some historical interest but will not provide information on profit margins or the operational efficiency of the business. Equally, if a proportion of the business income has been within the black economy, then any accounts may be misleading.

In general, management accounts (in a North European sense) tend not to be drawn up by businesses in Spain. This is odd, as management accounts act as a vital report for the future and are one of the only ways of assessing accurately the true workability and potential of a business.

It may be that owners of Spanish family-run businesses feel they know their businesses intimately and can do without an accountant's analysis. Whatever the case, it makes buying an existing business a hazardous matter and one reliant upon believing what you are told – often with little reliable, concrete evidence available to prove matters one way or another.

Working Life

The routine of working life varies depending upon where you live in Spain. Certainly, working life in big cities such as Barcelona, Madrid and Valencia is quite different from that in provincial towns and villages. The siesta, for example, is hardly adopted in major cities but tends to be de rigueur elsewhere, particularly in Mediterranean areas.

Siesta, where it does exist, will influence your working day irrespective of your occupation. Siesta lasts all year and is roughly between 14.00 and 16.00 every day. It is a time during which no work is undertaken, with shops and offices closing and many Spanish workers returning home to their families. The major meal of the day will be consumed at this time and a rest of some kind taken.

The impact of siesta on life in Spain is considerable as it significantly lengthens the working day. Indeed, depending on local custom, the working day may be as follows:

08.00   Work starts. Bars/cafes open
09.30   Breakfast
10.00   Work recommences. Shops open
14.00   Siesta starts. Bars and restaurants remain open
16.30   Siesta ends. Work starts again. Shops reopen
20.00   Work finishes. Shops close
24.00   Bars/Cafes close

So, appreciate that the schedule you may be used to in the UK may not exist in Spain – despite any desire or efforts to achieve the contrary. Certainly, few people who end up running bars and cafes understood beforehand the lengthy working hours of their industry.

Meanwhile, working in a business that combines British and Spanish relationships can be tough as well. For example, estate agents or surveyors can find themselves working through siesta as well as late into the evening. This can be exacerbated by weekend work.

Recognise that your working day may be considerably longer than it was in the UK

As an employer, you may find the rhythm of Spanish life frustrating. The continual breaks in the working day can be disruptive and it can take a year or two to adjust to siesta. Certainly, normal business cannot be conducted during siesta and any attempt to do so will fail. Making a business telephone call at 15.00, for example, is considered the height of ill manners unless the matter concerns something of genuine urgency.

Of course, change is constant and the siesta may become less important. Some of the Spanish themselves find siesta exasperating and would prefer – and sometimes are willing – to work the conventional hours of Northern Europe. However, as long as schools keep siesta hours, any change would be impractical for parents and is unlikely in the foreseeable future.

As in many other Mediterranean countries, August is considered a holiday month. Even if your staff do not go on holiday, you may find business in the last two weeks of August devastatingly slow (unless your company is tourist orientated). In fact, the last fortnight of August can be compared to a UK Christmas period. Few people are at work, decisions are hard to obtain, most people are soporific, and there is a general lack of interest in business matters.

Spain also has a mind-boggling array of fiestas throughout the year. These are often quite unlike those in Northern Europe and many last a full week. During this time, you can find it hard to function efficiently unless you have a bar, shop, restaurant or hotel that benefits directly from the fiesta. Every village and town will have at least one full week's fiesta during which work becomes, to all intents and purposes, impossible – with employees expecting to have time off. Some fiestas, of course, last only a day and are similar to a UK bank holiday.

Finally, Spain has a reputation for a *mañana* (tomorrow) mentality when it comes to getting things done, and workers have a reputation for being charmingly slow but somewhat lazy. This myth has continued perhaps because of the more relaxed appearance of the Spanish at work. Business dress is generally (outside the major cities) smart/casual and it is common to enter a professional office and hear a radio playing in the background. Equally, meetings often take place late at night or in bars and cafes, and the personal network of family and long-term contacts is considered priority. However, this should not be mistaken for a lack of seriousness about work.

Ensure you are not assessed for tax
in both the UK and Spain

In fact, the Spanish toil as hard as anyone and there is a high degree of professionalism. Appointments are kept and participants are expected to be on time. Apart from the lacklustre construction industry (as in most countries!), Spain has a well-functioning business environment.

Without doubt, working life in Spain is different from that of Northern Europe. To work efficiently you need to make an effort to adapt to the rhythm and customs of the country. If you do this and take on patiently any idiosyncrasies, you will enjoy yourself thoroughly – and be enriched greatly by the challenges faced.

For more detailed information, you may wish to have a look at a book that I have co-written that deals specifically with working and making a living in Spain called *Make a Living Abroad – in Spain,* also available from Summertime Publishing.

Healthcare

Spain, to its great credit, is a very healthy country. Longevity rates are some of the highest in Europe with the life expectancy of women being 82 and men, 76. Of course, this may have more to do with the Mediterranean diet and outdoor lifestyle than outstanding medical care. However, the health system in Spain generally works well and can be relied on without having to turn to private health care.

Certainly, the Spanish healthcare system is extensive. There are some 800 hospitals and 2,700 medical centres (*centros de salud*) throughout the country. Almost every village will have a doctor (*medico*) who will attend his medical centre daily (even if it is just for a few hours before he goes to the next village or district). Normally a nurse (*enfermera*) will be in attendance and often a patient can see his doctor the same day. Meanwhile, there is a network of hospitals across Spain with accident and emergency (A&E) departments (*urgencias*).

Children under 14 must be seen by a paediatrician (*médico de paediatrica*), rather than a GP (*médico de familia*). There are, therefore, medical clinics specifically for children, which deal with their particular medical needs. These are located normally in towns and often within the main health centre.

Spain also has private healthcare, to which a significant minority of the Spanish population subscribes. As a consequence, there are many private clinics and hospitals. Some state hospitals (as in the UK) also have private healthcare sections. Many of the private clinics and hospitals have a walk-in facility and rooms, thus enabling you to see a doctor almost straight away and, if necessary, to stay for care. That said, these facilities can lack full A&E departments.

Unfortunately, many who come to Spain abuse the system – this is as true of tourists as it is of those who have relocated. Often the latter expect to receive free healthcare but don't contribute to the Spanish state or bother to obtain the correct documentation. As a result, the healthcare system has problems clawing back the significant costs of treatment provided to those not entitled to it. This, of course, has a direct impact on funding, particularly given the vast number of foreigners who come to Spain.

Free Healthcare in Spain

Free healthcare is provided as of right to Spanish citizens and to those foreigners who are:

- **Registered as employed:** If you are employed you must contribute to the Spanish social security system. If you are self-employed (*autonomo*) you will have to make monthly social security payments by direct debit. If you are employed, your employer will have to contribute to the social security system.

- **Pensioners:** If you are a pensioner (over 65) then you must apply to obtain free healthcare.

Once you are eligible for Spanish state healthcare, you will be provided with a *SIP (Sistema de Informacion Poblacional)* card. This is like a credit card and displays your details and *NIE* number. You must show this card whenever you attend a medical centre, whether for an appointment or treatment. You will also need it when you go to a pharmacy to obtain your prescription.

Healthcare Out of Spain

If you are permanently resident in Spain, and decide to travel out of Spain and within the EU, you must obtain a European Health Card (EHC) to receive free healthcare. If you do not have an up-to-date EHC you may be charged for any healthcare provided. So, in effect, once you are in the Spanish social security system (because, for example, you make social security payments in Spain or are a Spanish tax resident), you are considered 'out' of the UK healthcare system, even if you are a UK national with a UK passport.

If you are resident in Spain, you will need to obtain an EHC to receive free healthcare if you travel out of Spain and to any country in the EU (including the UK) – even if you are a British citizen

The Spanish equivalent of the EHC is called a *Tarjeta Sanitaria Europea* and can be applied for at your local Spanish social security office (INSS). These cards have to be renewed annually.

Temporary Travel to Spain

You will be granted free healthcare in Spain as a visitor. However, to obtain this you must have a European Health Card (EHC) before you leave the UK. This can be obtained from *www.dh.gov.uk/travellers.*

European Health Card (EHC) parameters

You should note that the EHC is not a substitute for medical travel insurance and that it will not cover medical repatriation, ongoing medical care, specific medical treatment, or treatment that is not urgent. It will, of course, not cover any private healthcare received.

Private Healthcare

Of course, one of the downsides to opting only for Spanish state healthcare is having to rely on finding medical staff who speak English – unless you are fluent in Spanish.

Certainly, there are no official interpreters in hospitals and medical centres. So, you will have to take a Spanish-speaking friend with you or pay for a private interpreter.

Without doubt, making yourself understood is rarely more important than when you are ill. Equally, being abroad and sick can mean that you can feel more vulnerable than you would do in the UK and therefore that you crave greater urgency in your treatment. The answer, of course, is to have private healthcare insurance.

There are a wide range of private healthcare facilities in Spain that offer English-speaking doctors and medical staff. Indeed, private healthcare insurance packages are offered by major insurers (like Sanitas and AXAPPP Healthcare) and are worth investigating. Often these packages can be significantly cheaper than private insurance in the UK and therefore of real value, particularly during the first few years of coming to Spain. After that period you may be sufficiently fluent and confident to rely only on state care (if you are a pensioner or tax resident) or have a reliable network of translators to assist you.

Dentists, Opticians, Physiotherapists ...

As you would expect, Spain has a full complement of highly skilled medical professionals, as well as holistic practitioners. Obviously, finding fluent English speakers is important. Fortunately this is far less difficult than you might imagine, particularly in the coastal regions. Spanish practitioners have long recognised the importance of the foreign market and many speak English. Equally, there are some British professionals who live in Spain and are properly registered and insured to practise there.

If you want treatment from an English speaker then it is worth looking in free local papers or joining a blog or forum local to your area and making a relevant enquiry.

Invariably, fellow nationals in the area will be able to recommend someone.

Of course, establishing good from poor practitioners is much the same in any country! Recommendations and personal experience will, over a period of time, provide you with a selection of professionals to turn to.

Pharmacies

Pharmacies can be found across Spain, in even the smallest villages. Most medium-sized towns also have a 24-hour pharmacy. Though this is a reasonably new phenomenon, it is likely to become increasingly common.

Pharmacies are invariably well stocked and sophisticated. They are recognisable by their luminous green cross signs and prescription parameters for drugs and treatment appear to be wider than in the UK.

Residential Homes

In Spain, residential homes (*residencias*) are a relatively new phenomenon as, traditionally, the Spanish have cared for elderly relatives within the home environment. However, increasingly, residential homes are becoming more common. Normally they are privately owned, though some residents may be state sponsored. However, the Spanish and British concepts of residential homes are quite different.

A residential home in Spain is much closer to a hospital than a home and residents tend to be those who need high levels of care. As a generality, Spanish residential homes are therefore not appropriate for someone who is looking for a homely environment.

However, increasingly foreign businesses are investing in creating the types of residential homes found in the UK.

These are springing up in some coastal areas and will probably become a major growth industry – and one on which elderly expatriates will be able to rely.

Schools and Education

Few matters make relocation more complicated than when children are involved. Almost every decision you have to make will be influenced by their welfare and it will, no doubt, be your single most important concern. Indeed, your children may define whether or not you move at all and undoubtedly will exert a defining influence on where you go and the type of property you buy.

Certainly, the happiness of your children in Spain will be critical to the success of your relocation. If children are unhappy, this can place tremendous stress upon the adults within a family –strain a previously sound relationship. So, ensuring the relocation works for your children is crucial.

The Law

In Spain, education for children is compulsory from the ages six to 16. Primary education (*primaria*) lasts six years followed by four years of compulsory secondary education (*ESO*) at the end of which a certificate of education is received. The stages of education include:

Kindergarten	(0–3 yrs)
Pre-school/*Infantil*	(3–6 yrs)
Primaria (Compulsory)	(6–12 yrs)
ESO (Compulsory)	(12–16 yrs)
Bachillerato/ *Ciclos formatives de grado medio*	(16–18 yrs)
University (*diplomatura* 3 yrs)/ *Ciclos formativos de grado superior*	(18–20 yrs)
University (*licenciatura* 2 yrs)/ University post degree (2 yrs)	(beyond)

School Timetable

Times will vary from one region to another and will be affected also by what a child is studying, their level and their particular school. So, the following should be treated only as a guideline:

- The school year is divided into three terms with a long summer holiday break of almost three months:

  - Winter term (September to December)
  - Spring term (January to Easter)
  - Summer term (after Easter to late June)

- The school day for primary schools can vary, but is normally:

  - 09.00–12.00 and 15.00–17.00

- For *ESO* or *Bachillerato*, the school day is usually:

  - 08.00–15.00 or
  - 08.30–14.00 and 15.30–17.30 (one or two days a week)

Note: Both private and state primary schools normally look after a child from the beginning to the end of the school day (09.00 until 17.00). However, secondary schools usually do not look after children during the *siesta* break. This is an important factor to consider should your child be unable to return safely and easily to your home in this time. If this is the case, then you will have to arrange to collect and drop off your child before and after *siesta* – a significant interruption to your weekdays!

It is compulsory for children between the ages of 6 and 16 to attend school

Schools

There is a wide range of schools in Spain.

Primary state schools
- Primary education

Secondary state schools
- *ESO – Bachillerato – Ciclos formativos*

Semi–private schools
- Primary – *ESO – Bachillerato*

Private schools
- Primary – *ESO – Bachillerato*

Sometimes private and semi-private schools offer *Ciclos Formativos*.

State primary schools (6 years to 12 years)

These are known as *escuelas* or *colegios* (although the latter term is applied sometimes to semi-private and private schools that take pupils from primary to *Bachillerato/Ciclos Formativo*).

Virtually every village will have a primary school, as well as all towns. These schools vary considerably in size and sophistication, but often provide a caring and kindly environment for small children. Most will take children from the age of three, although there are some exceptions. Children younger than three (*preescolar or infantil*) are not usually catered for by the state and are looked after only by private kindergartens.

> *Concentrate on ensuring excellent schooling for your child as an unhappy child will stress any relationship and lead to an unsuccessful relocation*

Some state schools in some areas of Spain only teach in the dialect of the given region – as opposed to in Spanish. So, in Catalonia, Galicia, Valencia or the Basque country, subjects are taught in, respectively, Valencian, Gallego, Catalan or Basque. This is not always the case but is something to investigate carefully, as it will mean that your child will be taught in the regional dialect before learning Spanish. That said, most children master both the local dialect and *Castellano* (Spanish) as part of their general schooling.

Entry to a primary school depends on the catchment area in which you live. So, make sure you find a satisfactory school *in the area* before buying a property – otherwise you may find your child is not eligible to go to the school of your choice.

State secondary schools (12 years to 18 years)

All towns and cities have secondary schools, generally known as *institutos*.

There are excellent state schools and others that are 'sink' schools with a proportion of (for example) recently arrived immigrants to whom Spanish is a second language. This can place considerable stress on a school (particularly in the big cities) and can result in the academic progress of classes being held back. However, the standard of teachers is generally good, the school curriculum impressively rigorous and all state teachers highly qualified.

Like primary schools, some secondary schools teach subjects in the regional dialect rather than in Spanish. This can create problems as it means your child will have to learn two languages simultaneously while also undertaking increasingly difficult academic work.

> *Be extremely cautious before placing a child of*
> *12–13 years old into a Spanish state school,*
> *unless your child is already fluent in Spanish*

Obviously, you must research secondary schooling with the same rigour that you would in the UK. At the best of times, this can be a difficult process, but personal recommendations are often the best way of finding out the truth about a given school. Local estate agents tend to be sensitive to local schools particularly if they have children of their own in the educational system. Indeed, there is probably no better proof than another parent of your nationality being happy with the local schooling of their child.

Entry to a secondary school also depends upon the catchment area in which you live.

ESO

Secondary education up until *Bachillerato/Ciclo formativo* level (see below) is known as *ESO*. So, a child of 13 (who has not failed a year) will be in second *ESO*, a child of 15 in fourth *ESO*, and so on.

At the age of 16 a child should attain a Certificate of Completion of Secondary Education (*Titulo de Graduado en Educación Secundaria*) if he has passed (*aprobado*) his examinations (*examen* or *control*). If a child has not been successful then he will leave school with a *Certificado de Escolarización*. Once children have achieved the *Titulo de Graduado en Educacion Secundaria* they can:

- Leave school
- Continue their education by studying for the *Bachillerato* (essential for university)
- Continue to attend their school by taking a vocational course (*Ciclo Formativo*)

Bachillerato

The academically demanding *Bachillerato* takes two years and is roughly equivalent to the UK's A Levels, although it is considered to be more rigorous and is certainly more highly regarded. There are several variations of *Bachillerato*, each of which is biased towards a given area, for example, the arts or the sciences. Nine subjects are studied and the yearly exam results of each subject aggregated to provide an overall mark out of 10.

So, if a student in their first year achieves a grade of 7.4 (across all subjects) and, in the following year, a grade of 8.2, the final *Bachillerato* grading will be a creditable 7.8 (7.4 + 8.2 = 15.6 ÷ 2 = 7.8).

A pass at *Bachillerato* level will allow a student to take university entrance examinations (*selectivo*). However, the overall grade gained at *Bachillerato* is important and, subject to how well a student does in their *selectivo* examinations, will define what they can study at university.

Selectivo is attended after the completion of *Bachillerato* and is supervised by the state. The student will take seven or eight examinations over three days that mimic their *Bachillerato* examinations. They will be provided then with an aggregate score out of 10 (as in the *Bachillerato* system). This will be combined with their *Bachillerato* score to provide the overall university grade – although the school *Bachillerato* exam results will account for 60% of the final aggregate; the *selectivo* 40%.

Ciclos Formativos

The vocational courses provided by *institutos* are intended to provide practical training for skills such as plumbing, electrical work and hairdressing. These vocational courses last four years and result in qualifications universally recognised across Spain. There are two parts to the *Ciclos Formativos*:

- *Grado Medio* – this lasts two years and provides a basic level of training.

- *Grado Superior* – this lasts a further two years and can only be started when a student is 18 years old. If a student passes his *Grado Superior*, he obtains access to the university system. *Grado Superior* is open also to direct entry from students who have passed their *Bachillerato*.

It is worth noting that there are also private *academias,* which offer additional teaching at all levels. These operate after school hours and during holidays. Their purpose is to help students who may be struggling in a given subject. So, they help with revision/homework (*repaso*) and can be of critical help if a student is heading towards failure (*suspendido*) of an exam.

Certainly, many parents seek additional help for their children and the use of *academias* is common. Equally helpful are a number of teachers who offer their services for private homework (*repaso*) classes. These can be particularly important to British children during their first years of Spanish education.

State universities and polytechnic universities

There are state universities throughout Spain that provide 'degree' (*diplomatura*) and professional qualifications (*licenciatura*) as well as post-degree education. Confusingly some universities are called polytechnic universities, which suggests they are biased towards the sciences. However, this is not always the case and there is no difference between their status and that of a more traditional university.

Currently, the Spanish system is being harmonised with the rest of Europe. This is likely to result in a system similar to that of the UK with three to four year degrees and two-year Master's qualifications.

Note: Spanish state universities appear not to use the tutorial system – a cornerstone of British universities. Students are expected to be highly disciplined and are treated as a 'number', which can be a tremendous shock in their first year. Indeed, the consensus is that private schools do not always prepare students well for the harsh self-discipline required to achieve success in an environment devoid of mentors. That said, state university qualifications appear to stand up well against their European counterparts.

Note that grants are available and are means tested and dependent upon the family income.

Other schools include:

- **Kindergartens**
  These are private and similar to those of the UK. If properly registered, they are subject to stringent health and safety regulations and must be fully insured. The latter should be checked should you wish to place your child in a kindergarten.

- **Semi-private Spanish schools**
  These schools require fee-paying but the fees are nominal. These are generally desirable places for a child and are almost always run by the church. There is often considerable competition among parents to obtain the few places available. These schools can provide both a primary and secondary education.

- **Private Spanish schools**
  Most large towns will have one or two fully private (fee paying) schools. These schools sometimes have a

nursery facility and will take children from the age of 18 months until they pass their *Bachillerato* examinations. Furthermore, these schools normally teach only in Spanish, the regional dialect being an obligatory second language alongside English. Children usually have to wear a uniform until they reach secondary school.

The fees of Spanish private schools vary greatly but tend to be much less than the fees of their UK counterparts.

- **International schools in Spain**
  There is a scattering of international schools throughout Spain. These are found normally in the big cities and coastal regions. They provide education in English and the curriculum is British. Often pupils are accepted from pre-school age all the way through their education, until they are 18.

  Interestingly, a large proportion of students in an international school might be Spanish. This is because Spanish parents recognise the importance of English and endeavour to ensure their children are completely bilingual from an early age.

- **Private universities**
  These are fee-paying universities that provide the same qualifications as state universities. However, they provide a much higher level of personal supervision and a better post-graduation network of contacts.

Age Sensitivities

Without doubt, the younger a child is, the easier it is for them to assimilate Spanish and therefore to come to grips with academic work if attending a school within the Spanish system. Most children pick up the language with an ease that is infuriating for any adult struggling to become bilingual.

However, this is a far more difficult for older children. Experience has shown there is an age at which children find it impracticable to learn a new language and deal with the demands of increasingly complicated academic work.

Be aware of over-stressing your child should they need to learn Spanish at the same time as being taught in a regional dialect

The danger time for moving children into a Spanish school (if they do not speak Spanish) is around 12–13 years old, and older, when it may become extremely difficult for them to keep up with their peers. This can be demoralising and damaging at this already vulnerable time in their lives.

Certainly, if you are considering relocating under these circumstances, you may have to consider placing your child at an international school. The issue is not so much that your child will be unable to learn the language quickly – just that they may risk falling behind academically at a critical time.

Passing the Academic Year

You should note that in Spain, both in primary and secondary school, students are expected to pass the year. If they fail exams throughout the year, they can be made to repeat the year. This is no idle threat and quite a few children in every school repeat a year. This can be an unwelcome experience for a British child, although in reality it makes good sense. There is little to be gained from a child becoming ever more stressed by being pushed beyond their capabilities. Repeating a year, therefore, can be necessary to provide a child with the time to catch up.

If your child is nearly 11 or 12 years old and is not particularly academic, it is worth preparing both yourself and them for a potential repeat year at some stage. However, this can be looked at in a positive way. If your child leaves school completely bilingual (in two of the most widely spoken languages in the world), it is a small penalty to pay for leaving school a year later than planned.

State, Private or International Schooling?

You need to assess carefully your child and his capabilities together with the schools available and your own budget. There is much to be said for buying a cheaper house and investing or setting aside money for the long-term private education of your children if you think that will best for them. After all, if they are happy and settled, this will make a substantial difference to the overall success of your move.

At secondary level, a private Spanish school is worth considering. You will be paying for a high standard of attention and you will have a far greater say in your child's education than you would in a state school. In the latter, there is a real danger that your child will be left sitting at the back of a classroom for a year or so while learning Spanish painfully. This is not to say that mechanisms are not available within the state secondary system to provide assistance where required.

Interestingly, state teachers are well regarded by the Spanish themselves. It is certainly not easy to become a teacher and the examinations to enter the profession are rigorous. This is reflected also by the considerable difficulty a teacher faces in obtaining a permanent contract with a state school. Indeed, to do so involves some terrifically hard civil service examinations called *oposiciones*.

> *Prioritise the education of your children,*
> *recognise the move will be challenging*
> *and consider providing them with an*
> *edge through private education*

If your child is starting Spanish schooling at secondary level and is not fluent, he will need significant care and attention during the first year. Additional tuition in Spanish may be needed. But also recognise that some subjects (such as mathematics) have different symbols and different methods to those used in the UK.

Our own children went to a Spanish private school that delivered a superb academic education within a loving environment. Neither dropped a year and both achieved their academic potential. We believe the money spent had incalculable value and contributed significantly to the success of our relocation.

There are some fine international schools that teach in English and follow the British curriculum. These are particularly appropriate for older children so they can continue with the curriculum they have been studying in the UK.

Of course, private schools may have a further advantage in that your child's peers are likely to come from wealthy or influential backgrounds. This means your child is likely to develop a potentially useful network of contacts for later in life. However, there are also some important negatives to bear in mind.

Private schooling tends to take children out of the local community and place them in an artificial social 'island'. Many of the children in your child's school will come also from outside your area. Friends can be therefore from a far more scattered geographical region than is the case at local schools, where pupils are from a particular catchment area. This means it can be difficult for your child to make friends easily in your locality, particularly if you live outside a town and on an *urbanización*.

Finally, an important consideration is the school timetable (as discussed previously). Seemingly endless drop-offs and collections can make life a nightmare if you both work and do not live close to your child's school. So, if you need an uninterrupted working day and your child is of secondary school age, you may have to consider private schooling, where children are looked after the entire day, including during siesta time.

Sport

One difference to the UK that seems to follow across Spanish schools is the lack of extensive sports facilities. Though sport is pursued within schools, it tends to be undertaken at a very low level.

Make the time to take your children to sports activities so they can integrate with a wide circle of children

Towns and villages throughout Spain generally have very good sports facilities and competent professional coaching. However, these facilities are primarily for use after school and it is therefore up to parents to take their children to the facilities. So, if you want to involve your child in sport, you will need to find out what is on offer at the local sports centres and arrange this personally.

English Language

English language tuition is obligatory throughout Spanish schools. English is also considered universally important, with the Spanish state increasingly placing pressure on schools to maximise tuition in the language. Obviously, this is of help to any British child, who will have always something of value to offer his new classmates!

Summary

Spain can provide an excellent level of education from primary to university level. However, choosing the right school is an even more delicate process than it is in the UK. Much depends on your child, his fluency and his particular needs. These also need to be assessed in light of the (potentially disruptive) timetable inherent to state schools.

Having a child of school age should not put you off relocating to Spain. Far from it! Your children can gain a tremendous amount from the experience. They will become quickly bilingual and benefit from being exposed to another culture, which will broaden their minds immeasurably. Furthermore, your child will be living within a healthier and more child-friendly environment than that of Northern Europe. These are all benefits that should yield positive results for the rest of their lives.

Domestic Animals and Wildlife

Despite its climate being quite different, Spain is suitable for most North European pets. Certainly most animals quickly get used to the more extreme heat of summer with few or no ill effects. Meanwhile, various potential animal health problems common to Spain, such as ticks and tapeworm, can be kept under control. Rabies, although present in other EU countries, does not currently exist in Spain.

There are excellent vets throughout the country, with appropriate medicines and high-quality treatment easily available. In short, there is no reason not to relocate with your pets or for them not to enjoy life in Spain as much as you!

Taking Your Pet(s) to Spain

If you wish to take your pets to Spain, however, you must make sure that you comply with EU regulations for transporting pets to another country. This centres upon obtaining a pet passport, which is a booklet identical throughout all EU countries. In essence, it is a certificate of health particular to a specific and identifiable animal (a microchip with a unique code is inserted into the animal's neck).

While obtaining a pet passport can involve some expense, the most important factor to bear in mind is *timing*. A pet passport is not something obtained instantly, as you have to allow time for the vaccination process and blood test. Accordingly, you need to plan well ahead if you are to take your animal with you when you move.

A pet passport is available for both cats and dogs, although the animal concerned must be over three months old before it will be allowed to enter Spain. The process of obtaining a pet passport can be broken down into four stages, all of which need to be conducted by a Licensed Veterinary Inspector (LVI):

- Micro-chipping. Your pet will have a microchip inserted with an individual identification code fitted. The code and date of insertion will be logged in your pet's records.
- Irrespective of any previous rabies vaccination, your pet will be vaccinated for rabies.
- 30 days after the rabies vaccination, your pet must have a blood test. Note that you will have to give your pet regular rabies booster inoculations – the passport will no longer be valid if these are missed.
- Subject to your pet's blood test being clear, your animal will gain his passport.

Returning Your Pet to the UK

Once your pet has his passport then you can transport him from Spain and back to the UK again should you so wish. However, should your animal be returned to the UK then he will need:

- An anti-rabies booster
- A further blood test (30 days after the vaccination, and six months before your return trip)
- Proof of treatment against ticks and tapeworm between 24–48 hours before departure from Spain
- Examination and health certification by a vet

Owner's Liability in Spain

As in the UK, all liability for your animal will lie firmly with you. If your animal causes an accident or hurts someone, then you will be responsible for any resulting damage or injury. So, make sure that you have adequate insurance cover. This often comes part and parcel of a household insurance policy, but you should check that this is the case. Of course, if you are renting somewhere, then it is highly likely that you will not have any cover – in which case you should take out specific insurance.

Vet bills, as in the UK, can be expensive, so it is a good idea to take out a separate pet insurance policy that covers any treatment. There are a number of different policies available and details and sales brochures are often found in the clinics of vets. Alternatively, you can contact your insurance broker or any of the major insurance companies for details of their policies.

Note that it is mandatory in Spain to keep your dog from distracting the driver of a car. So, you must either have a screen between dog and driver or the dog must be placed securely in a harness that will prevent it coming into contact with the driver.

Finally, a dog owned by you must have:

- An identification microchip.
- Current (annual) inoculation against rabies – although this is not obligatory in all the regional areas (*communidades*) of Spain.

Public Areas

Despite all appearances to the contrary, it is:

- Illegal for a dog to be walked on Spanish beaches.
- Obligatory, in all public places, for a dog to be kept on a lead – and this includes within the countryside.
- Obligatory for a dog classified as a 'dangerous dog' (*perro peligroso*) in any public place to wear a muzzle. This classification includes such dogs as Alsatians, Pit Bull Terriers and Rottweilers.

Common Diseases and Problems for Pets

For both, cats and dogs make sure that they have specific annual vaccinations (against viruses and bacterial problems). Specifically, you must protect them against:

- Mosquitoes (*mosquitoes*), which cause *leishmaniasis*, a fatal disease. However, the symptoms of this disease can be treated to provide any affected pet with a better and longer life than would otherwise be expected.
  Use a preventative collar and a treatment such as Frontline Spot On.

- Ticks (*garrapatas*), which are a constant problem and can cause diseases such as canine *Babesiosis* and *ehrlichiosis*. You should inspect your pets regularly and remove any ticks as soon as you see them.
  Use a preventative collar and a treatment such as Frontline Spot On.

- Fleas (*pulgas*), which transmit worms and allergies.
  Use a preventative collar and a treatment such as Frontline Spot On.

- Tapeworms (*lombriz*), which affect the overall health and well-being of an animal.
  Preventative treatment with tablets every three months.

For cats beware:

- Feline *leukemia*
  Vaccinate your cat

- Immune deficiency
  No cure

- *Peritonitis*
  No cure

Advice from Spanish Vets

A summary of general advice for foreigners coming to Spain:

- When you come to Spain, seek the advice of a vet to establish any common problems or peculiarities within your given area. Conditions differ hugely from one region to another and therefore so do the specific animal healthcare requirements.

- Keep all animal vaccinations up to date.

- Ensure that your animal is provided with healthy, good-quality food (but do not overfeed!).

- Ensure you treat all intestinal problems promptly.

- Wherever possible, keep your animal inside at night to avoid the worst affects of mosquitoes.

- Avoid taking your animal to areas where there is an obvious mosquito problem (such as in marshes).

- Never leave an animal alone in a vehicle. Even in winter the sun in Spain can be very hot, causing an animal to quickly overheat and die.

Spanish Attitude to Animals

There used to be a notion among the British that the Spanish were a cruel people, particularly with respect to animals, but there is little evidence to suggest this is the case now. Indeed, having pets and looking after them as an integral member of the family is common. Evidence for this can be seen from the profusion of vets in every town and city and the number of Spanish walking and playing with their dogs in the parks.

There are exceptions, the most usual of which is the use of guard dogs in country areas. Sometimes these are tethered alone to look after a property. Bored and aggressive, these poor animals are sometimes fed on automatic feeders and become maddened by their solitary existence.

Equally, strays on urbanisations are reasonably common and are occasionally dropped off by town dwellers in the hope that they will be taken in and given a home by a soft-hearted resident. Often the trouble is that a cute puppy became a high-maintenance dog too large to be housed in a modest town flat. That said, sometimes dumped pets are blamed on the Spanish, when, in fact, Britons returning permanently to the UK, are to be blamed.

Meanwhile, the controversy around the national sport of bullfighting continues – and does little to alter any perception of the Spanish and their concern for the welfare of animals. In fact, it appears that, very gradually, the popularity of bullfighting is declining, and this seems markedly true of the younger generation. That said, bullfighting can be seen regularly on Spanish TV and many towns and villages have their own bullfighting rings.

To the great credit of British expatriates, there are many animal charities throughout Spain that have been started and that are run almost entirely by expatriates. Indeed, many relocating Britons tend to get their pets from these charities and support them with both their money and time. To some extent this works well for all parties: distressed animals receive invaluable care and those helping receive a meaningful addition to their lives.

Animal Rescue

To their credit, many North Europeans take in stray dogs or help to run or fund animal rescue centres. If you would like a pet, then there is much to be said for trying to get one from an animal rescue centre.

Dangerous Animals of Spain

Spain has few dangerous creatures and you would be unlucky indeed to be badly hurt or killed by any animals in the wild. Although there are bears and wolves in Spain, these are extremely rare and attacks on humans rarer still.

Perhaps one of the most dangerous commonly encountered creatures is the processionary caterpillar, which is armed with poisonous hairs that can cause respiratory problems and severe skin rashes. The caterpillars can also kill smaller animals such as dogs if the latter eat them mistakenly or inhale the hairs. However, these caterpillars are usually around only for a month or so a year and most animals avoid them.

Spain has snakes (13 types), but only five of these are poisonous. In fact, although you may see quite a few snakes, particularly on the roads, it is very unusual to encounter one in close proximity and the danger of dying from snake bite is less than the danger of dying from bee stings. Evidently, only around three to six people a year (out of a resident population of some 45 million and about 50 million foreign holidaymakers annually!) are killed by snakes.

Meanwhile, there are some 1,700 different types of spiders! However, only three are harmful, with the most dangerous (though not lethal) being the black widow. Scorpions are also prevalent but will give you nothing more than a very painful sting. A similar danger exists from a very large centipede that occasionally you may see in your garden.

Mosquitoes are as common as elsewhere in Europe but are not malarial. More of a problem is ticks, which can be a constant nuisance for dogs and cats.

Along the coast, the most unwelcome animals tend to be jellyfish. In the summer, these can invade beach areas. Normally, beach patrols sound the alert when jellyfish are around the shoreline.

Vehicles, Motoring and Transport

As driving in Spain is done on the left-hand side of the road, it is best to own a left-hand drive car. After a very short time you will become as confident as you are when driving on the right in the UK. Certainly a car with a left-hand drive makes overtaking easier and motoring safer.

UK-registered Car

You can elect to keep your UK car in Spain, so long as you formally import and register it with Spanish registration plates. This must be done should your car remain in Spain for 183 days or longer. This is a somewhat complicated and expensive process and the most sensible action is to employ a *gestor* to do the paperwork.

> *Remember that UK motor insurance will normally expire 30 days after you leave the UK!*

Note that your car insurance, when driving your UK car abroad, lasts normally for only 30 days. After this time period, you will need to approach a specialist insurer to insure the car for its remaining time in Spain. There are a number of insurers who do this, with brokers throughout Spain (particularly in foreigner-dense areas). Most specialist brokers, not surprisingly, speak English. If your MOT runs out while you are in Spain, you can attend a Spanish *ITV* (MOT) centre and voluntarily '*ITV*' your car. If it passes, you will receive certification that should be acceptable to your insurer – although this should be checked independently.

Legal Requirements

It is obligatory to have all the original paperwork in your vehicle, including:

- Insurance certificate
- Proof of payment of insurance certificate
- Car registration papers/log book
- A copy of your *NIE* number
- Two safety triangles
- Two high-visibility reflective jackets (which should be in the main body of the car, not in a closed boot)
- A spare pair of glasses (if you wear them)
- A bulb replacement set

Make sure you have all your original documents in your car at all times

Car Ownership

Spain, like any country, has a wide selection of garages selling new and used cars. Indeed, outside any major town you are likely to find a light industrial or commercial estate with a range of car manufacturers' showrooms and garages. There are also likely to be garages that sell used cars, from almost-new models to the cheapest and oldest on the road.

You can also buy second-hand cars privately. These are advertised in much the same way as in the UK and can be found in car magazines and local papers and on websites, one of the most important being *www.segundamano.com.*

Transfer of vehicle ownership is complicated but crucial to get right – so use a gestor if you have any doubts about what you are doing

However, buying a car in Spain is anything but simple. There is considerable paperwork involved not least because purchase tax is payable to the Spanish state by the buyer (whether the car is new or used). As a consequence, almost certainly you will need to employ a *gestor* to ensure that the necessary paperwork and any tax or debts on the car are dealt with correctly.

Certainly, be wary of buying second-hand cars in Spain on the open market (as opposed to from a reputable garage), as any debts attached to the car will be passed on to you. Indeed, you may find yourself liable for the accumulated parking fines of the previous owner, or worse, a hire-purchase debt.

Most reputable garages will undertake the necessary transfer of ownership for you as part of their sales service. However, you should check this is the case before agreeing to buy a car. Meanwhile, it is worth noting that diesel cars tend to be significantly cheaper to run in Spain than those powered by petrol – so it may be worth buying one (even if the initial cost is sometimes greater).

Motor tax and MOT (Inspeccion Tecnica de Vehiculos)

If you own a car in Spain, this must be registered with your local town hall – to which you will pay an annual road tax. This tax, at the time of writing, is considerably cheaper than in the UK.

As in most of Europe, you must have a valid MOT (*ITV*). This is unnecessary for a car that is less than four years old. After that time though, an *ITV* must be renewed every two years until the car is 10 years old – at which time it will need an annual *ITV*. Commercial vehicles need to be tested every six months.

An MOT (ITV) is mandatory for any vehicle over four years old

ITV's are undertaken at dedicated *ITV* centres, which are normally on the outskirts of most large towns and within industrial estates. Normally you can turn up on any working day with your vehicle and join any existing queue.

Before the test, you will need to go to the *ITV* office with the relevant paperwork and pay a fee. Your car will then be inspected thoroughly. After the test you will be provided with a form stating whether it has passed or not, and any reasons for a failure. If your vehicle has passed, you will be provided with a sticky label that shows the due date of your next *ITV*. This sticker must be placed inside your front windscreen. If your car fails the test then, obviously, you will have to correct the problem and retake the test.

Spanish Driving

Obviously, you must have a valid driving licence from your own country to drive in Spain. However, after 180 days in Spain you should apply for a Spanish driving license *(licencia de conducción)*. Though many people neglect to change their driving licence, you may face a significant fine for this.

The easiest way of changing your current UK driving licence for a Spanish one is to use a *gestor*. They will undertake the necessary paperwork, which involves applying for and obtaining your driving licence from the provincial traffic headquarters *(jefatura provincial de tráfico)*. You must provide them with:

- Your current UK driving licence (both the card and paper licence). In return, you will receive a stamped note acknowledging your application for a licence. This note can be produced as proof of a valid licence if you are stopped by the police.
- *NIE* number
- *Certificado de ciudadano de la unión* (Certificate proving that a person has been registered on the Registro Central de Extranjeros)
- *Certificado de empadronamiento* (proof of address)
- Two recent (passport-sized) photographs

You should note that you can sometimes encounter problems hiring a car in the UK if you have only a Spanish driving licence.

If you do not have a driving licence (or your children need to get one), you will need to take a test. The driving test is in two parts: a written theoretical test and a practical driving test. Both need to be passed before you can obtain your licence. The theoretical test is reputed to be particularly difficult. However, there is a profusion of driving schools in most towns, and all will take care of the application process for you.

Note: You will need to take a medical examination before you can apply for your driver's test.

It is worth noting that a learner driver cannot drive even when accompanied by someone holding a valid driving licence. The learner may only drive with a registered instructor. This can make obtaining practical experience difficult.

The Spanish driving test system is considered generally less effective than that of the UK. Typically, students struggle with rather ambiguous questions in the theory examination (often having to retake the test). Once that is passed, a student might pass the practical driving test after driving only a very limited circuit of a local industrial estate and part of a town. Certainly, it is not uncommon to hear from members of both the Spanish and immigrant communities that you can sail through the practical test process if you are willing to pay 'extra', irrespective of your knowledge and driving skills. This may account for some of the driving on Spanish roads, which can, at times, be less than impressive.

A driving licence can be obtained for a vehicle under 50 cc at the age of 16 For a driving licence for a car, you need to be at least 18 years old.

Finally, when you have your licence you must display a green 'L' sign (meaning probationary driver) for the first year of driving.

Motoring

One of the joys of Spain is that, outside of the cities, you can experience the pleasure of motoring. The roads are almost devoid of traffic and there is an exceptionally fine network. Indeed, the roads and motorways of Spain are renowned for their quality – albeit due to huge amounts of EU money (to which you may have contributed!).

Though toll motorways do exist, these are mainly on the coast. Elsewhere, driving is normally free, with a wide range of well-located (and generally high-quality) service stations.

Spain has a zero tolerance policy to drunk driving – so never drink and drive!

The Spanish police are quick to act if you use a mobile telephone while driving and you must never use your mobile telephone at a petrol station. Spain also now has a zero tolerance policy to drunk driving. Equally, despite appearances to the contrary, it is mandatory to wear a crash helmet when you are on a motorcycle and you will be penalised by the police for not doing so.

Spain has a points system similar to that in the UK. Drivers have a clean licence 'score' of a maximum of 12 points – unless they have just passed their driving test, in which case they have eight points for the first three years. Points are deducted for offences and your driving licence is withdrawn for a year if you lose all your points. To get your licence back, you have to retake the driving test.

Note: Spain has a growing number of traffic cameras, so the days of carefree speeding are rapidly coming to a close!

Traffic Accident (accidente de trafico)

Spain has had a poor record for road safety so there is a chance you may either witness or be involved in a traffic accident of some kind. If an accident occurs:

- Stop immediately.

- Put on one of your high-visibility reflective jackets and place your warning triangles to the front and rear of your vehicle.

- If anyone is injured, call the emergency services on 112 immediately and provide basic first aid (but try not to move badly hurt or unconscious casualties unless it is essential to get them away from immediate danger).

- Avoid moving any vehicles until the police arrive. If for some reason you have to move a vehicle, then take extensive photographs beforehand or at least an accurate sketch. If possible, get this signed by any witnesses and include their names and addresses.

- Exchange details with the driver of any other vehicle involved in the crash. You must make sure that you provide and obtain:

- The registration number of the vehicle(s) involved
- The names, addresses and insurance companies of all parties

Note: The Spanish have identity cards (*documento nacional de identidad* or *DNI*) from which you should take their details. From non-Spaniards, you should seek verification of their identity from their passport.

- Try always to ensure that you have details of any witnesses and try to take down the registration numbers of their vehicles if they are reluctant to stop.
- Advise your insurance company straightaway that you have had an accident.

Note: If the accident has not been serious and there have been no injuries, it is not mandatory to call the police. However, you must concentrate on making sure you obtain clear details of what happened and the parties involved so that any insurance claims can be processed easily.

Do not sign any document of any kind unless you are absolutely clear about the contents and agree with them!

Public Transport

Spain has an extensive public transport network linked by rail (RENFE), numerous national and regional bus companies, and several airlines (although most domestic flights are operated by Iberia). Prices, obviously, vary greatly according to the route and time of year. Generally, however, Spain's public transport system is both efficient and affordable, with train travel a bargain compared to that in the UK.

Letting Your Property

For some people, the possibility for letting out their property is important. This provides a potential 'get out' if they decide subsequently not to stay in Spain and rather to use their property as a potential income-earning investment. Alternatively, as many Spanish villas have independent apartments, the option may exist to earn an income from renting out this excess space.

Be extremely wary of renting your property

The Dangers

Letting property in Spain is extremely hazardous. Tenancy law is strict and complicated and can provide tenants with protection against eviction – a landlord's nightmare. In certain circumstances, a tenant may even obtain rights to remain for up to five years.

Spanish law grants inalienable rights to tenants, irrespective of the intentions of a landlord and despite any contract terms to the contrary. Removing a reluctant tenant can be very difficult – even if he is in breach of an agreement (such as not paying rent). Any enforced removal will require a court order, which can take significant time to obtain (up to six months depending on the local court) and involve unwelcome expense. Meanwhile, you may find you have an embittered tenant who stoops to causing damage and the possibility of any recompense unlikely.

In short, letting a property in Spain is not something to take lightly. This is the case particularly when the letting time exceeds more than a short holiday period.

249

If you decide to let your property, you must go to a tenancy lawyer who specialises in property and take advice on any potential letting agreement and its implications. Obviously, any contract should be drafted only by an experienced lawyer and should be in writing and always signed by all the relevant parties.

Many people let their properties in Spain. The Spanish frequently let their flats on long-term agreements, while North Europeans often subsidise their pensions through letting to holidaymakers. Usually, during July and August there is a high demand for virtually every type of property (particularly those with a swimming pool) situated near the coast. During the rest of the year some properties seem always to be in demand from North Europeans who want to enjoy Spain's winter sun.

Always use a qualified property lawyer to draft out a written tenancy agreement

However, many (if not most) holiday lets in Spain by North European property owners are illegal and income not declared to the Spanish tax office. Furthermore, many rentals probably do not comply with Spanish health and safety regulations. These are enforced for B&Bs (*casas rurales*) and hotels but, under new laws, can be applied also to underbuild apartments and any other accommodation that is rented out.

Regularly, the English language newspapers in Spain warn that Spanish tax authorities are cracking down on owners of rental properties who do not declare their income. Though the actions of the authorities to date have not been very effective, this should not be taken for granted.

Finding landlords who are not properly registered as a business is hardly difficult given how extensively they use the big web portals specialising in holiday rentals.

These sites display the details of vast numbers of flats, villas and houses for rent, as well as the location and owner details, which makes owners easy to track down.

Many people who rent their properties to holidaymakers do so casually, claiming the people staying are non-paying family and friends. Within limits, this can be a sound way of proceeding. However, if this is combined with public advertising, then it can become less convincing to the tax authorities, who may impose a fine on the basis of assessed earnings!

In addition to the issue of tax evasion, there is also a considerable fine for letting out any holiday accommodation without a proper license. A large number of owners have already suffered fines (typically around €30,000) that have more than wiped out the income gained from past rentals. Nonetheless many people, rather stupidly, take the risk and continue to rent their accommodation unofficially.

Business Registration in Spain

The problem with letting your property in Spain is that being properly registered can be an expensive process. If you are resident in Spain then you will have to become tax resident and register your letting business. This will involve, inevitably, the help of a lawyer or tax consultant (*asesor fiscal*) and will include:

- A possible formal inspection of the premises to be let. This may mean that you have to spend money to ensure your premises comply with all relevant Spanish health and safety requirements.

- Registration as a business. Most likely you will be advised to become *autónomo* (self-employed), which involves:

- Paying monthly social security contributions of at least €250–300
- Delivering proper invoices
- Accounting for *IVA* (VAT) either monthly or quarterly
- Paying your lawyer or tax consultant's fees
- Obtaining public liability insurance

Take care of renting your property illegally
– the Spanish authorities will impose
heavy sanctions if they find out

Note: In reality a properly registered rentals business is not financially viable unless the net profit from the rental exceeds €350+ a month.

Marketing

If you choose to rent your property, there are a number of ways of obtaining tenants, depending on your market. The principal marketing undertaken by most people revolves around:

- Advertising on some of the major property rental web portals such as *www.villarentals.com* and *www.ownersdirect.com*. Some websites are extremely efficient and have automated booking charts, and both take and pay deposits upon your agreement. Sites may charge one-off fees for registration of your property while others will take a percentage of the booking fee.

- Setting up your own website to advertise specifically your property. This may be complemented by banner advertising in papers or magazines.

- Networking. This can involve simply telling everyone you know that you do rentals and getting friends to circulate this information by e-mail or verbally to other friends or work colleagues.

- *Se Alquiler* (For Rent) boards. These can be effective in attracting local people.

Finally, be sceptical when a seller tells you that your intended property (or an extra apartment on the property) is rented out regularly for high returns. Always ask for proof of this. Equally, be aware that a rentals business is not always as stable as it appears. Economic fluctuations can significantly harm international holiday letting with the consequence that rents can plummet. You will have to be prepared also for the inconvenience and, sometimes, considerable disturbance of people on your property.

Money and Pensions

Few things will destroy the success and happiness of your relocation more savagely than encountering money problems. The stress of being short of money is also always worse when abroad. You will feel more vulnerable and have less of a support system to fall back on than you would in your own country. Family and friends will not be present to help out and you will be away from a business network that you may have belonged to for most of your working life.

Control your finances and do not overspend –
particularly during your first year in Spain

Many newcomers to Spain are not sufficiently careful about their finances. Some people mistake capital wealth for income. Also, they make no allowance for potential exchange rate fluctuations and thereby the purchasing power of their pension or investments. The natural volatility that occurs with differing economic conditions can also significantly decrease unearned income streams.

All too typically, people who relocate will overspend during their first year in Spain. An understandable desire to make a dream real, coupled with the optimism inherent in starting a new life, can lead to all caution being suspended. As a consequence, property budgets are exceeded and this is swiftly followed by over-exuberant purchases of brand-new furniture and an upmarket car. Undisciplined daily spending and the mistaken belief that Spain is dirt cheap can further aggravate matters. After a couple of years, financial problems inevitably loom.

Personal Discipline

When it comes to money, the secret of relocation is to:

- **Underspend on your property:** Set a budget of less than you can afford and then keep to this. Be disciplined and remember that an inanimate object (even a lovely house) will not guarantee you happiness in the long term. Financial problems, on the other hand, are absolutely certain to provide you with heartbreak and intolerable stress.

Avoid exceeding your budget when buying property – and remember, it is not inanimate objects that make life fulfilling for the long term

- **Avoid any borrowing, whether mortgages or otherwise:** Keep your fixed costs and overheads to a minimum. Cash is king – unless you are financially very sophisticated.
- **Budget for the worst possible income return on existing investments or pensions:** As 2008 showed, sterling can crash. Equally, the value of pensions and other investments can drop as radically as they can rise. Nothing is absolutely certain and you must build in a conservative factor to your anticipated long-term income. Make sure that you can live comfortably should your predicted income drop by 20%–30%.
- **Be precise about the property you buy:** Make sure that your new home is right for you and that you will not have to move again. The additional costs of buying property in Spain are considerable (around 10% of the purchase price) and capital gains tax is payable (with exceptions) on the sale of your property, whether it is your primary residence or a second home. If you buy a property that is not suitable for some reason and then sell up and buy again, you will have lost:
    - At least 20% of the gross value of the properties bought (2 x 10% purchase costs)

- The amount of capital gains tax payable
- Fees due to estate agents
- The ancillary costs of moving (such as removals)

This is a fine way of wasting a lot of money very quickly.

- **Allow at least three years for any work or new business to start providing a satisfactory income:** Businesses are invariably much slower to produce a proper income than first anticipated (irrespective of the country!). There are exceptions, of course, but be very cautious – even pessimistic – with your predictions of expenditure involved and the time it will take to receive a viable income.

- **Make a contingency budget for unexpected problems:** Unanticipated difficulties occur as surely as night follows day and can involve expense beyond that ever considered. So, always earmark several thousand euros as a contingency budget – to be used *only* in cases of emergency.

> *Be pessimistic about the time it will take for any work to become financially viable – and have a good contingency plan in place*

Some people fall into the trap of letting their ego run riot over common sense. Indeed, it is amazing how many retiring couples use their purchase in Spain as a status symbol to show off to occasional visitors. This results in many couples living in vast, high-maintenance villas that prove to be nothing more than a burden. In many cases, it is much cheaper to rent a local villa, apartment or even hotel room for visiting family and friends. Unless you can afford a gardener, pool cleaner, maid and handyman, stretching your finances to buy the biggest villa possible can prove to be a mistake.

Without doubt, financial caution should be uppermost in your mind when relocating. Set sensible and conservative budgets and stick to them at all times. Everyone has finite resources, however wealthy they are. Nonetheless, few people are capable of being disciplined and realistic when in holiday mode or free from the constraints of their normal lives. The penalty for not being extremely careful can be devastating, and destroy an otherwise perfectly attainable dream relocation.

Financial Affairs

You will be deemed resident in Spain if:

- You have been in Spain for over 183 days (continually or in part) during the course of a given year.
- Your main and primary residence is in Spain.

If you are resident in Spain, your world wealth (irrespective of your wishes) will become taxable by the Spanish state. You must therefore annually declare your financial situation to the Spanish tax authorities. Just like in the UK, this can be a complicated matter, particularly if you are to avoid being over-taxed or (worse still!) taxed by two countries at the same time. Equally, it is important to make a tax declaration (and a correct one) even if it is a nil return to prevent the possibility of financial sanctions and penalties being applied by the Spanish state. Almost certainly you will need the advice and help of a *gestor* when it comes to ensuring that your financial affairs are in proper order.

Gestors

Gestors are of considerable importance and a profession not really comparable to anything in the UK. A *gestor* is a qualified Spanish professional who acts as the interface between the state and the private sector. G*estores* are multi-problem solvers and will do your tax return, company accounts and *IVA* returns. They can advise you on your financial situation and be employed to undertake a raft of functions – from obtaining your *NIE* to helping you get your *SIP* card, from converting your driving licence to a Spanish one to helping you complete the paperwork on a car you wish to buy.

Omnicapable and normally having a superb network of local contacts, *gestores* are absolutely essential to anyone in business. Even if you are not involved in business, a friendly and efficient *gestor* will probably prove a valuable resource at some stage.

Gestores are present in all towns and cities and often have large offices with a variety of specialists ranging from state administrative experts to tax and accountancy specialists to employment law consultants. This means that a sophisticated *gestor* can act as a one-stop shop for an array of problems or administrative matters.

> *Always have a good gestor – he will be almost as important as your lawyer*

Of course, you must find a *gestor* who has someone in his office who is fluent in English. This is essential as you are likely to be seeing a *gestor* on matters that either concern financial issues or complicated bureaucratic paperwork. Precise instructions and a clear understanding of any advice received will be vital.

As with lawyers, make sure your *gestor* is properly qualified and insured. Equally, you should only choose a *gestor* who is independent of any business that is in direct local competition to your own.

Pensions

One of the oddities of pensions is how little Britons tend to know about them – including where the pension is held, its value and what to do to maximise its effectiveness. There is a saying in the pension industry that ignorance about a pension is much like 'owning a house but not knowing where it is and how much it is worth' …

In fact, there can be considerable benefits to moving abroad if you have a pension and manage it wisely. After five years of living abroad, for example, all restrictions and regulations concerning your UK pension fund disappear. Indeed, it is possible to reposition your pension fund within QROPS (Qualifying Regional Overseas Pensions Schemes) so that you can take advantage of:

- An immediate lump sum payment
- Greater investment choices
- The ability to pass on unused funds to whoever you want, free of UK tax
- Tax efficiencies between the UK and Spain
- Potential inheritance tax avoidance
- An annuity (i.e. income for life) by the age of 75

Take professional advice regarding your pension – you may find that you can rearrange its effectiveness

Obviously, to arrange for these benefits you need expert advice. This you must choose extremely carefully. Indeed, if you are considering a change to your pension, you must ensure that you take advice only from:

- A UK-registered (and insured) pension specialist
- A professional who is an up-to-date and qualified IFA (Independent Financial Advisor)
- Someone who has access to a wide selection of QROPs
- A specialist in pension funds between the UK and Spain

Residency

The importance of residency within the EU is often misunderstood by Britons moving to Spain. While most Britons fully appreciate that they have the right to live and work in another EU country, they do not understand how this right transfers into reality. Misunderstand residency issues and you may find you have moved to Spain under a false illusion of what it can offer you.

The Law

As an EU citizen you can visit Spain for up to three months without any form of paperwork – although, should you wish to buy a property, you must apply for your *NIE* number (as discussed in *Finance and Enabling)*. Without this you cannot sign the *escritura* ('complete' in UK terms) on a property – whether that property is to be an investment, holiday home or permanent home. Furthermore, you will be unable to sign a contract for electricity, water or any other fiscal matter (which may endanger any intention you have to rent a property for a long term period).

If you do not intend buying (or long term leasing) a property, of course, there is little point in applying for a *NIE* number. Possessing a *NIE* number is not obligatory and obtaining it will gain you little or nothing during your stay. Also, it has nothing whatsoever to do with 'residency'.

However, if you remain in Spain for longer than three months, you are obliged by law to register yourself on the National Register of Foreigners (*Registro Central de Extranjeros*). This could be considered as 'logging on' to the Spanish state.

Know the difference between being a
resident in Spain and being tax resident
– the two are not the same!

Registering on the National Register of Foreigners is only an administrative action – it does not follow that you will receive free healthcare or Spanish tax benefits and inheritance tax exemptions and so on.

However, note that you will be deemed to be *tax resident* (*residente fiscal*) in Spain (whether you like it or not!) if you spend over 183 days within the country, whether those days are consecutive or not.

In that case you must file an annual income tax return with the Spanish tax authorities declaring your worldwide wealth.

Reality

You will not receive free healthcare or tax benefits (including inheritance tax exemptions) unless you are *tax resident* – even if (and this is worth repeating) you are registered on the National Register of Foreigners.

The only exception to the above is if you are 65 or over (a *pensionista*), in which case you will be provided with free healthcare, subject to having registered yourself properly.

In essence, when you relocate to Spain permanently, you obtain rights as well as obligations. You must contribute to the Spanish state financial system (normally as an employee or self- employed person) if you want the benefits offered by the country. If you do not pay tax or file an annual income tax return with the Spanish authorities you will not be considered tax resident – and you cannot expect (and will not receive) all the same benefits as a native Spanish national.

Of course, for many people coming to Spain, the 'benefits' of being tax resident appear almost pointless. If your children have grown up and you have private healthcare, you may ask why should you bother becoming tax resident. However, if you do not declare yourself tax resident:

- You are breaking the law (which *deems* you to be tax resident after 183 days). Accordingly, in principle, you could face sanctions for not paying tax (or, at the very least, for not making a proper annual income tax return to the Spanish state).

- If you sell your property you will have to pay the 3% capital gains tax (*Impuesto sobre la Renta de no Residentes*) that is exercised on the full sale price of a property sold by a foreigner who is not tax resident. Additionally, you will be unable to avoid any further CGT (applied at 19%) due on the sale of your property. As a tax resident this can be avoided by buying another Spanish property of the same or greater value within two years of your sale.

- You will not receive the potentially significant benefits applicable under Spanish inheritance tax law (See *Wills and Inheritance Tax*).

Naturally, you may think that once you are *deemed* tax resident you can automatically enjoy all the benefits of a Spanish national, even if you do not pay any tax or make any annual tax returns. Again, you *must* make a tax return or pay tax to be considered tax resident. If you cannot show *proof* of having done so, you will not be eligible for any tax (or other) benefits!

Situation Normal ...

What tends to happen is that Britons reside for years in Spain without fulfilling the above-mentioned tax resident requirements. They either deliberately avoid paying tax and social security payments or make one of the following errors:

- Confuse the concept of tax residency – with that of formally acknowledging their presence in the country by registering themselves as a foreigner (under the EX16 residencia form).

- Believe that possessing an *NIE* number grants them tax residency.

- Expect free healthcare – despite paying no tax to the Spanish state.

Be aware of the tax implications on any sale of your Spanish property if you are not tax resident

Typically, a Briton intending to sell his property is then horrified to find that he has to pay a non-negotiable 3% of the sale price of his property in capital gains tax on the day of signing the *escritura*. Worse still, notwithstanding that this property is his only home, he is amazed to find that he has to pay capital gains tax on any gain that he has made.

Furthermore, the non tax resident finds that he cannot claim 'free' healthcare for his family as he did in the UK. Finally, should the non tax resident Briton die, his inheritors are horrified to discover the severity of Spanish inheritance tax of the deceased's Spanish assets.

So, if you want 'free' healthcare, tax benefits, inheritance tax exemptions and so on in Spain, you effectively have to pay the Spanish state for these.

Action

It makes sense for anyone thinking of relocating to:

- Apply for an *NIE* number straight away. There is nothing to lose by doing this as it involves only a very small fee and compromises none of your rights within the UK.

- Register on the National Registry of Foreigners. This can be done at the same time as applying for an *NIE* number and at the same offices (the *Oficina de Extranjeros* or *Comisaria de Policia*). The process is a little more complicated than applying for an *NIE*. However, it is easily tackled with patience or in conjunction with your lawyer, agent or *gestor*.

If you are coming to Spain permanently or for longer than six months, then (depending on your work status), you should arrange to make an annual income tax return, pay social security payments and become properly tax resident.

Speak to your lawyer, who will be able to advise you further – often they can recommend a tax advisor (*asesor*). Alternatively, see a *gestor*. Any of these professionals will be able to help you fulfil your obligations, assist you to make your annual tax return or set up your social security payments.

Paying Tax

If you pay tax to the Spanish state and thereby make national insurance contributions, you and your immediate family (your partner/spouse and children) will be eligible for free healthcare and welfare payments (depending on what you have paid!) Your national insurance contributions will also provide you with a pension, although you have to work for 15 years before this comes into effect!

You should note that just because you are paying tax, it does not follow necessarily that, for example, your wife is classed as tax resident. This factor can have great significance should she die before you. In this case, her estate could end up bearing the full brunt of any inheritance tax on her Spanish assets (see *Wills and Inheritance Tax*).

It is advisable to make a common (rather than individual) income tax return. A common income tax return will include your partner and thus make him or her tax resident.

Wills and Inheritance Tax

Whenever you have to deal with tax issues or wills it is vital to know, right from the start, your current tax residence status in Spain (see *Residency*). This is of primary importance as it has profound implications upon how you will be treated by the Spanish state.

For example, if you die as a tax resident (*residente fiscal*) of Spain, your estate may be eligible for significant Spanish state inheritance tax benefits and exemptions.

However, if you die as a non tax resident, your estate may (depending on the nature of the bequests) be subject to a high Spanish inheritance tax. As a result, your estate may be penalised with a severity far harsher than that of the UK. This may create horrendous hardship for your surviving spouse. It may also result in the Spanish taxman receiving far more of the value of your estate than ever you intended – or was necessary.

> *"In this world nothing can be said to be certain, except death and taxes"*
> **(Benjamin Franklin)**

Intestacy

Astonishingly, many people die intestate (without having made a valid will). Indeed, a reputable probate advisor in Spain states that this is the case for around half of the estates with which he deals. This can lead to great stress for surviving family members.

So, whatever else you do, make a will – preferably both a UK will (for your UK assets) and a Spanish will (for your Spanish assets). This is particularly important if you have assets or property in Spain. It is not obligatory to make a will, but if you don't have one your estate will:

- Be subject to excessive bureaucratic delays.

- Incur enormous expense – as translations and certifications of documentation are required, as well as excessive (and probably international) legal expertise.

- Potentially accrue penalties if the due inheritance tax has not been paid within six months of the death.

- Possibly create major inconvenience and financial embarrassment as joint bank accounts are frozen until resolution of the estate (although sometimes direct debits for services can be paid).

If you have property in Spain and die intestate, then (whether you are tax resident or non tax resident) your estate will be liable to Spanish inheritance tax (IHT) on your death. Furthermore, you may find that Spanish IHT also applies to your worldwide assets. Obviously, there is no difference in the amount of tax applied by the Spanish tax authorities depending upon whether you died intestate or with a valid will.

Make both a UK and a Spanish will before, or at least as soon as, you own property or assets in Spain – otherwise you may leave your heirs and executors with terrible problems

The Law

Spanish inheritance law is a very complicated subject. Worse still, it is very region (*comunidad autónoma*) sensitive. The central government of Spain has devolved powers to the 17 *comunidades autónomas* and two autonomous cities, so that each can decide on the inheritance tax rate and exemptions for their given regions. So, this makes any definitive guidance almost impossible to provide. You must always seek advice from a tax professional with detailed knowledge of the law in your region.

However, of one matter you can be certain: as a non tax resident you will not be entitled to any inheritance tax exemptions. This means that the full, unmitigated force of Spanish inheritance tax will be unleashed on the assets you own in Spain. This may also mean:

- Your assets in Spain have Spanish inheritance tax applied without (effectively) a nil rate tax band. In the UK, by comparison, you will not be taxed on the first £325,000 of your assets (as at 2009/2010).

- There is no such thing as nil rate inheritance tax on the disposition of your Spanish assets between you and your spouse upon the death of either.

The consequences can be devastating as considerable tax is applied to assets owned by the deceased. The implications for a surviving spouse can be dreadful – as they may have to pay maximum inheritance tax on (say) half the marital home. This can create significant problems unless the surviving partner has substantial money of their own.

Be aware of the severity of Spanish inheritance law – if you are not tax resident – and the potential for high tax liabilities on your Spanish assets

The obvious solution would be for the surviving spouse to sell the marital home or to raise a mortgage on it to pay any inheritance tax due. However, the home cannot be sold (or charged) *until* the estate of the deceased has been finalised and all tax paid. And until then, any bank accounts of the deceased will be frozen as well as any joint accounts. This catch-22 can lead to real hardship for the surviving spouse.

Critically, by Spanish law, it is the individual inheritor who is taxed, rather than the estate. This means that the amount of tax to be paid will depend on the status and relationship of the of the individual to the deceased – with certain circumstances leading to a major reduction in the tax payable. However, any reduction and inheritance tax exemptions are in turn dependent upon the deceased having been officially tax resident!

If the deceased was a Spanish tax resident then (depending upon the *comunidad autónoma*), the estate will effectively benefit from significant tax reductions. However, these reductions depend upon:

- The exact relationship of the inheritor to the deceased (such as testator and spouse, or testator and nephew, or testator and friend).

- Whether the beneficiary is handicapped or not.

Not surprisingly, the further the relationship of the beneficiary to the testator, the higher the tax to be paid by the beneficiary. So, there will often be little relationship between the amount of tax applied on a bequest to a son (for example) and a friend. The latter will be taxed highly and the former much less so. More importantly (again, this depends upon the *comunidad autónoma)*, the reductions – if the deceased was tax resident – can amount to an almost nil rate tax on bequests between spouses.

So, for example, in the *Comunidad de Valencia,* inheritance between husbands and wives has a tax exemption on amounts up to €40,000 (as at 2009). Furthermore, there is a further tax discount available of up to 99%. This means that effectively there is no inheritance tax between spouses in this region.

Obviously, a problem for many spouses is that one party is often not tax resident. So, for example, the husband may be tax resident, and his wife not. Should the latter die, the bequest of her assets will not have any inheritance tax exemptions or reductions applied! So, the party making the annual income tax return should always make an income tax return that includes their spouse.

Spanish law imposes absolute terms upon its citizens as to whom they must leave their property and assets. By law, a testator must leave two-thirds of his estate to certain heirs (*la legitima*).

However, as a British citizen you are exempt from this particular regulation and can leave your assets to whoever you wish. In any event, any asset out of Spain should be covered expressly by your British will and state that this asset will be subject only to British inheritance tax law.

A further advantage to a British will is its flexibility. Whereas a Spanish will (once it has been certified) cannot be adjusted by the beneficiaries on the death of the testator, a UK will allows this, with the consent of the beneficiaries. This is important as it allows beneficiaries to potentially avoid certain taxes.

With a British will, for example, beneficiaries may 'gift' an inherited property to a UK limited company. In this event, no Spanish inheritance tax is payable. Indeed, all that will be required in Spain to satisfy the tax office is a UK Grant of Probate and Death Certificate that has been duly translated, notarised and apostilled.

Types of Spanish Wills

Spanish wills can be *common* (holographic, open or closed) or *special* (for the military, people at sea and wills made out of Spain). However, the most usual wills are:

- **Open will** (*testamento abierto*), in which the provisions of the will are not concealed.

- **Closed will** (*testamento cerrado*), in which provisions are secret. This will is placed into a sealed envelope in front of a *notary*.

- **Holographic will** (*testamento ológrafo*), which is handwritten. Upon the death of a testator the will has to be executed within five years, but must first be authenticated by a judge – a process that can delay the execution of the will.

> *Before you make a will: seek expert advice on how to mitigate the potential tax liabilities of your estate upon your death*

Making a Spanish Will

The vast majority of wills made are *open wills*. These should be drafted by a qualified and experienced bilingual, Spanish probate lawyer. An *open will* needs to be:

- Signed by you (the testator)

- Signed by a notary

- Provided to you (the testator) as an authorised copy with a further copy kept by the notary

- Registered by the notary at the Central Registry of Wills (*Registro Central de Ultimas Voluntades*)

- If you are not Spanish the will should be both in Spanish and English

All of the above can be completed quickly and costs very little – and is the very least you can do to avoid leaving behind any significant problems should you die.

Tax Avoidance and Inheritance Tax Avoidance

Of course, one of the preoccupations of anyone making a will is how best to dispose of their assets without paying too much inheritance tax. This is an extremely complicated matter as much depends upon the law at any given time. So, always obtain professional advice from a sophisticated (and trustworthy!) tax avoidance expert, will specialist, or canny lawyer who understands both Spanish and UK tax laws.

> *If you go to a tax advisor, make sure that he is properly qualified and check – and double-check – his bona fides and his understanding of English!*

At the moment, there are ways of reducing your tax liability and these should be looked at closely. For example, there are some arguments for taking full advantage of corporate ownership of your Spanish property. This can be advantageous at the time of buying, as well as if you already own a property and should you wish to reduce your potential Spanish inheritance tax liability. This is certainly important if you are non tax resident and have no intention of becoming Spanish tax resident.

Furthermore, a recent UK law provides some help to those owning property abroad. If the difference between your earnings and your mortgage payments (per annum) is negative, you can deduct the difference from your CGT allowance on your UK taxes. This can be particularly useful should you own a holiday home in Spain.

Summary

Certainly, making a will and attending to potential inheritance tax liabilities is important. It is, however, something that often is forgotten or left for 'another time' (which inevitably does not come around).

So, make a will both in the UK and Spain either before or immediately after you buy a property in Spain. It is a remarkably simple and pain-free process that also costs very little and could save your partner and heirs from some horrendous problems should the worst happen.

It is certainly worth taking tax advice before you come to Spain from a specialist in Spanish tax, as this can, sometimes, provide you with considerable protection and sometimes help you to avoid the worst of some Spanish property and inheritance related taxes.

Finally, understand the critical difference between being tax resident and non tax resident in Spain. If you are unsure of your classification, check with your lawyer. Certainly, if you are non tax resident, consider either becoming tax resident or removing your assets out of the reach of Spanish inheritance tax laws.

Contracts and Disputes

If you ask experienced litigation lawyers in any country in the world how best to avoid disagreements, they will reply:

- Always have a clear and precise agreement in place right from the start of any transaction

- Ensure that the details and exact intentions of any agreement are provable and are in writing

If you do not operate on the above principles then, more than likely, you will become embroiled in ugly and often unnecessary disputes – whether you are in Spain or anywhere else.

Of course, it stands to reason that you should never enter into an agreement unless you understand exactly what you are agreeing to and all the implications thereof. So, under no circumstances enter into any agreement if you have the slightest doubt about any aspect. This is critical when you will be involved in agreements (both oral and written) that are invariably in Spanish.

Always take legal advice before entering into an agreement – or if you are unsure about any aspect of it

Asking for Trouble

Unfortunately, for some bizarre reason, many English-speaking people who come to Spain enter into contracts in a fashion that is positively cavalier. Indeed, litigation lawyers in Spain are constantly amazed by the sheer lunacy displayed by mature and experienced foreigners once they are in Spain. For some reason, common sense is often discarded and agreements entered into when, from the outset, the person concerned had little or no idea of what they were agreeing to.

To compound matters, contracts are often made with little to nothing in writing and blatant conflicts of interest on the part of others accepted as a matter of course – astonishingly, on the rare occasions legal advice is sought, many Britons allow their lawyer to act for both parties.

It would be no exaggeration to state that English-speaking people in Spain who ignore the basic rules of entering into contractual relationships have become something of a phenomenon. This is extraordinary given that most people in their own countries exercise great care.

Certainly, be under no illusion as to your freedom to make a binding contract in Spain. If you are of full age and have full legal capacity then you have the freedom, with limited exceptions, to bind yourself to whatever you and the other contracting party decide. Furthermore, it is a fundamental rule of Spanish contract law that it is the individual responsibility of the contracting parties to understand exactly the details of the agreement. This means that if you enter into a contact (that later turns out to be something other than you imagined) you will have difficulty escaping from its terms and conditions.

Never sign something you do not understand –
consult a lawyer and/or a properly qualified,
independent interpreter

It is fundamentally important to be aware of the consequences and implications of contract law in Spain. Every day you spend here will involve contracts of one sort or another, whether you go shopping for groceries, agree to the building of an extension, buy a villa, or hire a car. You must know therefore what elements a contract comprises, how to ensure it is enforceable, and what to do when either you or the other party breach an agreement.

You must appreciate that Spanish law is different from that of the UK. In Spain, civil law is based on the Napoleonic Code as opposed to the combination of statute and common law of the UK. There are, therefore, fundamental differences.

Certainly, the conduct of court cases is somewhat different, with far more emphasis placed on written rather than oral evidence. There is also no distinction within the legal profession between barristers and solicitors, although certain lawyers do specialise in advocacy rather than in the overall preparation of cases. Moreover, judges in Spain do not have to practise law (as lawyers) before being appointed. Indeed, to be a judge is a specific profession for which a Spaniard would train just as if he wanted to become an engineer, *gestor* or doctor.

Equally, when your lawyer is conducting your case, he must appoint a *procurador* to act for you. A *procurador* is the communication link between your lawyer and the court, and has no comparable counterpart in the UK. Your lawyer will have to appoint a *procurador* in each of the jurisdictions in which your case is likely to be heard, from your local court right through to the Supreme Court, if applicable.

Outline of Contract Law

In Spain there are three types of contract:

* **Oral agreement**
  This is when different parties enter into an agreement without any written evidence. However, for the agreement to be considered binding there must be the following components:

1. An offer to do or supply something that is defined
2. An acceptance – consensus from the other party to do or supply the defined 'thing'
3. Consideration – a reward (normally money)

This type of contract is as binding as a written contract. However, without supporting paperwork it can be often difficult to define clearly the reality of the agreement.

Indeed, major caution must be exercised with any oral contract. Never forget that, in the event of a court dispute, your success will be dependent on the quality of the evidence your lawyer can submit to the court. So, always commit everything to do with an agreement in writing. Back up every step you take with written confirmation. If you pay money, get a receipt; if you make a bank transfer, keep the transfer documentation; if you agree something over the telephone, back it up with written correspondence.

- **Written agreement**
  A written agreement must have the three critical components of offer, acceptance and consideration. A written agreement is far better than any oral agreement because, by its very nature, the terms between the parties are recorded in writing and therefore tend to be easier to prove. However, much depends on how well the agreement has been drafted. So, it is always advisable to use a lawyer to ensure that all the fundamentals of a contract are present and that your intentions are properly and clearly expressed.

- **Notarised agreement**
  This is a written and formalise agreement that the parties place before a notary for his approval. It is a binding agreement, but does not need to have the same basic components as an oral or written agreement. An

example of a notarised agreement would be the purchase of a property or a company – in which case there would be a formal deed of sale (*escritura de compaventa)*, authorised by a Spanish *notary*.

Obviously, some contracts are quite clearly more important than others and can have important long-term implications. Indeed, whenever in doubt, you should ask the advice of a lawyer. Unfortunately, few people do so and do not appreciate the trauma that can occur when even a seemingly minor contract goes wrong. Certainly, not seeing a lawyer is a mistake: for a small outlay, a contractual dispute can be avoided that could cost a fortune and last years.

> *If a contract is important, always use a lawyer either to draft, or check the full implications of, the proposed agreement*

Certainly, it is the experience of most litigation lawyers (both in the UK and Spain!) that the vast majority of contractual disputes occur because of genuine misunderstandings and miscommunications between the parties involved. Indeed, few contracting parties ever set out to breach contracts deliberately. However, differing expectations and a lack of initial clarity about the detail and performance of an agreement endlessly provide lawyers with work. Invariably, this could have been avoided had a precise agreement been drafted beforehand. This takes on an even greater importance in Spain should you not be fluent in Spanish and your knowledge of Spanish law be minimal.

Certainly, your primary aim should be to avoid contractual disputes. These are difficult enough to resolve at home, but doing so in a foreign country can be little short of a nightmare. So, having a specialist litigation lawyer on hand is important.

Obviously, the key to minimising contractual disputes is to prevent them from happening in the first place. This can be achieved through ensuring that, whenever you make an agreement, you take it seriously and always consider the worst that could possibly occur.

> *Recognise that the majority of disputes occur because of misunderstandings. Make sure you have a good interpreter and always write down the precise details of any agreement*

Of course, much depends on how a contract is drawn up and the clarity and precision of definitions of the various contractual clauses. It is in the latter that many contractual problems arise and where a good lawyer is absolutely necessary.

Written Contracts

Certainly, few people specify clearly what they want, exactly when and how they want it done, and the importance of some clauses in relation to others within a contract. As a consequence, court action is often likely, despite the initial good intentions of the contracting parties. So, before you enter into any contract:

- Understand all components of a contract in Spain

- Ensure that any contract of importance is detailed and sets out an agreement clearly, precisely and in writing

- Use a lawyer!

A written contract in Spain will comprise a number of sections:

- **Clarification of the contracting parties**: The parties involved need to be clearly identified by their names, addresses, passport numbers and fiscal numbers (*NIE* if you are an individual or *CIF* if you are a company).

- **Legal capacity**: There should be a declaration stating that the parties are legally capable to enter into the contract.

- **The core of the agreement**: This is the critical substance of the contract and will set out – in clauses – what is agreed between those party to the agreement.

- **Implied terms**: These are terms that are implied by Spanish state or EU law and that are binding irrespective of whether they are or are not contained within a contract.

- **Severance clause**: Normally there will be a clause that states that if any clause in the contract is invalid, then the contract should proceed as if the invalid clause had never existed.

- **Dispute resolution**: A contract should provide a clear route to dispute resolution. This is usually through stating the route to a defined type of mediation or arbitration. If that fails then the law that will regulate the contract (normally Spanish law) is stated.

- **Jurisdiction clause**: This should state the courts that have jurisdiction over the contract; for example Spanish Law and the courts of (say) Valencia if this is your local area.

- **Signatures**: These are always on the last page of the contract, although in Spain the contracting parties should also initial each page of the agreement.

- Finally, attached to a written contract may be pertinent documents specifically referred to in the main body of the contract.

Note: A contract should be written always in Spanish for ease of use in the Spanish courts. This is to avoid the considerable problems that can arise over interpretations that can change entirely the meaning you originally intended. The correct thing to do is to have the document drafted in Spanish and then translated by a properly qualified legal translator into English. The translation is vital for you, but it will be the Spanish document that will prevail at all times.

*Always ensure the agreements you make
are placed in writing*

When you relocate, probably the most important contracts you make will revolve around your home and any building, whether new or renovation. These are areas fraught with problems and require close attention from both an industry professional (such as an architect or surveyor) and a good lawyer. Given the high stakes involved, you must ensure that any contract is watertight and specific in every area. You should leave nothing out, right down to the type of windows you want, the quality of the fittings, the height of ceilings, the number of sockets in each room, the type of paint finish, and the penalties for late completion of the project.

Sadly, few people take the trouble to have extensive professional contracts drawn up for building work. Rather than go to any trouble and expense, they accept bland and loose builder's or developer's contracts. Some do not even commit an agreement to writing and pay everything in cash without getting receipts –simply madness. As a consequence, the scope and detail of the work, right from the very start, is often unclear to both the contracting parties. This is great news for lawyers – but is an entirely avoidable error.

Disputes

The first rule is to believe that any contract that you make will end in a dispute! So, having made a proper written contract (preferably through a lawyer!), it is fundamental to keep proper records of everything relating to the contract and its implementation.

Certainly, there is no point complaining about the inadequacy of lawyers if you do not provide them with the basic tool they need, which is, in a word, *proof*. Indeed, clear, unequivocal evidence is king in any court action. Any "he said, she said" should always be replaced with "he wrote, she wrote".

The importance of keeping full records cannot be over-emphasised. In order to do this properly, open a paper file right from the start of contractual negotiations. Print out all emails exchanged pre- and post-contract, and during the implementation of the contract. All documents (of every nature) should be kept for safekeeping and originals should be retained in a dry, safe place in a plastic folder.

> *Keep proper and full records of a contract from start to finish. Keep them in a safe place*

The second rule of disputes is to try to settle them as quickly as possible and without going to court. Notwithstanding the best preparation for a court case, it is impossible to have absolute certainty (even from an expert lawyer) as to a judge's final decision.

That said, always ask your lawyer to provide a realistic opinion as to the chances of a successful outcome before you embark upon a court case. Equally, ask for an estimate of the probable fees and costs involved. These may be different at the end of the case due to complexities encountered, but it is vitally important to know roughly how much a court action may cost. After all, you may not be able to afford to run the case all the way to completion – or the case may simply not be worth the expense involved.

In fact, the vast majority of cases tend to settle before the final hearing. This is often due to a combination of common sense, loss of nerve and an end to posturing from one or another party. Nonetheless, the journey to this point can be exhausting, costly and, sometimes, unnecessary. So, always try to settle a dispute before it escalates.

If you are involved in a dispute:

- Carefully, and unemotionally, establish the core problem of the matter and distil your dispute down into its most vital and objective issues. All too often, ancillary matters and emotions cloud judgment and blur the real problems.

- See a litigation lawyer and make sure you know exactly your legal position from the start. Depending on the circumstances, it can be a good tactic to deal with the matter directly, with the lawyer watching from the sidelines; in other words, without having him physically present. That said, recognise your limitations and immediately involve a lawyer if you find yourself out of your depth. Equally, never sign any settlement without getting advice on what is being proposed and the implications this may have on the matter going forward should you have to go to court.

- In some matters it is wise to have your lawyer present from the outset as he will add gravity to negotiations and may balance the situation should circumstances be weighted against you.

Note that the concepts of 'without prejudice' or 'off the record' do not exist – so be careful of what you say or write down during negotiations!

- At any face-to-face meetings, make sure that you have an agenda and keep it short, concise and concentrated purely on the key points. Vitally, note that the idea of 'without prejudice' does not exist in Spain – so never sign a draft settlement agreement until you have taken legal advice and considered every detail carefully.

- It may be an idea to have a mediator present – perhaps even a mutual friend, if applicable.

- If you are dealing with people who speak a different language, always use an interpreter. Although common sense, this step is often overlooked. Though you may fare all right ordering lunch and carrying out basic transactions in Spanish, never be foolhardy and overestimate your aptitude for Spanish when complicated matters are being negotiated.

- If you cannot settle your dispute, try to reach agreement with the other party as to the exact nature of the core problems between you.

- After any meeting, coldly assess what occurred and analyse the stakes involved should the dispute continue. Sometimes, even when you are in the right, it is only pragmatic to draw a matter to a close – even if this means loss of face and an overwhelming sense of injustice.

- Remember that your case may be statute barred if you do not bring proceedings within the correct time. In some cases the time frame can be as little as six months to one year. Always check this point with your lawyer.

Formal Mediation

Many contracts contain a clause stating that, in the event of a dispute, both parties must seek formal arbitration before turning to legal action. The exact type of arbitration is normally stated within the contract and will depend on the nature of the agreement.

Legal Action

Formal legal action should never be taken lightly and you should only ever undertake it having exhausted all other remedies. In particular, before you take any legal action consider carefully:

- Does your opponent have a viable counter-claim that may endanger you and potentially negate your success?

- Is the time and cost of your case sustainable? If you cannot fund a court case all the way to the trial, then you may find yourself forced to settle the matter – whatever the merits of your case.

- Is your opponent capable of paying any debt should you win the case? If he has no money, or money will be difficult to obtain, then any successful judgment may be time-consuming to enforce.

- If the case relates to forcing your opponent to undertake an action (in the UK 'specific performance'), would you really want this to be undertaken by your opponent after a bitter court battle?

Assess the taking of legal action dispassionately. Can you settle the matter without risking lengthy and costly court action?

Outline Civil Action

If you decide to take someone to court, first ensure that you provide your lawyer with the best instructions possible. This will involve a consultation with your lawyer as to the merits of the case and the likely costs. Allow your lawyer time to review all the documentation and then seek a follow-up meeting to discuss everything in detail.

Depending on the nature of a dispute you may need to arrange:

* Photographs to be sworn by a *notario*

* Expert reports from professionals such as surveyors, architects, doctors, or engineers

* The attendance of witnesses (some of whom may no longer be in Spain)

Note that there may be a time limit to bringing your claim to court. In many situations, you have as little time as one year in which to start proceedings. So, ensure that you allow your lawyer sufficient time to prepare your case and quickly supply him with all the reports and information required. Act too slowly and you may find that your 'winnable' court case cannot be brought to court because of your delay in prosecuting it!

Once your lawyer has all the documentation from you to fully support your case, he will then draft the court pleadings (*demanda*). It is a good idea to meet with your lawyer prior to the filing of the case so that you can assess it one more time. Subject to this meeting, the *demanda* will be lodged at the appropriate court by your *procurador*.

Unlike in the UK and Ireland, it is not the job of a lawyer to serve or notify the defending party of court proceedings against him. This is done by the court, when it serves the *demanda* on the defendant.

Once the *demanda* has been served on the defendant, he has some 20 days to reply. The reply is then passed onto to you or your lawyer by the *procurador* and from then on your case will proceed according to the court administrators' procedures. Unfortunately, there is no way of knowing how long it will take for your case to come to a hearing, as this depends on how busy the court in question is and varies greatly from region to region. However, it is not unusual for it to take 14 to 20 months before a case reaches a final hearing.

Typical court proceedings proceed in two phases:

- **The preliminary hearing:** This is the last official chance for you and your opponent to settle your case (without major cost implications) before it goes forward to a full hearing. If the matter is to go to a full hearing, the lawyers will set out the evidence they will be relying on and will also list the witnesses they wish to call.

- **The full hearing:** The setting of the full hearing differs quite a lot from that of the UK. Spanish courtrooms tend to be smaller, less formal and greatly less intimidating than you might expect.

  It is important to listen to your lawyer leading up to the case so that you can manage your expectations as to the outcome. If you are called as a witness, prepare carefully and check your records in advance. When giving evidence, answer truthfully and exactly, and to the best of your knowledge.

  If you are speaking through an interpreter, speak slowly and clearly. Remember that your accent may be hard for the interpreter to understand – so be careful to pronounce everything with that in mind.

- **Judgment:** Be aware that you will not obtain the court judgment on your case immediately at the end of the final hearing. A court's judgment in Spain is given in writing and is issued some time later by the court service via your *procurador*. Indeed, the timescale of any judgment can vary considerably and depends on the complexity of the matter, the speed of the judge concerned, and the efficiency of the court service.

Normally, there are three eventualities:

  - You win your case outright.
  - The judgment is not one with which you are entirely satisfied.
  - You lose your case.

- **Appeals:** When you receive the judgment it is worth considering the outcome carefully. If you are not satisfied, then you can appeal – but be aware that there is a time limit in which to do this. Miss the deadline and you may be barred from appealing your case. So, always go through a judgment carefully and assess your potential options as soon as possible after receiving it.

Take care to make a decision to appeal a judgment you do not like – before you are time barred

If you appeal, remember that normally you cannot introduce new evidence (i.e. evidence that was not presented to the original court) and you cannot set down new facts before the court of appeal. The appeal court will be concerned with the conduct of the proceedings of the original court and will assess the way in which the law was applied to your particular case. Finally, the number of appeals permissible depends on the type of court case concerned and the circumstances of the dispute.

If you have a successful action and the other side does not appeal and does not comply with the court judgment, then you may have to enforce the judgment. This will involve taking advice from your lawyer, who will inform you of the options available to you. Enforcement orders invariably require further legal work from your lawyer and need to be looked at carefully to ensure that the most effective solutions are employed.

- **Legal costs:** As in the UK, a court's decision regarding legal costs follows the judgment. In other words, the outcome of the case influences any costs awarded – not the other way around. Normally, if you win a case, then the losing party has to pay your costs. However, it is not uncommon for a court to order that everyone pays their own costs. This may occur when a judge takes the view that both parties were responsible for the dispute.

Finally, note that even if the other party has to pay your costs, this is unlikely to fully reimburse you for all your legal expenses. So, always make sure that, when you sue someone, you can afford it! It is rare, even for a successful litigant, to find your court action has cost you nothing.

The better you prepare, the better the result.
Keeping good records at all times will give
you a fighting chance in the courts

Your Lawyer

If you are involved in a dispute, it is critical to employ the right lawyer. Litigation (*litigio*) is complicated and specialised, and should not be undertaken by a lawyer involved mainly in conveyancing, commercial or criminal work. Litigation requires very particular skills together with considerable experience of how the courts work and the basis upon which they make their judgments.

Certainly, you must be extremely careful about choosing the right lawyer and making sure he is fluent in English. This is vital given the importance of accurate and precise evidence. Without doubt, any misunderstandings between you and your lawyer could be potentially disastrous.

Unfortunately, finding an experienced, assertive, fluent English-speaking litigation lawyer in Spain is no easy matter. This is particularly true in provincial areas of Spain, where most lawyers tend to have small general practices. Although these practices can deal with most matters at a low level, they are not suited to sophisticated contractual problems or corporate work. So, it pays to spend time finding a competent contract lawyer.

Finally, before you embark on a court case you must obtain some idea from your lawyer about the likely worst-case scenario costs. These can vary considerably. Additionally, you should try to establish the time it will take for your matter to reach a conclusion, should it go all the way to trial.

Police and Emergency Services

The Police

Few matters are more confusing initially to someone coming to Spain than the array of police forces around the country. It can be difficult to know who to go to when you are in trouble and why one police force will attend to a crime in one place and another police force elsewhere.

> *For all emergencies, call 112 – and say*
> *"¿Hablas ingles?" if you need to report the*
> *emergency to an English speaker*

Essentially Spain has three police forces: the *Guardia Civil*, the *Policia Nacional* and the *Policia Local*, each of which has its own specific jurisdiction and clearly defined working parameters. However, in reality, only the *Guardia Civil* and *Policia Nacional* have the extensive powers and resources that would be recognised of a police force in the UK.

Guardia Civil

Perhaps most distinctive is the *Guardia Civil*, dressed in green and a highly disciplined military force that has internal regulations and a command structure similar to the army. It was founded in 1844 by Queen Isabella II after the first Carlist war (1833 – 1839) and was originally created to restore and maintain security in the bandit-ridden countryside of the time. Now the *Guardia Civil* are primarily responsible for rural areas, with a remit that covers all crimes within the countryside, including those in towns and villages with a maximum population of around 20,000.

If you need the Guardia Civil, call 062

Most commonly, you will see the *Guardia Civil* controlling and inspecting traffic on the highways, roads and borders of Spain, although their police stations (*casas cuarteles*), with their distinctive flag, can be seen in many small towns and large villages.

There are around 73,000 *Guardia Civil* agents, of which around 2,500 are women. These agents operate from some 2,100 police stations throughout Spain and are controlled from 50 provincial departments, overseen by 17 divisional headquarters. The *Guardia Civil* is under civil authority during peacetime and is directed by the Ministry of the Interior. However, in time of war or an emergency, the Ministry of Defence takes over. Under normal circumstances, some 40% of the Spanish population live under the protection of the *Guardia Civil*, although this percentage rises to around 65% during the summer holiday season, when many urbanites leave the towns and cities.

If you have a problem or are a victim of a crime, and are in the countryside or a small town, then it is to the *Guardia Civil* police stations that you should go. The *Guardia Civil* will attend to your problem, react to an emergency, and investigate a crime exactly the way you would expect of any professional police force. Indeed, the *Guardia Civil* are well resourced, highly trained and well regarded by the Spanish for their honesty and efficiency.

Policia Nacional

However, the remit of the *Guardia Civil* does not extend to intensively populated urban areas. Any town or city with a population of over 20,000 is controlled by the *Policia Nacional*, a force that was amalgamated in 1986 with the disliked 'secret police' (the higher police force). It has a trade union and, unlike the *Guardia Civil*, is a civil (rather than military) force.

If you need the Policia Nacional, call 091

The *Policia Nacional* is responsible for crimes and general policing in large towns and cities. It is to them that you go if you have suffered a crime or if there is an emergency within an urban area. Note that, should you need to obtain an *NIE* number or register as a foreigner, then you will need to go to the *Policia Nacional* (not the *Guardia Civil*) – irrespective of where you live.

The *Policia Nacional* has some 60,000 officers located within 1,700 municipalities. This provides roughly two police officers for every 1,000 people living in urban areas throughout Spain.

Policia Local

Finally, there is the *Policia Local*. This force is recruited, funded and controlled by local town halls and is responsible to the elected mayor (*alcalde*). The *Policia Local* respond to minor crimes and mostly deal with local authority enforcement matters, together with urban traffic control and any associated violations. Crimes are not investigated and any serious matter is immediately handed over to either the *Guardia Civil* or *Policia Nacional* as appropriate.

If you need the Policia Local, call 092

Other Police and Intelligence Forces

Of course, there are exceptions to the rules above. The Basque country, Catalonia and Navarra all have their own regional police forces in place of the *Policia Nacional*.

Furthermore, Spain has an intelligence service (with whom, hopefully, you are unlikely to come into contact!) called *the Centro Nacional de Inteligencia (CNI)* that, unusually, deals with both inland and external intelligence matters.

To Spain's credit, the country has made a remarkable transition from the dictatorship of General Franco to that of a modern, first world democracy. This is nowhere more apparent than in its police forces, which have a generally good reputation. Indeed, the US State Department 'Country Reports on Human Rights Practices 2006' gives Spain virtually a clean bill of health.

On a day to day basis, most expatriates tend to find the *Guardia Civil* and *Policia Nacional* helpful and efficient, if a little remote and macho at times. Certainly, they have a reputation for dealing with trouble in a no-nonsense fashion and it is unwise to be aggressive towards them. Meanwhile, *Policia Local* officers are usually charming and often provide considerable assistance to tourists and foreigners.

> *To report a crime, call 902 102 112*

Recognising the Spanish police

Guardia Civil

- Green uniforms (can be seen in a tricorne hat at ceremonies)

- Distinctive insignia on their white and green vehicles and outside their police stations (*casas cuarteles*) – an emblem of the Royal Crown of Spain with a sword and fasces (birch sticks bound together with an axe protruding)

- Normally encountered on highways, in rural areas and small towns, and at customs controls

- Operate in pairs (*pareja*)
- Regarded as honest and efficient

Policia Nacional

- Black uniforms with white shirts (but can be dressed in blue military style uniforms)
- Blue and white vehicles
- Operate in urban areas with a population over 20,000
- Police stations are called *comisarias*
- Also encountered when applying for your *NIE* or foreign registration

Policia Local

- Blue uniforms with white shirts
- Only found in villages and towns
- Deal with minor crimes – mainly traffic control and associated violations
- Blue, white and yellow cars

If a Crime Occurs:

- Go to your nearest police station (*Guardia Civil* or *Policia Nacional*)
- Make a *denuncia* (statement), giving all the relevant details
- Obtain a copy of your *denuncia* (statement) in case of an insurance claim
- The *Policia Nacional* or *Guardia Civil* will then investigate the matter

Rights Upon Arrest

Note: Under certain circumstances, the rights below can be suspended (i.e. for investigations relating to terrorist actions).

- You must be released or brought before a judge within 72 hours of arrest.

- You must be advised in your own language of why you have been arrested.

- You have a right to remain silent and to plead not guilty.

- You have a right to ask the police to make a telephone call to a third party, nominated by you, to advise of your arrest.

- You have a right to an interpreter and to be examined by the court doctor.

- Your consulate must be advised of your arrest, if you so request it.

- You have a right to appoint an independent lawyer and if you do not do so, a court-appointed lawyer will act for you.

A *juez instructor* (examining magistrate) will be in charge of investigating your case, preparing proceedings and transferring the matter to the appropriate court. He has the power to dismiss the case, release you without charge, detain you further or bail you. Local criminal courts are presided over by a single professional judge who hears cases in which the maximum punishment is five years in prison. More serious cases are tried by a panel of three professional judges. Certain offences (such as embezzlement and murder) are tried by a nine-member jury, presided over by a single judge.

Fire Service (Bomberos)

Spain has a highly trained fire service. It is used primarily for fires, and emergencies such as traffic accidents and rescues. It is also responsible for putting out fires in the countryside and for this purpose it has water-carrying helicopters and aircraft.

If you need the Fire Service, call 080

Ambulance Service (Ambulancia)

As with the fire service, this is a national organisation that is both reliable and effective.

If you need an ambulance, call 061

Accident and Emergency Departments

Most hospitals have an A&E department that will provide any urgent medical help irrespective of whether you have the correct paperwork on you or not. They are normally highly efficient and have the capacity to transfer a patient to specialist units.

Emergency Telephone Numbers

For all emergencies:	112
To report a crime:	902 102 112
For the *Guardia Civil*:	062
For the *Policia Nacional*:	091
For the *Policia Local*:	092
Medical Service:	061
Fire Service:	080

Note: Most emergency services have some English-speaking operators so ask: *"¿Habla Ingles?"* (Do you speak English?). Repeat this clearly until you are passed to someone to whom you can explain the nature of the emergency.

In Perspective

It is easy to read a book like this and become alarmed at the complications involved in moving to Spain or buying property here. Worse still, you can end up feeling overwhelmed by the multitude of guidelines – and daunted by the constant warnings to be careful.

However, moving to Spain is not a giant leap into the unknown. It is more akin to a large step over rocky terrain – easily undertaken but requiring an element of prudence.

Certainly, you cannot come to Spain and expect it be like the UK. Spain has substantial differences that extend to every aspect of life. Some of these differences are what makes the place so wonderful – and so tremendously life enhancing. Other differences can be potentially ruinous if not understood properly.

Without doubt, the greatest troubles for most people revolve around property and for this, Spain has had (justifiably) terrible press coverage. However, as much as there is property abuse on the part of the Spanish, there is also sheer idiocy on the part of many incoming foreigners.

A prime example of the lunacy displayed by many Britons (but rarely publicised by the UK press) is not using a lawyer to undertake the conveyancing of a property. This has been accompanied by a general (and very peculiar) failure to instruct a surveyor to check that a given property is sound.

In the UK, this would be inconceivable. Yet, time and again, people come over to Spain and do not employ professionals to assist them. Yet surely greater care is required when buying a property in another country than in one's own?

Compounding this recklessness is a tolerance of blatant conflicts of interest on the part of others, even though every sentient Briton understands the dangers of this. So why is it that, when in Spain, people allow their conveyancing lawyer (when they do use one!) to act for both the seller and the buyer? Or why do they agree to 'free legal work' from an estate agent or developer as part of the buying package? This is an obvious and predictable recipe for disaster. It would be in the UK – and it certainly is in a foreign country.

There is also a tendency for people either buying or moving to Spain to treat the whole matter with a worrying lack of attention to detail. Often properties are bought with little more rigour than would be used when choosing an upmarket washing machine. Meanwhile, the sheer delicacy of the matter of location is overlooked – whereas, in the UK, infinite time and care would be invested to ensure that any move was to exactly the right area – and even to the correct side of a particular street.

Certainly, almost all the problems inherent in buying property in Spain or moving to the country can be easily negated by the application of simple common sense. In fact, the advice provided in this book could be virtually summarised in a few brief words:

Do not throw caution to the wind, just because you are in a foreign country. In fact, be more careful then ever – particularly when any action has financial consequences.

If you would normally employ a lawyer when you buy a property in the UK (and even if you would not!), use one in Spain. If you would normally use a surveyor, use one. If you would not tolerate a conflict of interest, do not allow this in Spain either. If normally you would be extremely careful about where you are moving to, do the same. If usually you double-check what you are told, do so in Spain. If normally you would scrutinise the independence, ability and credentials of a professional before using them, then always do so in Spain …

An addendum to the above is to be alert to anyone who states 'but it does not happen like that in Spain'. They may be right – but all too often these are weasel words. Your alarm bells should ring out loud and clear, until you can categorically prove the statement is correct.

Certainly, a naive belief in the essential goodness of people involved in business transactions is absurd, whether in Spain or elsewhere. This follows for the commonly held conviction that, because a fellow Briton is met abroad, he will share a common bond of integrity.

Anyone involved in business, whether a compatriot or otherwise, is out for what they can get. On odd occasions, you may meet someone who acts altruistically and who has iron integrity. However, these qualities are as rare in Spain as they are in the rest of the world and any 'brotherhood' based on nationality, when it comes to business, is a myth. So, just as in the UK, be sceptical and do not be overly trusting just because you may be dealing with a fellow Briton.

It is, of course, easy to be condemnatory of Spain with regard to its property abuses and overall property development. However, in a way this is to be expected. After all, only 35 years ago, Spain was a relatively impoverished dictatorship. Since then its development has been explosive, with new wealth and colossal amounts of money pouring into the country. It is little wonder then that a previously poor people have taken every opportunity to make money irrespective of legalities and aesthetics. The latter, certainly, are a luxury for the wealthy and are rarely of interest to an impoverished farmer turned property developer.

This is not to say that Spain has been universally 'trashed'. That would be misreading the country completely. Indeed, it would be like equating the whole of Britain to an area of urban blight in London, and dismissing the many fine developments and beautiful landscapes of the country. Spain is mostly composed of gorgeous areas, with some boasting more sensitive new developments.

Certainly, Spain has produced some of the best and most renowned architecture in the world. An example of this is the Gothic-influenced organic styles of Gaudi (seven creations have UNESCO World Heritage status, including the Sagrada Familia in Barcelona). More recently, there are the stunningly futuristic and gravity-defying designs of Calatrava (for example, the City of Arts and Sciences in Valencia).

The architectural influences of the built environment in Spain have a dramatic and fascinating history. There are Roman aqueducts, Moorish castles, ancient fortified towns and fine old squares with elegant townhouses. Throughout the country there is a steady occurrence of traditional features and classical design that have influenced buildings of all types. This is sometimes tastefully interspersed with beautiful and carefully located modernist buildings.

Unfortunately, a significant proportion of Spanish architects are not in the same league as their masters. Many have been let loose on townscapes and urbanisations with little thought or proper planning control. Indeed, sometimes it seems the first time a community learns of an ugly new development it is when construction starts.

Certainly, Spanish controls on building design are less rigid (with the exception of some historic or tourist zones) than those of the UK. Although clear building regulations do exist, their implementation has been nothing if not patchy. Indeed, there has been far too much 'have a go' architecture that is likely to scar some localities for a century or more, with buildings that simply do not work within their environment.

Tragically, the 'style' of some of the worst apartment blocks, constructed mainly in the 1970s (and widely considered blots on the landscape), has started to rear its ugly head again. Once again, many Spanish villages and towns are suffering the ideas of what some lacklustre architects perceive communities and buyers want. This commonly includes drab, grey facades, limited external space (sometimes no balconies are provided at all!) and generally unappealing buildings. These are not only difficult to sell, but also often devalue some of the nearby, better designed buildings. Not surprisingly, their lack of appeal can also make them difficult to rent – thus encouraging low monthly rental rates and a cycle of long-term poverty and dispossessed residents.

Although some regions have managed to resist detrimental practice, this has generally not been the case for areas of recent major construction. These regions now need to bring an abrupt halt to their poor architectural design, before irrevocable damage occurs. In this respect, the market downturn of 2008 may be a good thing. It may, finally, force Spanish architects, developers and town planners to be more careful about what they build next. With luck, some of the worst offenders may go out of business and learn the meaning of unsustainable development.

Ironically, it is probably easier to find fine examples of recent Spanish revival architecture (whether 'Hispanic' or 'Mediterranean') in California or Florida in the USA than in modern day Spain. This is despite the fact that the majority of people (over 75%, reportedly) prefer traditional designs to bastardised modernist ones.

Naturally, the argument between architects and the public over modern development is an old one. However, it seems fair to make a plea to architects to appreciate that classicism is not just a style in itself. It is more akin to a set of proven design principles that have influenced the built environment of a particular area or country in a positive way over centuries. Certainly, the utilisation of classic principles or even influence from nature (however subtle), will often make the difference between a building looking attractive and 'right' or blatantly 'wrong' to the majority of people.

Of course, it is not too late to change and Spain has the opportunity to combine the best of traditional and modern architecture to build a better future (and overall environment). This will be vital for the native Spanish, not least to ensure the innate beauty of Spain is preserved. Certainly, this is critical if Spain is to continue to maximise its appeal to tourists and foreigners wishing to relocate to Spain. Both are massively important industries and mainstays of the Spanish economy. On their own account, they justify more sensitive development – alongside the enforcement of stringent planning and design controls.

It is true to say that Spain needs to take a clear look at the overall operation of its property industry and to clean it up, fast. At present, the property industry does no justice to a country that claims to be developed. Poor building control, town hall corruption and an unregulated real estate sector with indifferent conveyancing lawyers hardly engenders confidence in those wishing to buy in Spain.

Indeed, it should be unnecessary to write a book on how to move or buy *safely* here. However, this book will continue to be necessary until the Spanish government acts forcefully to tidy up the property industry.

Of course, Spain is not alone in having a poorly operating property industry. Indeed, it is probably better here than in many Mediterranean or emerging countries, where property tales can be nightmarish. The industry in Spain is not overly chaotic – just extraordinarily badly managed, with professionals poorly supervised and regulations not enforced properly.

Nonetheless, with the right knowledge, you can buy safely and enjoy a superb life here. To do so, you need to act with far more care than you would in the UK. So, be sensible and cautious, and get knowledgeable – and soon you will revel (as we do!) in the sheer joy of Spain.

Good luck!

Nick Snelling

In Perspective

Terms and Definitions

Abogado(a)	Spanish lawyer
Academia	Private study college
Accidente de tráfico	Traffic accident
Adosado	New terraced house
Administrador	Administrator
Agua Potable	Mains drinking water
Alcalde	Mayor – elected and has significant local power
Ambulancia	Ambulance
Animales domésticos	Pets
Apartamento	Beachside or mountainside apartment
Aparejador	Building engineer
Aprobado	Passed
Agente de la Propiedad Inmobiliaria (API)	Registered Agent
Arquitecto	Architect
Asesor financiero o fiscal	Financial advisor
Autónomo	Self-employed
Auto Promotor	Self-builder i.e. someone who builds his own house – rather than use a professional developer
Aseguradora	Insurance company

Ayuntamiento	Town Hall
Bachillerato	Equivalent to UK A Levels
Banco	Bank
Basura	Rubbish
Bombero	Fireman
Campo	Countryside
Caja	Savings bank
Cargas	Charges and encumbrances (as in mortgages, rights of way, and so on, on a property)
Casas Cuarteles	*Guardia Civil* barracks
Casa de la Cultura	Cultural centre
Casa Rural	B&B in the countryside
Caserios	Mansion
Casita	Single-storey house often built as a summer country retreat
Castellano	Spanish language
Catastro	Property register
Cedula de habitalidad	Old name for the *Licencia de Primera Ocupación* (see below)
Centro de Salud	Health centre
Centro Nacional de Inteligencia (CNI)	Spain's intelligence service

Certificado de Escolarización	Certifies that a student has finished secondary education – although he did not pass the final examinations
Certificado de Fin de Obras	Construction project completion certificate
Certificado de Empadronamiento	Certificate of residency within an area controlled by a specified town hall
Certificado de Ciudadano	Registration certificate for an EU
de la Unión	citizen
Certificado de Residencia	Certificate proving Spanish residency
Ciclos Formativos	Vocational studies taken voluntarily after the completion of secondary education
CIF number (Codigo de Identificación Fiscal)	Corporate fiscal number
Chalet	Villa
Colegio/Escuela	Primary school
Colegio de Arquitectos	Architects association and regulatory body
Comisaría de Policia	*Policia Nacional* station
Comunidad Autónoma	Regional area of Spain (there are 17 and two autonomous cities)

Comunidad de Bienes (CB)	Partnership
Conserje	Caretaker
Constructor	Builder
Contrato	Contract
Contrato de Arras	A contract stating that the seller has to pay back twice the amount of the buyer's deposit if he (the seller) reneges on the deal
Contrato Privado	Private contract
Contrato indefinido	Permanent (employment) contract
Contrato temporal	Temporary (employment) contract
Control	Test or examination
Corredor	'Runner'/informal real estate agent
Cortijos	Huge landowner's property, normally in Andalucía
Cuotas de Autonomos	Self-employed social security payments
Demanda	Legal summons to start a court action
Denuncia	Legal statement/formal complaint
Dentista	Dentist
Depósito de agua	A water reservoir

Diplomatura	Equivalent to a UK degree qualification after 3 years' study. After 5-6 years' study the qualification achieved is called a *licenciatura* or *ingeniería*
Director	Director
DNI (Documento Nacional de Identidad)	Spanish personal identity card
Economista	Economist
Electricista	Electrician
Enfermero(a)	Nurse
Escritura de Propiedad	Property deeds
Escuela	Primary school
Escritura de Compaventa	Deed of purchase
E.S.O	Secondary education
Examen	Examination
Experto de construcción	Building surveyor
Extranjeros	Foreigners
Finca	Farmhouse (or block of flats – the building – in the Valencia region)
Fontanero	Plumber
Funcionario	State employee/civil servant
Garrapatas	Ticks

Gestor	A professional who deals with state-related paperwork and tax returns. May also have lawyers and accountants within his practice
Gota Fría	Intense and sustained rainstorms that can last several days
Guardia Civil	Police in charge of rural areas/borders and urban areas under around 20,000 people. A military force
Hacienda	Spanish tax office/Inland Revenue
Hipoteca	Mortgage
Hospital	Hospital
IBI (Impuestos de Bienes Inmuebles)	Local authority rates
Impuesto de Sucesiones	Inheritance tax
Impuestos sobre la Renta de no Residentes	3% CGT retention on sale of a property by a non-resident
INE (Instituto Nacional Estatisticas)	National Institute for Statistics
Infantil	Child of 3–6 years
Inmobiliaria (API)	Estate agent
Inmobiliaria	Real estate/property
Instituto de Enseñanza	Secondary school that also provides *Bachillerato* and

Secundaria	Vocational courses
Instituto de Formacion Prefesional	School for vocational studies only
ITV (Inspecion Técnica de Veculos)	Spanish Vehicle MOT
IVA (Impuesto sobre el Valor Añadido)	Spanish VAT
Jefatura de Tráfico	Provincial traffic headquarters
Jefe	Boss/owner/manager
Juez Instructor	Examining magistrate/judge
La legitima	Obligatory heirs
La Renta	Capital Gains Tax
Licencia de conducir	Driver's licence
Licencia de Primera Ocupación	First Occupation Licence or occupancy permit
Licenciatura	Professional qualification achieved after 5–6 years of university study
Litigo	Litigation
Masía	Huge landowner's property – normally Valencian/Catalan country house
Mañana	Tomorrow
Médico	Doctor
Médico de Familia	General practitioner

Memoria de calidades	Specification
Memoria de trabajo	Schedule of works
Metres constuidos	Total m² of a property (including all space taken up by internal walls and supporting pillars etc.)
Metros útiles	m² area of a property that is useable space
Mosquito	Mosquito
Nómina	Salary/payroll
Nota simple	Certificate issued by the Property Registry describing a given property
NIE (Numero de Identificatión de Extranjero)	Individual fiscal number for non- Spaniard
NIF (Numero de identificacion fiscal)	Spanish ID number
Notario	Professional who certifies documents as legal
Obras menor	Small works
OCT (Organismo de Control Técnico)	Building Control
Oficina de Extranjeros	Foreigners' Office
Pareja	Pair (*Guardia Civil*)
Parcela	Plot of land
Pazos	Huge landowner's property, normally in Galicia

314

Pediatra	Paediatrician
Pensionista	Pensioner (over 65)
Perito de obras	Building surveyor
Perro peligroso	Dangerous dog
Piso	A flat or apartment that is normally not on the beach front
Poder Notarial	Power of attorney – formal and notarised authorisation for someone (normally your lawyer) to act for and sign documents on your behalf
Plan Parcial	Development plan for a specific local area
Planeamiento Urbanistico	Urban development plan
Policia Local	Police (with restricted powers) appointed by the local town hall
Policia Nacional	Police in charge of urban areas
Póliza de seguro	Insurance policy
Preescolar	Child of 0–3 years
Procurador	Communication link between your lawyer and a court
Protegido	Protected (as in land)
Proyecto de la Ejecución	Formal construction project

Pulgas	Fleas
Primaria	Primary education
RENFE	National railway
Registrador	Registrar
Registro Central de Extranjeros	National Register of Foreigners
Registro Central de Ultimas Voluntades	Central Registry of Wills
Registro de la Propiedad	Land Registry
Repaso	Homework/additional study
Residencia de tercera edad	Residence for the elderly
Residente fiscal	Tax resident
Rústico	Agricultural land
Selectivo/Selectividad	State university entrance examination
Se Alquila	For Rent
Se Vende	For Sale
Seguridad y Salud	Health and safety
Seguro Decenal	10-year structural faults' insurance backed guarantee
SIP (Sistema de Informacion Poblacional) card	Spanish national health card
Solitaria	Tapeworm
Sociedad Anonima (SA)	Public company

Sociedad Limitada (SL)	Limited Company
Sociedad Limitada Unipersonal (SLU)	Limited Company with a single share-holder
Solar	A fully urbanised building plot
Sótano	Under-build
Suspendido	Failed (as in examination)
Tasación	Valuation
Tasador	Bank valuer/assessor
Tarjeta Sanitaria Europea	European Health Card (EHC)
Testamento Abierto	Open Will
Testamento Cerrado	Closed Will
Testamento Ológrafo	Holographic Will
Titulo de Graduado en EducaciónSecundaria	Certificate of secondary education (like UK's O levels)
Trastero	Store room
Urbanización	Housing estate
Urbanizable	The legal designation of land as it changes from *rústico* to *urbano*
Urbanizado	Where a full infrastructure has been installed (mains water, electricity, landlines telephone, mains drainage, pavements, lights etc.)
Urgencias	Emergencies

Usufructo	A right to use/live in a given property
Valor Catastral	Value as calculated by the town hall
Veterinario	Veterinarian surgeon
Villa	Detached villa for permanent living

Useful Contacts

Building Surveys

www.surveysspain.com
English building surveyor based in Spain

Currency Transfer companies

www.currencies.co.uk
Currency transfer and exchange specialists

www.currenciesdirect.com
Currency transfer and exchange specialists

Governmental Information

www.dh.gov.uk/travellers
Health travel cards information

www.ine.es
Web site of the Spanish National Statistics Institute

www.registradores.org/principal/indexx.jsp
Web site to buy Nota Simples

www.ukspain.com
UK government advice about Spain

Information on Pets

www.defra.gov.uk/animalh/quarantine/pets/
Pet passports

Insurance Companies

www.ibexinsure.com
Specialists in insurance in Spain

Lawyers

realyjust@gmail.com
English speaking Spanish conveyancing lawyer

www.povedahayes.com
Valencia litigation lawyers

Newspapers and Information Sites

www.britishexpats.com
Forums and useful articles

www.costablancanews.com
English language newspaper for Costa Blanca

www.costablancauncovered.com
Information website for Costa Blanca region

www.culturespain.com
For all things Spanish

www.euroweeklynews.com
English language newspaper

www.expatfocus.com
International web site

www.expatica.com
Information web site

www.eyeonspain.com
Information web site

www.Guide2Valencia.com
Information and property web site

www.practicalspain.com
Information web site

www.roundtownnews.com
English language newspaper

www.thesentinella.com
English language newspaper

www.thespainforum.com
Web site Forum

www.thinkspain.com
English language newspaper

www.spain-football.org
Everything about football in Spain

www.soltimes.com
English language newspaper for the Almeria region

www.spanishpropertyinsight.com
Property Information web site

www.thespainforum.com
Web site with popular Forum

www.thisisspain.com
Information web site

Pensions and inheritance tax advice

www.qrops.es
UK pension transfer specialists

www.winchamiht.com
Tax and inheritance tax avoidance

Property Portals

www.casalasafor.com
Properties around Gandia

www.Girasol.com
Spanish property portal

www.idealista.com
Spanish property web portal

www.kyero.com
Biggest English language property website in Spain

www.spain-property.culturespain.com
Property in Spain

Property Rental Sites
www.ownersdirect.com
Rentals web portal

www.villarenters.com
Rentals web portal

Second hand goods
www.segundomano.com
Spanish website for second-hand goods

Spanish Language Courses
www.donquikote.org

Contributors

Carolina Just Miro *Abogada (Spanish lawyer)*
Carolina is a Spanish lawyer specialising in conveyancing. She speaks fluent English and has extensive experience of the Spanish property market and the complexities of the buying and selling process. She has an international client base and is frequently called upon to analyse and resolve property-related disputes.

(0034) 96 287 6843
(0034) 627 567 139
realyjust@gmail.com

Mark Paddon BSc Hons Building Surveying. MCIOB. FAS. CAAT *(Building surveyor)*
A Spanish-speaking British building surveyor who has been based in Spain for seven years, Mark writes for a local paper and has acted as consultant and contributor to Channel 4's 'Selling Houses Abroad'. He has a detailed knowledge of Spanish properties, both old and new, and carries out structural surveys for buyers. Mark also assesses building defects for existing owners, to whom he provides detailed remedial solutions and expert witness reports for court actions and insurance claims.

www.surveysspain.com
(0034) 96 280 7247
(0034) 653 733 066
markpaddon@terra.es

Alberto Diaz Reya *Ingenerio Superior. M.Sc (Asset management)*
Alberto has worked as an international management consultant and, for many years, successfully ran his own real estate agency. He has also worked as a property developer and been involved in the renovation of properties and the construction of new villas and flats. He has an intimate knowledge of both the Spanish real estate and construction industries.

a_diaz_raya@hotmail.com

John Pointon *BA MIM (Marketing and management consultant)*
Based in Spain and Malta, John is a director of an international construction consortium and was previously an advisor to the UK government. He is the CEO of an international management and marketing consultancy and also has a company providing investment opportunities in established fast-food restaurant and retail store group franchises worldwide.

Sonia Garcia Fernández *Veterinaria (Veterinarian surgeon)*
Sonia has worked as a vet for many years and specialises in the treatment of domestic animals. An experienced surgeon, she has an extensive knowledge of animal ailments and health problems in Spain. She works from a mixed practice that comprises both Spanish and international clients.

vetsonia.@yahoo.es

Dra. María Soriano Carreras *Médica Pediatra (Paediatrician)*
Maria is a consultant physician specialising in children's healthcare. She works for a busy practice with a wide variety of international and Spanish patients. She has worked extensively within the Spanish healthcare system and is permanently based at a children's clinic within the Valencia province.

Beatriz Gonzalez Menendez *(Professor of Classics)*
Beatriz has taught since 1982 and is currently head of department at her school and a member of several education committees. She was an assistant head teacher for two years. She speaks fluent Spanish, Valenciano, German, English and Modern Greek.

momentobea@hotmail.com

Jose Ivars Lopez *(Marketing and property expert)*
Jose is Spanish, an international property development specialist and a member of the RICS Royal Institute of Chartered Surveyors). He has worked as the UK managing director of a major Spanish development company and is now head of marketing for an international foreign exchange company based in London. He is also on the board of directors of a well-known UK charity connected with Spain.

Robert Burns *BA (Hons.) (Accountant)*
Robert is a qualified accountant trained at Coopers and Lybrand and now permanently based in Spain, having been a finance director and financial controller for several businesses in the UK. Currently, he works in partnership with a firm of Spanish-based independent financial advisors who specialise in assisting expatriates with their UK pension funds and investments.

www.qrops.es

The Author

Nick Snelling *LLB*

Nick worked as a litigation executive before founding and running a UK construction company specialising in high-profile central London renovations and structural remedial works.

In Spain, Nick has worked as a management consultant to two Spanish estate agencies and is currently a director of an international agency. He writes investigative articles on all aspects of Spain, is a specialist in property matters, and is the author of the influential blog Culture Spain - www.culturespain.com.

Nick is married with two children and lives in the mountains above Gandia in the Comunidad de Valencia. A keen climber, he spends his free time suspended high above crags around Spain!

Published books:

Home Ownership, 1861080670
Taking the Heat, 1905430469
How to Sell your Spanish Property in a Crisis, 1-905430523

Lightning Source UK Ltd.
Milton Keynes UK
UKOW06f2158061115

262262UK00014B/232/P